NATIONAL BESTSELLER

"A heartbreaking memoir, beautifully rendered…
A wise, thoughtful, and ultimately loving portrayal."
—*SEATTLE TIMES*

"Revelatory."
—*ENTERTAINMENT WEEKLY*

"The sleeper critical hit of the season."
—*VULTURE*

"Writing with enlightened panache and dry humor…
[Brennan-Jobs] has built her own house in memoir form…It's alive
in all the rough edges of its feelings, and it's home."
—*WALL STREET JOURNAL*

"Exceptionally written."
—*GQ*

"Shockingly honest and beautifully understated."
—*VOGUE* (UK)

"An ambitious and artful project."
—*LOS ANGELES TIMES*

"A beautifully wrought, often devastating account…
Intimate and unsettling."
—*BUZZFEED*

"Captivating…This engrossing memoir about
identity and adolescence is relatable to anyone familiar with
complicated family relationships."
—*NPR*

Praise for *Small Fry*

"Entrancing . . . Brennan-Jobs is a deeply gifted writer . . . Her inner landscape is depicted in such exquisitely granular detail that it feels as if no one else could have possibly written it. Indeed, it has that defining aspect of a literary work: the stamp of a singular sensibility . . . Beautiful, literary, and devastating."

—*New York Times Book Review*

"An intimate, richly drawn portrait . . . *Small Fry* is a memoir of uncommon grace, maturity, and spare elegance . . . The reader of this exquisite memoir is left with a loving, forgiving remembrance and the lasting impression of a resilient, kindhearted and wise woman who is at peace with her past." —*San Francisco Chronicle*

"Extraordinary . . . An aching, exquisitely told story of a young woman's quest for belonging and love." —*People*

"Mesmerizing, discomfiting reading . . . A book of no small literary skill." —*New Yorker*

"It's gratifying to see [Ms. Brennan-Jobs] assert her authority as the owner of her narrative. Writing with enlightened panache and dry humor, she's as keen a witness to the ambience of the Bay Area in the 1980's and 1990's . . . as she is to the behavior of the adults around her . . . Never having felt safe in any of her father's houses, [she] has built her own house in memoir form, a repository of her love and anger and mourning . . . It's alive in all the rough edges of its feelings, and it's home." —*Wall Street Journal*

"A heartbreaking memoir, beautifully rendered . . . It's a love story for the father that she had, flaws and all . . . A wise, thoughtful, and ultimately loving portrayal of her father." —*Seattle Times*

"[*Small Fry*] is a story of a girl growing up in 1980s and '90s California trying to fit into two very different families and not belonging in either. It's the story of her single mother trying to keep it together and often not succeeding. It's the story of a family that is as imperfect as every family, things complicated by wealth, fame and, in the end, illness and death."   —*Associated Press*

"Beautiful and restrained . . . Startling transitions, diamond sharp images and brutally efficient short chapters . . . An ambitious and artful project."   —*Los Angeles Times*

"Exceptionally written."   —*GQ*

"Revelatory . . . Her exquisitely written prose allows Brennan-Jobs to—painfully, complexly, heroically—reclaim her own story."
                    —*Entertainment Weekly*

"Captivating . . . This engrossing memoir about identity and adolescence is relatable to anyone familiar with complicated family relationships."   —*NPR*

"The sleeper critical hit of the season."   —*Vulture*

"A masterly Silicon Valley gothic . . . The bohemian landscape she captures will be virtually unrecognizable to anyone who equates this slice of Northern California with Teslas and tiger moms . . . Of the book's myriad achievements, the greatest might be making [this] story her own."   —*Vogue*

"An exquisitely written book about, first and foremost, growing up in a complicated family structure."   —*Refinery29*

"A beautifully wrought, often devastating account of a life spent yearning for a distant father's love . . . Intimate and unsettling."
                    —*Buzzfeed*

"Brennan-Jobs skillfully relays her past without judgement... staying true to her younger self. It is a testament to her fine writing and journalistic approach that her memoir never turns maudlin or gossipy. Rather than a celebrity biography, this is Brennan-Jobs's authentic story of growing up in two very different environments, neither of which felt quite like home." —*Booklist* (starred review)

"Here is a literary coming-of-age memoir of the highest order, the story of a child trying to find her place between two radically different parents, identities, and worlds. Compassionate, wise, and filled with finely-wrought detail, *Small Fry* is a wonder of a book, and Lisa Brennan-Jobs is a wonder of a writer." —Jamie Quatro

"As clear-eyed, amusing, honest, unsentimental, and sad as any memoir I've read in years. The prose sparkles, the vision behind it is ruefully compassionate and wise. No other book or film has captured Steve Jobs as distinctly as this one has. The love between father and daughter, thwarted and baffled as it often is, comes through beautifully." —Phillip Lopate

"A gorgeous, compelling work of art and a dazzling coming-of-age story. This is a lovely, sweetly intimate portrait, a story told through the eyes of a daughter whose father struggled with his own origins— and who almost became the father she hoped he would be." —Susan Cheever

SMALL FRY

SMALL FRY

LISA BRENNAN-JOBS

Grove Press
New York

The names and identifying details of some of the people mentioned in this book have been changed.

Printed in the United States of America

First Grove Atlantic hardcover edition: September 2018
First Grove Atlantic paperback edition: June 2019

This book was designed by Norman Tuttle at Alpha Design & Composition.

This book was set in 12 pt. Adobe Caslon Pro by Alpha Design & Composition of Pittsfield, NH.

ISBN 978-0-8021-4721-9
eISBN 978-0-8021-4651-9

Grove Press
an imprint of Grove Atlantic
154 West 14th Street
New York, NY 10011

Distributed by Publishers Group West

groveatlantic.com

19 20 21 22   10 9 8 7 6 5 4 3 2 1

for Bill

THIRD FISHERMAN. Master, I marvel how the fishes live in the sea.

FIRST FISHERMAN. Why, as men do a-land; the great ones eat up the little ones: I can compare our rich misers to nothing so fitly as to a whale; a' plays and tumbles, driving the poor fry before him, and at last devours them all at a mouthful. Such whales have I heard on o' th' land, who never leave gaping till they've swallowed the whole parish, church, steeple, bells, and all.

Shakespeare, *Pericles*

It was a curious experience to be the unrecognized source of this public attraction and to be standing in the sleet—it made one feel like a phantom presence.

Saul Bellow, *Humboldt's Gift*

Three months before he died, I began to steal things from my father's house. I wandered around barefoot and slipped objects into my pockets. I took blush, toothpaste, two chipped finger bowls in celadon blue, a bottle of nail polish, a pair of worn patent leather ballet slippers, and four faded white pillowcases the color of old teeth.

After stealing each item, I felt sated. I promised myself that this would be the last time. But soon the urge to take something else would arrive again like thirst.

I tiptoed into my father's room, careful to step over the creaky floorboard at the entrance. This room had been his study, when he could still climb the stairs, but he slept here now. It was cluttered with books and mail and bottles of medicine; glass apples, wooden apples; awards and magazines and stacks of papers. There were framed prints by Hasui of twilight and sunset at temples. A patch of pink light stretched out on a wall beside him.

He was propped up in bed, wearing shorts. His legs were bare and thin as arms, bent up like a grasshopper's.

"Hey, Lis," he said.

Segyu Rinpoche stood beside him. He'd been around recently when I came to visit. A short Brazilian man with sparkling brown eyes, the Rinpoche was a Buddhist monk with a scratchy voice who wore brown robes over a round belly. We called him by his title. Tibetan holy men were sometimes born in the west now, in places like Brazil. To me he didn't *seem* holy—he wasn't distant or inscrutable. Near us, a black canvas bag of nutrients hummed with a motor and a pump, the tube disappearing somewhere under my father's sheets.

"It's a good idea to touch his feet," Rinpoche said, putting his hands around my father's foot on the bed. "Like this."

I didn't know if the foot touching was supposed to be for my father, or for me, or for both of us.

"Okay," I said, and took his other foot in its thick sock, even though it was strange, watching my father's face, because when he winced in pain or anger it looked similar to when he started to smile.

"That feels good," my father said, closing his eyes. I glanced at the chest of drawers beside him and at the shelves on the other side of the room for objects I wanted, even though I knew I wouldn't dare steal something right in front of him.

While he slept, I wandered through the house, looking for I didn't know what. A nurse sat on the couch in the living room, her hands on her lap, listening for my father to call out for help. The house was quiet, the sounds muffled, the white-painted brick walls were dimpled like cushions. The terracotta floor was cool on my feet except in the places where the sun had warmed it to the temperature of skin.

In the cabinet of the half bath near the kitchen, where there used to be a tattered copy of the Bhagavad Gita, I found a bottle of expensive rose facial mist. With the door closed, the light out, sitting on the toilet seat, I sprayed it up into the air and closed my eyes. The mist fell around me, cool and holy, as in a forest or an old stone church.

There was also a silver tube of lip gloss with a brush at one end and a twisting mechanism at the other that released liquid into the center of the brush. I had to have it. I stuffed the lip gloss into my pocket to take back to the one-bedroom apartment in Greenwich Village that I shared with my boyfriend, where I knew, as much as I have ever known anything, that this tube of lip gloss would complete my life. Between avoiding the housekeeper, my brother and sisters, and my stepmother around the house so I wouldn't be caught stealing things or hurt when they didn't acknowledge me or reply to my hellos, and spraying myself in the darkened bathroom to feel less like I was disappearing—because inside the falling mist I had a sense of having an outline again—making efforts to see my sick father in his room began to feel like a burden, a nuisance.

For the past year I'd visited for a weekend every other month or so.

I'd given up on the possibility of a grand reconciliation, the kind in the movies, but I kept coming anyway.

In between visits, I saw my father all around New York. I saw him sitting in a movie theater, the *exact* curve of his neck to jaw to cheekbone. I saw him as I ran along the Hudson River in winter sitting on a bench looking at the docked boats; and on my subway ride to work, walking away on the platform through the crowd. Thin men, olive-skinned, fine-fingered, slim-wristed, stubble-bearded, who, at certain angles, looked just like him. Each time I had to get closer to check, my heart in my throat, even though I knew it could not possibly be him because he was sick in bed in California.

Before this, during years in which we hardly spoke, I'd seen his picture everywhere. Seeing the pictures gave me a strange zing. The feeling was similar to catching a glimpse of myself in a mirror across a room and thinking it was someone else, then realizing it was my own face: there he was, peering out from magazines and newspapers and screens in whatever city I was in. *That is my father and no one knows it but it's true.*

Before I said goodbye, I went to the bathroom to mist one more time. The spray was natural, which meant that over the course of a few minutes it no longer smelled sharp like roses, but fetid and stinky like a swamp, although I didn't realize it at the time.

As I came into his room, he was getting into a standing position. I watched him gather both his legs in one arm, twist himself ninety degrees by pushing against the headboard with the other arm,

and then use both arms to hoist his own legs over the edge of the
bed and onto the floor. When we hugged, I could feel his vertebrae,
his ribs. He smelled musty, like medicine sweat.

"I'll be back soon," I said.

We detached, and I started walking away.

"Lis?"

"Yeah?"

"You smell like a toilet."

Hippies

By the time I was seven, my mother and I had moved thirteen times.

We rented spaces informally, staying in a friend's furnished bedroom here, a temporary sublet there. The last place had become unsuitable when someone had sold the refrigerator without warning. The next day, my mother called my father, asked for more money, and he increased the child support payments by two hundred dollars per month. We moved again, to an apartment on the ground floor of a small building at the back of a house on Channing Avenue in Palo Alto—the first place my mother rented with her own name on the lease. Our new place was just for us.

The house in front of our apartment was a dark brown Craftsman with dust-covered ivy where a lawn might have been, and two bent-over scrub oaks that almost touched the ground. Cobwebs stretched between the trees and the ivy, collecting pollen that lit up bright white in the sunshine. From the street you couldn't tell there was an apartment complex behind the house.

Before this we'd lived in towns nearby—Menlo Park, Los Altos, Portola Valley—but Palo Alto is the place we would come to call home.

Here the soil was black and wet and fragrant; beneath rocks I discovered small red bugs, pink- and ash-colored worms, thin centipedes, and slate-colored woodlice that curled into armored spheres when I bothered them. The air smelled of eucalyptus and sunshine-warmed dirt, moisture, cut grass. Railroad tracks bisect the town; near them is Stanford University, with its great grassy oval and gold-rimmed chapel at the end of a palm tree–lined road.

The day we moved in, my mother parked and we carried in our things: kitchen supplies, a futon, a desk, a rocking chair, lamps, books. "This is why nomads don't get anything done," she said, hefting a box through the doorway, her hair disheveled, her hands flecked with white canvas primer. "They don't stay in one place long enough to build anything that lasts."

The living room had a sliding glass door that opened onto a small deck. Beyond the deck was a patch of dry grass and thistles, a scrub oak and a fig—both spindly—and a line of bamboo, which my mother said was difficult to get rid of once it took root.

After we finished unloading, she stood with her hands on her hips, and together we surveyed the room: with everything we owned, it still looked empty.

The next day, she called my father at his office to ask for help.

"Elaine's coming over with the van—we're going to your father's house to pick up a couch," my mother said a few days later. My father lived near Saratoga in Monte Sereno, a suburb about half an hour away. I'd never been to this house or heard of the town where he lived—I'd met him only a couple of times.

My mother said my father offered his extra couch when she called him. But if we didn't get it soon, she knew, he'd throw it away or rescind the offer. And who knew when we'd have access to Elaine's van again?

I was in the same first-grade class as Elaine's twins, a boy and a girl. Elaine was older than my mother, with wavy black hair and loose strands that created a halo around her head in certain lights. My mother was young, sensitive, and luminous, without the husband, house, and family that Elaine had. Instead, she had me, and I had two jobs: first, to protect her so that she could protect me; second, to shape her and rough her up so that she could handle the world, the way you sandpaper a surface to make the paint stick.

"Left or right?" Elaine kept asking. She was in a hurry—she had a doctor's appointment to keep. My mother is dyslexic but insisted that wasn't the reason she eschewed maps. It was because the maps were inside her; she could find her way back to any place she'd ever been, she said, even if it took her a few turns to get her bearings. But we often got lost.

"Left," she said. "No, right. Wait. Okay, left."

Elaine was mildly annoyed, but my mother did not apologize. She acted as if one is equal to the people who save them.

The sun made lace on my legs. The air was wet and thick and pricked my nose with the smell of spicy bay laurel and dirt.

The hills in the towns around Palo Alto had been created by shifting under the earth, by the grinding of the plates against each other. "We must be near the fault line," my mother said. "If there was an earthquake now, we'd be swallowed up."

We found the right road and then the wooded driveway with a lawn at the end. A circle of bright grass with thin shoots that looked like they'd be soft on my feet. The house was two stories tall, with a gabled roof, dark shingles on white stucco. Long windows rippled the light. This was the kind of house I drew on blank pages.

We rang the bell and waited, but no one came. My mother tried the door.

"Locked," she said. "Damn. I bet he's not going to show."

She walked around the house, checking the windows, trying the back door. "Locked!" she kept calling out. I wasn't convinced it was really his.

She came back to the front and looked up at the sash windows, too high to reach. "I'm going to try those," she said. She stepped on a sprinkler head and then a drainpipe, grabbed a lip of windowsill, and flattened herself against the wall. She found a new place for her hands and feet, looked up, pulled herself higher.

Elaine and I watched. I was terrified she would fall.

My father was supposed to come to the door and invite us in. Maybe he would show us other furniture he didn't want and invite us to come back.

Instead, my mother was climbing the house like a thief.

"Let's go," I called out. "I don't think we're supposed to be here."

"I hope there's no alarm," she said.

She reached the ledge. I held my breath, waiting for a siren to blare, but the day was as still as before. She unlatched the window, which scraped up and open, and disappeared, leg by leg, and emerged a few seconds later through the front door into the sunshine.

"We're in!" she said. I looked through the door: light reflected on wood floors, high ceilings. Cool, vacant spaces. I associated him that day—and later—with pools of reflected light from big windows, shade in the depths of rooms, the musty, sweet smells of mold and incense.

My mother and Elaine held the couch between them, maneuvered it through the door and down the steps. "It doesn't weigh much," my mother said. She asked me to step aside. A thick woven raffia frame held wide-weave linen upholstery. The cushions were a cream color spattered with bright chintz flowers in red, orange, and blue, and for years I would pick at the edges of the petals, trying to dig my fingernails under their painted tips.

Elaine and my mother moved fast and seriously, as if they might be angry, a loop of my mother's hair falling out of its band. After they'd shoved the couch into the back of the van, they went back inside and brought out a matching chair and ottoman.

"Okay, let's go," my mother said.

The back was full, so I sat in the front, on her lap.

My mother and Elaine were giddy. They had their furniture and Elaine wouldn't be late for her appointment. This was the reason for my vigilance and worry: to arrive at this moment, see my mother joyful and content.

Elaine turned out of the driveway and onto a two-lane road. A moment later two cop cars sped past us, going in the opposite direction.

"They might be coming for us!" Elaine said.

"We might have gone to *jail!*" my mother said, laughing.

I didn't understand her jaunty tone. If we went to jail, we'd be separated. As far as I understood, they didn't keep children and adults in the same cells.

The next day, my father called. "Hey, did you break in and take the couch?" he asked. He laughed. He had a silent alarm, he said. It had rung in the local police station, and four cop cars had sped to the house, arriving just after we left.

"Yes, we did," she said, a flaunt in her voice.

For years, I was haunted by the idea of a silent alarm and how close we'd been to danger without knowing it.

My parents met at Homestead High School in Cupertino, California, in the spring of 1972, when he was a senior and she was a junior.

On Wednesdays, through the night, she animated a student film in the high school quad with a group of friends. One of those nights, my father approached her in the spotlight where she stood waiting to move the Claymation characters and handed her a page of Bob Dylan lyrics he'd typed out: "Sad-Eyed Lady of the Lowlands."

"I want it back when you're done," he said.

He came the nights she was there and held candles for her to see by while she drew in between takes.

That summer they lived together in a cabin at the end of Stevens Canyon Road, my father paying the rent by selling what they called blue boxes that he made with his friend Woz. Woz was an engineer who was a few years older than my father, shy and intense, with dark hair. They'd met at a technology club and become friends and collaborators and would later start Apple together. The blue boxes emitted tones that made phone calls go through for free, illegally. They'd found a book by the phone company in the library that explained the system and the exact series of tones. You'd hold the box to the receiver, the box would make the tones, and the phone company would connect the call to wherever in the world you wanted. At that house the neighbors owned aggressive goats, and when my parents arrived home in the car, my father would divert the goats as my mother ran to the door, or he would run to her side of the car and carry her.

By this time, my mother's parents had divorced; her mother was mentally ill and increasingly cruel. My mother went back and forth between her parents' homes; her father was often gone, traveling for work. Her father didn't approve of my parents living together, but he didn't try to stop them. My father's father, Paul, was outraged at the plan, but his mother, Clara, was kind, the only one of the parents to come over one night for dinner. They made her Campbell's soup, spaghetti, and salad.

In the fall, my father left for Reed College, in Oregon, which he attended for about six months before dropping out. They broke up; they didn't really talk about things, she said, not the relationship or the breakup, and she'd started dating someone else. When he understood she was leaving him, he was so upset he could hardly walk, she said, but sort of slouched forward. It surprised me to discover that she was the one who broke it off with him, and I wondered, later, if this breakup was part of the reason he was vindictive toward her after I was born. He was aimless then, she said, a college dropout, longing for her even when she was beside him.

Both my parents went to India separately. He traveled for six months, she for the year after he returned. He told me later that he'd gone to India specifically to meet the guru Neem Karoli Baba, but when he arrived, the guru had just died. The ashram where the guru lived had let my father stay for a few days, putting him up in a white room with nothing in it but a bed on the floor and a copy of a book called *Autobiography of a Yogi*.

Two years later, when the company my father started with Woz, Apple, was just beginning, my parents were a couple again, living in a dark brown ranch-style house in Cupertino together with a man named Daniel who, along with my parents, also worked at Apple. My mother worked in the packing department. She had recently decided to save up to leave suburbia and leave my father, who was moody, and to get a job at the Good Earth in Palo Alto, a health food restaurant on the corner of University Avenue and Emerson Street. She had an IUD inserted, but it was expelled without her knowledge, as they are in rare cases soon after insertion, and she discovered she was pregnant.

She told my father the next day, when they were standing in the middle of a room off the kitchen. There was no furniture, just a rug. When she told him, he looked furious, clenched his jaw, and then ran out the front door and slammed it behind him. He drove off; she thought he must have gone to talk with an attorney who told him not to talk to her, because after that, he wouldn't say a word.

She quit her job in the packing department at Apple, too embarrassed to be pregnant with my father's child and also working at his company, and went to stay at different friends' houses. She went on welfare; she had no car, no income. She thought of having an abortion but decided not to after a recurring dream of a blowtorch between her legs. She considered adoption, but the one woman she trusted to help her at Planned Parenthood was transferred to another county. She got jobs cleaning houses and lived in a trailer for a while. She went to silent meditation retreats four times during her pregnancy, in part because the food was plentiful. My father continued living in the house in Cupertino until he bought the house in Monte Sereno, where we would later get the couch.

In the spring of 1978, when my parents were twenty-three, my mother gave birth to me on their friend Robert's farm in Oregon, with the help of two midwives. The labor and delivery took three hours, start to finish. Robert took photos. My father arrived a few days later. "It's not my kid," he kept telling everyone at the farm, but he'd flown there to meet me anyway. I had black hair and a big nose, and Robert said, "She sure looks like you."

My parents took me out into a field, laid me on a blanket, and looked through the pages of a baby-name book. He wanted to name me Claire. They went through several names but couldn't agree. They didn't want something derivative, a shorter version of a longer name.

"What about Lisa?" my mother finally said.

"Yes. That one," he said happily.

He left the next day.

"Isn't Lisa short for Elizabeth?" I asked my mother. "No. We looked it up. It's a separate name." "And why did you let him help name me when he was pretending he wasn't the father?" "Because he was your father," she said.

On my birth certificate, my mother listed both of their names, but my last name was only hers: Brennan. She drew stars on the document around the margins, the kind that are only outlines with hollow centers.

A few weeks later my mother and I went to live with her older sister, Kathy, in a town called Idyllwild in Southern California. My mother was still on welfare; my father didn't visit or help with child support. We left after five months, beginning our series of moves.

During the time my mother was pregnant, my father started work on a computer that would later be called the Lisa. It was the precursor to the Macintosh, the first mass-market computer with an external mouse—the mouse as large as a block of cheese—and included software, floppy discs labeled LisaCalc and LisaWrite. But it was too expensive for the market, a commercial failure; my father began on the team working for it, but then started working against it, competing against it, on the Mac team. The Lisa computer was discontinued, the three thousand unsold computers later buried in a landfill in Logan, Utah.

Until I was two, my mother supplemented the welfare payments by cleaning houses and waitressing. My father didn't help; my mother's father and her sisters helped when they could—not much. She found babysitting at a church daycare center run by the minister's wife. For a few months, we lived in a room in a house my mother found listed on a noticeboard meant for pregnant women considering adoption.

"You would cry, and I would cry with you; I was so young and I didn't know what to do and your sadness made me sad," my mother said about those years. This seemed like the wrong thing. Too much fusion. But nonetheless I felt it had shaped me, how I felt powerfully for others sometimes, as if they were me. My father's absence makes her choices seem more dramatic, like they happened in front of a black backdrop.

I blamed her, later, for how hard it was to fall asleep in a room with any noise at all.

"You should have made sure I slept in noisy places, too," I said.

"But there was no one else around," she said. "What was I supposed to do—bang pots and pans?"

When I turned one, she got a waitressing job at the Varsity Theatre, a restaurant and art house cinema in Palo Alto. She found good, inexpensive daycare nearby at the Downtown Children's Center.

In 1980, when I was two, the district attorney of San Mateo County, California, sued my father for child-support payments. The state wanted him to pay child support and also to reimburse the state for the welfare payments already made. The lawsuit, initiated by the State of California, was made on my mother's behalf. My father responded by denying paternity, swearing in a deposition that he was sterile and naming another man he said was my father. After this man's dental and medical records were subpoenaed and didn't match, his lawyers claimed that "between August, 1977, and the beginning of January, 1978, plaintiff engaged in acts of sexual intercourse with a certain person or persons, the names of whom the defendant is ignorant, but plaintiff well knows."

I was required to take a DNA test. The tests were new, done with blood instead of buccal cells, and my mother said that the nurse could not find a vein and instead kept jabbing at my arm as I wailed. My father was there too because the court had ordered us all to arrive at the hospital at the same time. She and my father were polite to each other in the waiting room. The results came back: the chance we were related came to the highest the instruments could measure then, 94.4 percent. The court required my father to cover welfare back payments of about $6,000, child-support payments of $385 per month, which he increased to $500, and medical insurance until I was eighteen.

It is case 239948, filed on microfiche at the Superior Court, County of San Mateo, plaintiff vs. my father, defendant. My father signed it in lowercase, a less-practiced version of the way he signed later. My mother's signature is pinched and wobbly; she signed twice, once below and once on the line. A third start is crossed out—had she finished that signature, too, it would have hovered above the others.

The case was finalized on December 8, 1980, with my father's lawyers insistent to close, and my mother unaware of why the case that had dragged on for months was now being rushed to a conclusion. Four days later Apple went public and overnight my father was worth more than two hundred million dollars.

But before that, just after the court case was finalized, my father came to visit me once at our house on Oak Grove Avenue in Menlo Park, where we rented a detached studio. I don't remember the visit, but it was the first time I'd seen him since I'd been a newborn in Oregon.

"You know who I am?" he asked. He flipped his hair out of his eyes.

I was two and a half; I didn't.

"I'm *your father*." ("Like he was Darth Vader," my mother said later, when she told me the story.)

"I'm one of the most important people you will ever know," he said.

♦

On our street, pepper tree seeds in pink casings dangled down from tree limbs low enough to touch, crackling apart when I rubbed them between my fingers. The leaves, shaped like fish bones, swayed in breezes. Mourning doves made calls like out-of-tune woodwinds. The sidewalk around some tree trunks was cracked and warped.

"It's the tree roots," my mother said. "They're strong enough to push up the cement."

In the shower with my mother, the droplets made their way down the wall. Droplets were like animals: they jerked and took winding paths, slower and faster, leaving a trail. The shower was dark and closed, tiled and curtained. When my mother turned the water to hot, we yelled, "*Open pores!*" and when it was cold, we yelled, "*Closed . . . pores!*" She explained that pores were holes in the skin that opened with heat and closed with cold.

She held me in the shower and I nestled against her and it wasn't clear to me where she ended and I began.

My mother's goal was to be a good mother *and* a successful artist, and every time we moved, she brought two large books with us: an album of photographs of my birth and a book of art she called her portfolio. The first I wished she'd throw away because it contained nudity, and the second I worried she might lose.

Her portfolio contained a series of her drawings encased in plastic. That it was called a *portfolio* gave it dignity. I would flip through the pages, enjoying the weight of them in my hand. In one pencil drawing, a woman sat behind a desk in a windowed office, a gust of wind lifting her hair up into the shape of a fan and scattering sheets of white paper all around her, like a storm of moths.

"I like her hair," I said. "I like her skirt." I couldn't get enough of this woman; I wanted to be her, or for my mother to be her.

She'd made this drawing sitting at a table, using a mechanical pencil, an eraser, and the heel of her hand, blowing graphite and eraser leavings off the page. I loved the low murmur the pencil made on paper, and how her breath got even and slow when she worked. She seemed to consider her art with curiosity, not ownership, as if she weren't really the one making the marks.

It was the drawing's realism that impressed me. Every detail was precise like a photograph. But the scene was also fantastical. I loved how the woman sat in her pencil skirt and buttoned blouse, poised and dignified amid the chaos of the flying papers.

"It's just an illustration, not art," she said dismissively, when I asked her why she didn't make more like it. (It was a commercial piece, and less impressive than her paintings; I didn't know the difference between the two.) She'd been commissioned to illustrate a book called *Taipan*, and this was one of the pieces.

We didn't have a car, so I rode in a plastic seat on the back of her bicycle over sidewalks under the trees. Once, another rider came toward us on the sidewalk on his bicycle; my mother steered away, the other rider did the same, and they collided. We flew onto the sidewalk, skinning our hands and knees. We recovered on a lawn nearby. My mother sat and sobbed, her knees up and her shorts hanging down, one of her knees scraped and bloody. The man tried to help. She sobbed for too long in a way that I knew must be about more than the fall.

One evening soon after, I wanted to take a walk. She was depressed and didn't want to go, but I begged and pulled at her arm until she relented. Down the street, we saw a leaf-green VW hatchback with a sign: "For Sale by Owner, $700." She walked around it, looking in the windows.

"What do you think, Lisa? This might be just what we need."

She wrote down the name of the owner and his telephone number. Later, her father brought her to his company's loan department and cosigned a loan. My mother talked about my dragging her out for a walk that night as if I'd performed a heroic feat.

As we drove, she sang. Depending on her mood she would sing Joni Mitchell's "Blue" or "The Teddy Bears' Picnic" or "Tom Dooley." She sang one about asking God for a car and a television. She sang "Rocky Raccoon" when she was feeling happy, feisty; it had a part where she went up and down the scales without real words, like scat, making me laugh, making me embarrassed. I was sure she'd invented it—it was too strange to be a real song—and I was shocked years later when I heard the Beatles' version playing on the radio.

These were the Reagan years, and Reagan had denigrated single mothers and welfare mothers—calling single mothers welfare queens taking government handouts so they could drive Cadillacs—and later she talked about how Reagan was an idiot and a crook and had designated ketchup a vegetable in school lunches.

Around this time, my aunt Linda—my mother's younger sister— came to visit. Linda worked at Supercuts and was saving for a condo. We were out of money, and Linda said she drove an hour to give my mother twenty dollars for food and diapers; my mother used it to buy food and diapers, and also a bouquet of daisies and a small pack of patterned origami paper. Money, when we had it, was quick-burning, bright, like kindling. We had just a little or not enough. My mother was not good at saving or making money, but she loved beauty.

Linda remembers walking in as my mother was sitting on the futon and sobbing on the phone, saying, "Look, Steve, we just need money. Please send us some money." I was three, which seems too young, but Linda remembers that I'd grabbed the phone out of my mother's hand. "She just needs some money. Okay?" I'd said into the receiver, and hung up.

◆ ◆ ◆

"How much money does he have?" I asked my mother a couple years later.

"See that?" My mother pointed to a ripped bit of white paper the size of a pencil eraser. "That's what we have. And see that?" she said, pointing to a whole roll of white kraft paper. "That's what he has."

This was after we'd moved back from Lake Tahoe, having driven there in the green VW to live with my mother's boyfriend, who had once been a renowned rock climber before a tendon injury and a botched operation in his right ring finger meant he could no longer climb. He'd started a company making outdoor gear, and my mother made illustrations of gaiters and other sports equipment for his company, and also worked as a waitress in a diner. Later, after they broke up, he would become a successful vacuum cleaner salesman and a born-again Christian, but those days he was still sometimes featured in magazine articles about rock climbing. One day, in the grocery store, my mother pointed to the cover of a magazine, a picture of someone hanging from a cliff. "That's him," she said. "He was a world-*class* rock climber." A tiny speck on the mountain—I could hardly make him out. I doubted it was the same man who took me on walks through the cedar forest in Skylandia Park that led to the beach.

"And this," she said, opening another magazine, "is your father." Now *here* was a face I could see. My father was handsome, with dark hair, red lips, a good smile. The rock climber was indeterminate, while my father was significant. Even though the rock climber was the one who took care of me, I pitied him now for his inconsequence, and also felt bad to pity him, because he was the one who was around.

We'd lived in Tahoe for almost two years when my mother wanted to leave the rock climber and move back to the Bay Area.

This was around the time the story came out, the "Machine of the Year," about my father and computers in *Time* magazine, in January 1983, when I was four, in which he'd hinted that my mother had slept with many men and lied. In it, he talked about me, saying, "Twenty-eight percent of the male population of the United States could be the father"—probably based on a manipulation of the DNA test result.

After she read the article, my mother moved in slow motion, the muscles on her face slack. She cooked dinner with the kitchen lights off, except for a dim light shining from under one cabinet. But in a few days she'd recovered herself and her sense of humor, and she sent my father a picture of me sitting naked on a chair in our house, wearing only those Groucho Marx joke glasses with the big plastic nose and fake mustache.

"I think it's your kid!" she wrote on the back of the picture. He had a mustache then, and wore glasses and had a big nose.

In response, he sent her a check for five hundred dollars, and that was the money she used to move us back to the Bay Area, where we would sublet a room for a month in Menlo Park in a house on Avy Avenue with a hippie who kept bees.

The day after we returned from Tahoe, my father wanted to show us his new house. I hadn't seen him for years, and I wouldn't see him for years after that. The memory of this day, the outlandish house and my strange father, seemed surreal when I thought of it later, as if it hadn't really happened.

He came to pick us up in his Porsche.

The house had no furniture, only many cavernous rooms. My mother and I found a church organ set up on a raised part of floor in a huge, dank room somewhere, a wooden shell of foot pedals arrayed below and two whole rooms with latticed walls filled with hundreds of metal pipes, some so large I could fit inside them, some smaller than the nail on my pinkie finger, and every size in between.

Each was held vertically in a wooden socket made specifically to hold it.

I found an elevator and went up and down it several times until Steve said, okay, enough.

The face you saw upon entering the driveway turned out to be the thin side, and on the other side, the one that faced the lawn, it was vast, huge white arches with hot-pink bougainvillea billowing off. "The house is shit," Steve said to my mother. "The construction's shit. I'm going to tear it down. I bought this place for the trees." I felt a stab of shock, but they continued walking as if nothing had happened. How could he care about trees when there was such a house? Would he tear it down before I had a chance to come back?

His *s*'s sounded like a match doused in water. He walked tilted forward as if he were walking uphill; his knees never seemed to straighten all the way. His dark hair fell against his face, and he cast it out of his eyes by jerking his head. His face looked fresh against the dark, shiny hair. Being near him in the bright light with the smells of dirt and trees, the spaciousness of the land, was electric and magical. Once I caught him looking at me sidelong, a brown sharp eye.

He pointed to three huge oak trees at the end of the large lawn. "Those," he said to my mother. "That's why I bought this place."

Was it a joke? I couldn't tell.

"How old are they?" my mother asked.

"Two hundred years." My arms could reach around only the smallest section of trunk.

We walked back up toward the house then down a small hill to a large pool in the middle of a field of tall, untended grasses, and we stood on the lip looking in where thousands of dead bugs webbed the surface of the water: black spiders, daddy longlegs, a dead one-wing dragonfly. You could hardly see the water for the bugs. There was a frog, white belly up, and so many dead leaves the water had turned thick and dark, the color of ink.

"Seems like you've got some pool cleaning to do, Steve," my mother said.

"Or I might just take it out," he said, and that night I dreamt the bugs and animals rose up from the pool as dragons, flapping violently into the sky, leaving the water a clear turquoise netted with white light.

A few weeks later, my father bought us a silver Honda Civic to replace our green VW. We went to pick it up at the lot.

Several months after that, my mother wanted a break and we went on an overnight trip to Harbin Hot Springs. On the way back it was night and raining, and on a freeway that wound through the hills, a couple of hours from home, she got lost. The wiper was better on her side; the one on my side was warped in the middle and left a streak. The windshield was chipped in front of my seat in the shape of a small eye where a pebble must have hit at some point and left a mark.

"There's nothing. Nothing," she said. I didn't know what she meant. She started to cry. She made a high and continuous mew like a bow drawn along a string.

At twenty-eight, and newly single again, she found it much harder than she'd anticipated to raise a child. Her family was unable to offer much support; her father, Jim, who lent her small amounts of money and would soon buy me my first pair of sturdy shoes, was not present in any larger way. Her stepmother, Faye, would later babysit me sometimes, but did not like babies in her house, mussing up her furniture. Her older sister, Kathy, was also a single mother with a small baby, and her two younger sisters were starting their own lives. My mother felt deeply ashamed to be unmarried and felt herself cast out of society.

We passed the same hills we'd passed in the daytime, when they'd seemed smooth and benevolent like camel humps. Now they made desolate black curves below a dark sky. She cried harder, in round sobbing gasps. I was stoic and silent. An oncoming car approached

from the other side of the freeway, and I glanced at her to see her face
as the strip of light from the headlights fell on her for a moment.

"I think we missed the exit. I have no idea." It rained harder
and she turned the windshield wipers to high. The rain filled in the
half-circles as soon as they were cleared.

"I don't want this life," she sobbed. "I want out. I'm sick of living. Fuuuuuck!" She screamed loud, a wail. A foghorn. I covered my
ears. "Fuck you! Fuck you!" she screamed at the windshield. As if
she were furious at the windshield.

I was four and strapped down by two belts in my car seat, facing forward beside her (this was before children sat in the backs of
cars). In the cars that passed and the ones around us, I imagined
peace, and I wished to be inside one of those cars instead. If only
she would be the way she was before, in the daylight. One version
of her was inaccessible to the other. As she was yelling, she said later,
even if she could not stop herself, she was aware that I was old
enough to remember this.

"I have nothing," she said. "This life is shit. Shiiiiit." She struggled
to catch her breath. "I don't want to live anymore! This shitty life. I
haaaate this life!" Her throat was like gravel, her voice hoarse from
yelling. "This hell life."

She pushed hard on the pedal when she yelled, so the car leapt
forward, ground down along the road, rain like spit flying, like she
wanted the engine to be part of her voice.

"Fucking *Time* magazine. Fucking fucking fucker." Fucker was
sharper than fuck, had a spark at the end. It poked my sternum. She
let out a yell, no words, shook her head side to side so her hair flew,
bared her teeth, slapped the dash with the flat of her hand, made
me jump.

"What?" she screamed at me, because I jumped. "Whaaaat?"

I remained stiff; I became the idea of a girl stiff in her car seat.

Suddenly she veered off the freeway with such violence I thought
we were driving off the road to our death, but it was a ramp.

She pulled over, jammed on the brakes, and sobbed into her folded arms. Her back shook. Her sadness enveloped me, I could not escape it, nothing I could do would stop it. In a few minutes, she started driving again, took a freeway overpass toward another road. She continued to cry, but with less violence, and at some point I asked the cracked glass eye, the nick in the windshield where the pebble had hit, to watch the road for me, a kind of prayer, and I slept.

At the height of her hopelessness and noise, I'd felt a calm presence near us, even though I knew we were alone in the watery hell, the car jerking. Some benevolent presence that cared for us but could not interfere, maybe sitting in the back seat. The presence could not stop it, could not help it, only watch and note it. I wondered later if it was a ghostly version of me now, accompanying my younger self and my mother in that car.

The next morning, the man who tended the bees wore a white crinkly suit with attached gloves and a hat with a net sewn in. The bees lived in a slatted box in the small backyard. From the side of the kitchen, an attachment at the back of the bungalow, we looked out at the yard. He called to me, motioning for me to come over and look.

"There's nothing to be afraid of," he said.

"She's fairly allergic to bees," my mother called to him. Once I'd stepped on a bee and my foot swelled up; I couldn't walk on it for a week.

"My bees are really happy," he said. "They're not going to sting." He removed his hat while he spoke so we could see his face. "These are honeybees; they're friendly," he said.

"But you're wearing a suit," my mother said. "She's in shorts. She has no protection."

"It's because I have to get in there, take their honey. Otherwise, I'd be dressed like you. They don't *want* to sting you," he said to me. "Do you know what happens to them if they do? They give up their life." He paused. "Why would they want to give up their life to hurt you when they're happy and you're not doing them any harm?"

"Are you sure?" my mother asked him again. The setup looked wrong, but what did we know about bees.

"Yeah," he said, putting on his hat. I'd never seen a hive up close.

"Okay . . ." my mother said, only partially convinced. I walked over to where he stood and looked down at the teeming, velvety mass. The bees made a shimmering brown carpet. Some flew higher, bobbing above like tiny balloons on strings. One landed on my upper cheek and began to walk in a circle. I didn't know this circling was a kind of preparatory dance. When I tried to swipe it off, it was affixed, then it stung.

I ran back to my mother, who pulled me into the kitchen. The open windows carried her voice.

"What were you thinking?" she yelled at him, opening cabinets one after the other, then grabbing the baking soda, mixing it into paste with water in a bowl. "How dare you." She squatted beside me, pulled the stinger out with tweezers, then patted the paste on my cheek with the pads of her fingers as it began to swell.

"What an idiot," she muttered. "In a full body suit. Telling a girl she wasn't in danger."

When we had a little money to spare, we drove to Draeger's Market, where a wall of rotisserie ovens behind the deli counter held rows of slowly turning meat. It smelled of sweet dirt and steam. You could tell the uncooked chickens because they were bright white with orange powder dusted on the surface; the cooked ones were brown and taut. She pulled a number.

"One half rotisserie chicken, please," she said when our number came up. A man used what looked like garden shears to cut the bird in half, the ribs making a satisfying crunch. He slipped the half into a white bag lined with silver.

Back in the car she put the bag between us on the emergency brake and ripped the bag open and we ate the chicken with our fingers as the windows steamed up around us.

When we finished, she crumpled the bag around the bones and wiped my oily fingers with a napkin, then examined my palm. The place where my hand folds made grooves across the surface like a dry riverbed seen from a great height. No two people have the same lines, she'd explained to me, but everyone has a similar pattern.

She tilted the plane of my palm to make the indentations catch the light.

"Oh, God," she said, wincing.

"What?" I asked.

"It's just . . . not so good. The lines tatter." Her face looked stricken. She went distant, quiet. We went over this same routine many times in different variations, accruing details as I got older, each time my mother making the same mistakes, as if it was new.

"What does that mean?" Panic in my chest, stomach.

"I've never seen anything like it. The lifeline, the curved one, this one—holes, bubbles."

"What's wrong with bubbles?"

"They mean trauma, fracturing," she said. "I'm so sorry." I knew she wasn't apologizing for the hand, but for my life. The start of my life that I didn't remember. For how hard things were. She might have assumed I didn't know what a family was supposed to look like, but once, around this time, as I'd chased a boy in a playground wearing a pair of too-big shoes, she overheard me say to him, scornfully, "*You* don't even *have* a father."

"What's that line?" I asked, pointing to the one that ran from below the pinkie finger.

"Your heart line," she said. "Also difficult." I was swept up in what felt like grief, even though we'd been happy a moment before.

"And this one?" The last one, straight through the middle of my palm, branching off the lifeline. Crisper than the others at first—oh, hope!—but then it drooped, then thinned and split, like a twig.

"Wait," she said, brightening. "This hand's your left hand?" She was dyslexic and had gotten them mixed up.

"Yes," I said.

"Okay, good. The left tells me the circumstances you were *given*. Let me see your right one."

I gave her my other hand and she held it carefully, tracing the lines, turning it to see. The residual grease from the chicken made the skin reflect. "This hand tells me what you'll make of your life," she said. "It's *much* better on this side."

How did she know? I wondered if she learned to read palms in India.

In India, people didn't use their left hand in public, she said. In social situations, the right was used exclusively. This was because they didn't use toilet paper, but used their left hand instead, washing it afterward. This horrified me.

"If I go to India," I said, whenever India came up, "I'll carry my own roll."

She told a story about India, how she went to a festival in Allahabad called the Kumbha Mela that happened only once every twelve years, this one located at the confluence of the Ganges and the Yamuna Rivers. There was a huge crowd. In the distance, a very holy man, sitting up on a parapet, was blessing oranges and throwing them into the crowd.

"He was so far that he seemed like he was only an inch tall," she said.

The other oranges didn't land close to her, she said, but then he threw this one orange and she could tell it was coming toward her and—*bam*—it hit her right in the chest, right in the heart, took the wind out of her.

It bounced off and a group of men jumped after it, she said, so she didn't get to keep it. But I knew it meant something special

about her, about us, that the holy orange thrown from so far away
had hit *her* in the heart.

"You know," she said, "when you were born you came shooting
out like some sort of rocket." She'd told me this many times before,
but I let her say it again, as if I'd forgotten. "I went to these birth
classes and all of them said I'd have to push and then there I was
and you were coming out so fast I couldn't stop you." I loved this
story—how, unlike other babies, I had not made her force me into
the air and this had saved her something, and meant something
about me.

All of this—the palm, the orange, the birth—meant I was going
to be just fine, as an adult.

"When I'm an adult, you'll be *old*," I said. I imagined myself
progressing down the lifeline; getting older would mean I was further
down the line.

We walked to Peet's Coffee around the corner, where the man
gave her a free coffee, and then we sat on the bench outside, where
it was warm in the sunlight. The double line of sycamore trees around
the square across from the coffee shop had been pruned down to
their stems almost and looked like playing jacks, short branches with
fat balls at the ends. The air smelled like raw trees.

"Like this?" She pretended to walk like an old lady with a cane,
slumped over with no teeth. She straightened. "But sweetie, I'm only
twenty-four years older than you are. I'll still be *young* when you're
grown up."

I said, "Oh," as if I agreed. But it didn't matter what she said, or
how she explained. I saw us as a seesaw: when one of us had power
or happiness or substantiality, the other must fade. When I was still
young, she'd be old. She would smell like old people, like used flower
water. I would be new and green and smell of freshly cut branches.

◆

Halfway through the school year I joined a kindergarten class in a public school in Palo Alto. Before this I'd gone to another school, but my mother thought the class there had too many boys, so I'd transferred here. On my first day, one of the teaching assistants led me out to the side of the building and took a Polaroid, which she tacked on the board near the photographs of other students, and wrote my name underneath. I had foolishly wrapped my hand around the top of my head because I thought it would look good, while the other students were seated in front of a blue backdrop. The image was light-saturated, makeshift. I felt it revealed not only that I had started late but also that I was insubstantial, washed out by light.

The teacher, Pat, tall and plump, had a singsong voice and wore jean skirts down to her ankles, sandals with socks, T-shirts that hung over her large bosom, and reading glasses on a string. During recess, we played behind the classroom on a wooden jungle gym with a series of planks connecting the parts. A rope net between two wooden platforms was called the humping pit. Humping, the way I imagined it, demanded an undulation and a catch, an undulation and a catch. There was something sickly about it. Soon after I started at the school, I fell inside the netted part, and others yelled, "Hump-ing! Hump-ing!" as I scrambled out.

This kindergarten put an emphasis on reading, but I couldn't read. For each book completed, students received a small teddy bear.

I memorized a book to trick one of the teaching assistants into handing over a bear.

"I'm ready," I said. We sat down on the floor with our backs against the bookshelf in the reading section, the book on my lap. I spoke the words I believed to be on each page, based on what I'd memorized and the corresponding pictures. Two pages in, her face hardened and her lips thinned.

"You turned the page at the wrong place," she said. "And you missed a word."

"Just one bear," I said. "Please."

"Not yet," she said.

Daniela had amassed twenty-two; I asked her if I could have one.

"You have to read a *book* to get one," Daniela said.

I began to feel there was something gross and shameful about me, and also to know that it was too late to change it, that nothing could be done. I was different from other girls my age, and anyone good and pure could immediately sense this and would be repulsed. One indication was the photograph. Another was that I could not read. The last was that I was meticulous and self-conscious in a way I could tell the other girls were not. My desires were too strong and furious. I was wormy inside, as if I'd caught whatever diseases or larvae were passed through raw eggs and flour when I snuck raw cookie dough. I felt this quality in myself, and I was sure it must show when people saw me, so whenever I passed a mirror, caught my reflection by accident, and saw that I was not as dirty or repulsive as I pictured myself, it gave me a start.

During the free reading period, Shannon and I snuck around the back of the kindergarten classroom, past the jungle gym, to a hidden area paved with rocks between thick bushes and elementary school classrooms. Shannon had white blonde hair, white whiskery eyebrows and lashes; she also could not read. Her trousers were twisted so the seam did not line up with the middle of her legs. We threw rocks at the classroom windows and then clutched each other as though we were humping and writhed around on the rocks together.

Pat had told us that a new boy was coming to join our class.

"Let's spit water on him," I said.

"Yeah," she said. "From the fountain."

I had a feeling it was going to be funny, that even *he* would find it funny.

On the morning the new boy arrived, we waited near the water fountain. He wore shorts and had dark hair and looked confident; I'd imagined him to be fragile and small.

We filled our mouths and caught him at the start of the path, under the tree. "Hey," Shannon said, the cup of her mouth turned up. I glanced at her, trying not to laugh; her neck was shaking, a rivulet of water streaming down her chin. It would be funny, funnier than anything I'd ever done, and also clever.

The boy looked up.

"Uh, uh, uh," we said, almost in unison. After the final "uh," we spat. Before his expression changed into shock—before his parents, walking behind him, rushed over and kneeled down and comforted him—and I realized we'd done it, I was full of high confidence.

Shannon and I were separated, our mothers were called to come pick us up.

On the way home my mother spoke continuously.

"How did the boy feel? How do you think he felt?"

"Bad," I said. A moment after spitting I had been aware that it was not in any way his joke, as it was when I imagined it beforehand. It was only our joke, and it ended when the water hit him.

"I'm embarrassed. I feel bad for that boy," my mother said, driving too fast. "But I also blame Pat. What did she expect? Pat and her stupid fucking bears."

◆

The next year I went to a different school, the Waldorf School of the Peninsula. It was new, founded that year. The parents had gathered over the summer to paint the walls of the classrooms, and to choose the wood, sand down, and varnish each of our desks for the start of first grade. The tuition was about six hundred dollars per semester, discounted for us, and my mother figured she could make it work if we didn't buy any furniture. But still, we were often behind on the tuition, my mother contacting my father and asking if he could send a small check, which he did twice.

One day, from our apartment on Channing Avenue, we drove to Los Altos, where my mother cleaned a house. Her friend Sandra used to have the cleaning jobs, but gave the houses to my mother before she moved away. Sandra liked us; she once saved a newspaper clipping about a mother and daughter driving in winter: the three-year-old girl had walked alone two miles through the snow and found help for her mother, who'd crashed into a snowbank and lost consciousness. "That's something Lisa would do," she told my mother.

The woman who owned the house in Los Altos showed me how to use mayonnaise on the leaves of her dusty ficus plant; I polished them into a glossy, deep green. When my mother finished and the woman paid her, we drove straight to the bank to make the deposit, and from there to University Art, a few streets away.

"Hello, I'm a member here," she said to the man behind the counter. Artists had memberships and received discounts. "I'm worried that a check I gave you a few days ago might have bounced," she said. She often talked about checks bouncing. I didn't know what she meant, only that it sounded good even though it wasn't. "I want to write you another one, but I'd like to get a few paints first?"

"Of course," the man said. "Come back when you're finished shopping and we'll take care of it."

The man smiled; we smiled back. My mother was earnest and charming. Together we brought light into rooms.

She moved slowly along the row, touching each tube, looking at colors she liked even if she didn't need them or couldn't afford them. Turquoise, carmine, burnt sienna, gamboge—all dangling by their necks, the tubes pristine and without dents. "Different colors are different prices," she said, "based on the ingredients." The ingredients were colored substances harvested from the earth. The brushes were made of nylon or animal hair, different hair for different purposes, expensive. They were enclosed in plastic tubes and shaped into hard sharp points that broke apart and became soft when used. After my mother used her brushes and cleaned them, she licked them into points herself so they would keep their shape.

That day, she bought a tube of burnt umber. She wrote the check for the full amount at the register. She didn't take a bag, but cradled the tube in her palm on the way back to the car.

From there we went to a bookstore around the corner from Peet's. The man behind the desk, who owned the shop, spoke with my mother; I could tell he was intelligent. He was old, bearded, with bushy eyebrows, like an unkempt God. I wanted him to pay attention to me.

"My father is Steve Jobs," I said to the man. I wasn't supposed to tell people who my father was. My mother watched, bemused—we were the only ones in the store.

"Oh?" the man said, and put his glasses on his head.

"Yes," I said. It was like the shine on the leaf, it made him look. "And I'm the smartest girl in the world."

♦

"We're going to the Ellens' house to swim," my mother said one afternoon when she picked me up from school.

This was mixed news: the Ellens swam in the nude.

"Do we have to go *there*?" I said.

"I need adult company," she said. The Ellens weren't her favorites either, but we didn't have other friends who hosted gatherings, and they had invited us to swim.

On the car radio on the way over, people talked of the depletion of the ozone layer. It was torn and thinning; I pictured it like ripped tulle in the uppermost part of the sky; without it we would burn under the sun.

The Ellens' house was large and dark-shingled, in Old Palo Alto, where the trees and the lots were larger. The inside was big and hollow, sepia-toned, with boxes in corners, dirty windows, dust. The pool was a turquoise rectangle inside a large yard surrounded by a tall, dark wooden fence, which, to my relief, blocked the view from the street. Around the pool, pale-skinned, naked adults sat on mismatched chairs or on the concrete lip, talking, occasionally dipping toes and fingers into the water. When women entered the pool, they did it slowly, spreading their hands out on the surface, bracing as they glided in deeper.

"Will you wear your bathing suit?" I asked her.

"I wasn't planning on it."

"Please wear it. Please."

"Don't be a grandmother, Lisa. It might be strange if I'm the only one wearing a bathing suit."

"Do it for me," I said. I felt safe when her body was contained.

"Fine," she said. "I'll do it for you, conventional as you are."

Hippies let dust collect in the corners of their houses. They did not replace old, brown furniture. They spoke with elongated vowels that drooped between consonants like wet sheets sagging on a line. "Heyy there," they said. They advertised freedom, but it wasn't the right kind of freedom. It was drifting or sinking. I was convinced that if we mingled with them, whatever feeling of escape, of getting toward the light and buoyancy I could tell some other people had, would be gone, swallowed up, merged with swamp. My mother was susceptible to hippies because she was lonely. She would settle for them. She yearned to get away from me sometimes, to be more free. But hippies gave me the creeps. When she suggested hanging out with them, I became a stick-in-the-mud, a dervish of conservatism: my mother's guardian and jailer.

But most hippies we knew were harmless, hapless even. I sometimes questioned her about one she'd dated for two months a few years before who apparently told her he'd keep dating her only if she gave me up for adoption. The parallels between hippies were evident, I thought—the long slow vowels, the dun-colored clothes, the dull eyes, the lack of normal jobs—and by bringing up this one, I hoped to show her plainly her lack of discernment.

What we were really talking about was not hippies, though, but how she hadn't been sure she wanted me when I was little, and even now I felt her fantasy of escape—from me, from her life with me—and I wanted to make her ashamed, and repentant.

"He was awful," I said, "that hippie boyfriend you had. I hate him."

"*Hate's* a strong word, Lisa. I don't think you *hate* him." She paused. "Though I did hear, after dating me, he was dating some woman who had a dog—she totally loved her dog—and he told her that he'd keep dating her only if she gave her dog away. Can you believe it? He found the one thing that was most important to a person and asked her to give it up for him. He was very troubled, Lisa. We don't need to hate him for it."

I hated him all the same.

Ada Ellen was thin, a sprite, with a pleasing, scratchy voice, luminous honey-colored skin, green eyes, and golden hair that flew out from her head in ringlet wisps. She was only five, almost two years younger than me, but mature for her age, maybe because she was home-schooled. She and I wore bathing suits.

We jumped into the pool. Afterward we got towels in the house beside the large tan washing machine, away from the group of adults.

"Shhh," she said, showing me a pack of Juicy Fruit gum hidden in her towel. I wondered how she'd gotten it. For both of us, sugar gum was forbidden.

We slipped past the naked adults and danced carefully over the rocks and pointy grasses to the one bush in the middle of the yard we might hide behind. I walked as fast as I could, finding the blank dirt patches in between tufts of sharp, dry grasses and stones. The bush had hardly enough leaves to give us privacy. We unfolded the silver paper and we chewed piece after piece, eating the powdered sticks like candy. The wads grew in our mouths, pillows of tooth-colored gum.

"What are you two doing over there?" my mother called.

Ada and I emerged from the bush and stood side by side, facing the naked adults, my mother in her suit, and continued to chew. Ada's triangle scapulae poked out of her back.

"Is that gum?" Anne, Ada's mother, asked. "Who gave that to you?" Anne's skin was a creamy yellow hue, like milk left out. Her breasts, small and flat at the top, collected into sacs at the bottom. She wore a batik cloth around her hips.

"Gum fools your stomach into thinking that food is coming down," Anne continued. "If your stomach thinks food is coming down, it starts to produce stomach acid to *prepare* for the food."

My stomach ached. It would not stop me.

A woman I didn't know who sat beside Anne, naked except for a towel, said, "The acid will eat away at the lining of your stomach."

Hippies were not bothered about clothing, I thought, but they sure had strict rules about sugar.

"It's true," my mother said to me.

"Right here," Anne said, cupping her hand for us to spit it out. "Spit it out."

Ada spit first, and I followed.

"Go brush. Both of you." We walked into the dark house, up the stairs to a bathroom on the second floor. I used Ada's toothbrush. She watched me go to all the sides of my mouth, and as she watched me, she unintentionally moved her mouth like mine, a weak mirror image, her upper left in motion with my upper right, as if she were brushing her teeth at the same time.

On one of these afternoons after my mother left, I stayed to play with Ada.

"Follow me," Ada said, slipping into a bare room at the top of the stairs.

Anne was sitting cross-legged on the floor in the middle of the room, facing the door. She had the batik cloth wrapped around her legs and was naked on the top. Her husband, Matthew, was fully dressed and stood against the two windows at the far side of the room. Ada stood on one side of her mother, facing me.

"Have you ever tried nursing?" Ada asked in an insistent, cheery voice I'd never heard her use before, as if it were a performance.

"Ada likes to nurse," Matthew said from the other side of the room. "You should try it too."

I stood facing all of them. "No, thanks," I said.

"It's great. I do it all the time," Ada said in the same oversweet voice that would be one of the most haunting parts of the incident, how my friend had changed, become robotic and artificial, turned against me. Anne's arm on her back.

"No, thanks," I said, again. "I just don't want to," but I could feel pressure building like the air before a storm.

"Show her," Anne said, and then to my surprise, Ada knelt down and lay sideways in her mother's lap and sucked at a breast.

Matthew took a few steps forward so he was standing behind Anne. "Just try it. You'll like it," he said. "Just once."

Ada stopped and sat on her knees beside her mother. "I love it," she said. "It's great."

At this point I understood that I would not be able to leave this room until I'd sucked on Anne's breast. Maybe not for long. It was a humiliating notion; I was glad no one else was there to watch.

"Okay," I said, and crouched down into Anne's lap like Ada had.

There was no milk at all, her skin was tacky, a few degrees colder than my mouth, and tasted bland. No salt. I wasn't sure how long it was supposed to last. If I stopped too soon, I might have to do it again. I closed my eyes. One one thousand, two one thousand, three one thousand, four one thousand, five.

"Thanks. That was great," I said, sitting up.

"The Ellens made me nurse from Anne," I told my mother a couple of weeks later. I'd just built up the courage. We'd already seen them again; I didn't want to get stuck alone with them and feared I would if I waited longer to tell. We were sitting in the car in the driveway about to go somewhere.

"*Nurse?*" She froze.

"I had to do it."

"They forced you to *nurse?*"

"They wouldn't let me leave." I hoped she wouldn't be ashamed of me for giving in.

She yelled, "*What?*" and turned off the engine and ran back into the house. I got out of the car and stood in the driveway near the bottlebrush tree. Over the next few days I heard her speaking to people on the phone. Often she was crying. Years later she said she'd called my father, who said she shouldn't have called the police, downplaying the seriousness of the incident. She called other people. I assumed her reaction and these phone calls meant I wouldn't have to be alone with the Ellens again, and in fact we did not see them again after that. I was relieved, although I worried about Ada. My mother's new boyfriend Ron said she should call the police, and she did, filing a report.

♦

Before Ron, my mother spent some time with a man who made art out of sticks.

I didn't like him, or the way she fluttered near him, sparkled, seemed to levitate and be made up of air rather than a comforting solid. He was aloof, spoke softly, as if he were hiding something, and was shy in a way that made me suspect he was sneaky. One night after dinner we followed him to his car and he opened the trunk. Inside, on a blanket, was a stick he'd wrapped in places with several bands of colored thread and string. Attached to one section was a crystal, and to another, a feather.

"So these are what I make," he said softly.

"It's beautiful," my mother said. I hoped she was faking.

"This is a powerful crystal," he said. "And I found the eagle feather on a walk."

"An *eagle* feather. That's incredible," she said. She took it in her hand, reverent.

"But you don't really like them, do you? The sticks?" I said, when he wasn't around.

"I do," she said.

"They're just sticks. He's not a real artist like you." I wanted to remind her of her talent, the calm woman in the windy mess of papers.

"I think they're more than that," she said. "I mean, he wraps them. It takes a lot of time. Certain sticks call to him. Nature speaks to him. I might even make one myself."

"Oh *brother*," I said.

"Really. I might."

"They're sticks, Mom. Sticks."

"Okay. Maybe they're a little silly," she said.

She was back.

◆ ◆ ◆

My mother worked a few afternoons per week as a waitress at a restaurant and patisserie nearby, where she'd brought me once. She told
me the secret: the owner, a pastry chef who sat in the back making
the petits fours, cut the strings of frosting between the cakes by using
his tongue to lick the metal nozzle of the frosting bag. When I came
to visit her there, I ordered a cake anyway. I wasn't usually allowed to
eat sugar and it was too delicious to care about germs.

"The world is made of more space than matter," she said a few
days later, when we were at home. She was reading a book about
quantum physics, and it put her in an expansive mood. She said the
atoms are so far apart that there isn't a difference between space and
matter, because matter is mostly made of space; even if it looks like
a body, a couch, a table, it isn't, it's space—and if you could *really*
see this, you could walk through walls.

My mother said that some enlightened mystics could propel
themselves through walls, as if walls did not exist; they knew something about quantum physics, even if only intuitively, of the vast
spaces between atoms—larger than football fields, she said. I'd never
seen a football field. These mystics were not prone to the same illu-
sions of divided space as we were, and because they understood the
false quality of solid matter they were no longer forced to abide by
physical laws. There were anecdotal reports, she said, of gurus being
in two places at once, speaking with two different groups of people
at exactly the same time.

She told me about this in our living room. I tried to imagine
the bedroom beyond the wall, to *believe* in the absence of matter so
thoroughly that it dissipated before me. For a breathless few hours
the next day—after I put my finger in front of my nose a few inches,
focused beyond it, and my finger faded to semitransparency—I
thought I could see through my finger. I was capable of miracles.
Walls would be next.

Lifelines

When I was in second grade, my mother taught a weekend art class for me and five other students. She drove us to a local farm called Hidden Villa where we would draw and paint from nature. "Two to a seat belt," she said.

I sat in the front, squished against Mary-Ellen, who had short hair and dimples and a steady, calm way of breathing I could feel against my back. My mother loaded our equipment into the trunk. Each student had a small folding easel, a Masonite board on which to clip or tape the paper, a watercolor paint set, a charcoal, an eraser, and a soft cloth.

"What are we going to draw?" Joe asked.

"I'm not sure," she said. "We'll find something when we get there."

She wasn't like the other mothers; she and I weren't like other families. I worried that, as our teacher, she would reveal us, how strange we were.

A few days before, I'd walked in on my mother squatting on top of the toilet seat, perched up high, her trousers around her knees like a curtain, her feet planted on the rim.

"What are you doing?" I asked, horrified.

"I learned it in India," she said. "It's a better position. Close the door."

The farm was inside hills covered in bay laurel trees with thin trunks dropping yellow half-moon leaves, a bright green strip of miner's lettuce along the road. The air was glassy and fragrant with the smell of the trees. It was a triangle of flat land surrounded by layers of hills, owned by a family that had made money on asbestos. My mother said asbestos was insulation that turned out to be a kind of poison, and I thought about this at the farm, how clean the air was, how lush the farm, yet built on the proceeds of poison.

We collected our equipment and followed my mother into a field near the parking lot, where a small, barky tree stood up in isolation. A few leaves clung to the branches, shoots of grass like whiskers grew around the base of the trunk, with dirt clods visible between the neon blades. This one, she said.

We arranged our easels in a semicircle. Past the tree was a fenced garden, a barn, some sheds; beyond those, hills wrinkled up together at the end of the narrow valley like pinched skin. Tree, green grass, blue hills, then purple hills, sky—it would be hard to get the whole scene onto my small piece of paper.

"Stick the easels deep into the dirt to stabilize them," my mother said. She went around and pushed our easels into the rough ground, adjusting them, displaying her natural authority and comfort with the physical world, her bold speech and movements new to me, even a little frightening. Once we'd taped the paper to our Masonite boards, she stood in front of us with a pointed brush in one hand, her other hand held up flat like a page. "I want to show you how to use a brush before we start," she said. "You don't want to press down, head-on, like this"—she demonstrated, making the hairs on the brush splay out on her palm like a mop—"but draw the bristles along the paper in one direction, moving with, instead of against, the hairs." I had known for years how to use a brush and was annoyed to be instructed like the others.

We began to draw. The square-edged conté crayons were brown sticks that looked something like the branches themselves. We would paint on top of the drawing, to add color. "Don't draw the tree you *think* you see," my mother said. "Draw the tree. Trust your eye."

I wasn't sure where on the page to make the tree begin, from where it should grow up through the gradations of hills to the sky—the ground with the grasses took up almost as much room as the hills, I noticed, now that I was really looking at the scene before me. I worried my tree might end up in a tiny spot in the center, surrounded by the blank white space I knew my mother abhorred.

"That first mark takes courage," she said, glancing at my blank paper. "And remember: there are no straight lines in nature."

I made a few straight marks.

"A spill on the ground can be more interesting than a drawing," she said. It was a phrase I'd heard her say before, from one of her teachers at community college. When she and I drew together, she wouldn't let me use the black paint that came with a set, insisting that black was not a color, and that if I looked harder, I would see something else. She didn't believe in the "bad guy" and the "good guy" in books or movies either, and became angry with me when I referred to characters that way. To me, such titles, such a color, offered relief because they seemed like ledges where one could rest.

She walked around among us as we worked, helping one student smudge out a part that wasn't right, helping another begin to draw the place where a branch shot out from the trunk. "May I?" my mother said before she took the crayon from Mary-Ellen, addressing her as if she were an adult.

"I want you to try to capture the spirit of the tree," she said. "Not just the way it looks, but the life force inside it." It surprised me that no one smirked at this, that everyone continued to draw with the focus I lacked. Earlier I hadn't wanted to be associated with her; now I hoped to be singled out as her daughter, the insider, possessor of knowledge the others didn't have. I thought she spoke in a language no one understood but me, and I was ashamed of understanding it myself; but the other students listened as if they, too, understood, and were not ashamed.

It was difficult to see the tree only as it looked. It felt like writing with my left hand. The *idea* of the tree kept creeping back into my fingers and into my eyes, so that I had to move fast when I saw something, before it became the idea of the tree again.

"Close one eye if it helps," she said. I tried it; the world flattened. And then something unexpected happened: the branch I was drawing didn't jut. It was no longer a branch but a shape made of light, inside other shapes made of light. A thrill to see it. The tree was just a shape, nothing to do with branches. I drew it quickly, the way it looked, not the way it was.

There, I was finished. I'd seen it for a moment. It was enough.

We began to use the watercolors, adding a layer of color to the drawings we'd made.

"Trees need sunlight, water, nutrients," she said. "But if they have too many, too abundantly, they also don't flourish. Some struggle makes them stronger, makes the fruit trees produce better fruit." She would repeat this idea many times over the years, past the point when I understood it was a metaphor.

"See colors as they are, not the ones they're supposed to be," she said.

She'd shown me once how an orange in a bowl can be blue, reflecting sky, or purple in shadow, or white with glare. When this sight happens, she said, it's a surprise; that's how you know it's true.

There's no such thing as a color without a color around it. Even the color of the paper is not nothing. Everything matters, not just of itself, but in relation to everything else. At some point she must have touched her face, maybe brushing a strand of hair away, and when I looked, she had a brown smudge across the ridge of her nose. "Mom," I said, "you have charcoal on your face."

"It doesn't matter, Lisa," she said.

Before the parents came, she went around and made comments, looking at our drawings. She called it "the Critique." "I love the composition," she said to one student.

"Beautiful, subtle," she said to another.

She found Joe's picture particularly impressive. "This part," she said, pointing to the hills, "is sublime. Wow."

In mine, she complimented the swishy movement of the tree but said it was incomplete. I'd finished too quickly, she said, drawing and painting impatiently, as if the whole exercise had been a race.

◆

"Steve's supposed to come over and bring the bed tomorrow." She said his name like we knew him. He'd offered to bring this bed over twice already, but then he didn't show. My mother had curtained the small alcove with a skylight off the living room, and this was where the bed would go, replacing the futon on the floor where I slept when I didn't share her bed. His girlfriend, whom we'd never met, had even called my mother to apologize, promising that this time he'd show up.

Steve. I knew so little about him. He was like those Michelangelo sculptures of men trapped in rough stone, half smooth, half rough, that made you imagine the part inside that had not yet come out.

"He didn't come last time," I said. We'd waited for an hour. Maybe he didn't know what bed to buy; maybe he didn't know how to find our house. Maybe my mother told him the wrong time.

"He's promised to come this time," she said. "So we'll see."

We waited inside first, and then we went outside to the asphalt circle and watched the street. I was so excited for his arrival that I'd worn my nice dress, given to me by the rock climber, and I was fluttery in my stomach. Cars passed outside the driveway. Each one held the possibility of being him. We waited. "I don't think he's going to come," my mother finally said after some time. We went back inside. I felt like I'd been emptied out. The day, charged with excitement, newness, extravagance, and mystery, unlike other days, changed back into a dull and ordinary day. Just us again, and nothing to do.

"Let's go for a skate?"

When my mother and I went roller skating, our favorite thing was to find the soft cement. If you were walking, the seam between one type of pavement and another was not obvious, but on skates you felt a clear difference between the two. We said the soft pavement was "like butter." Transitioning onto the buttery parts after the rough, jangly pavement—the roughest parts vibrating up through my knees and hips to made my cheeks shake and my eyeballs itch—felt like floating.

One section we'd found was near the lot on Oak Grove where we used to live. Our old detached studio, along with the main house, had since been ripped down and replaced with a brown-shingled Comerica Bank. "Your umbilical cord is buried in the dirt somewhere underneath that bank," she said when we passed it. This disturbed me; surely other mothers didn't bury umbilical cords in yards.

The soft cement was located in front of a faux-Palladian office building, with two swooping walkways curving up over a rock garden to an entrance door made of tinted glass. The cement on the ramps was silken, lined with curved iron banisters. We skated in a circle up one, down the other, and back up again.

She kept glancing at me as we skated; I didn't let on that I knew she was looking. "You know, you're just the daughter I wanted," she said. "Exactly the one. On the farm before you were born there was this little girl, three or four years old, with her mother. A little Taurus girl, precocious and smart. I thought, I want that."

"I know," I said. She'd told me the story before. ("I don't only love you," she'd said often. "I also *like* you.") "And he named a computer after me?"

"He pretended he hadn't, afterward." And then she told me the story—again—of how they'd named me together in the field, how he vetoed all her choices until she thought of Lisa. "He loves you," she said. "He just doesn't *know* he loves you." This was hard to grasp. "If he saw you, really saw you and understood what he was missing, how he wasn't showing up for you, it would kill him. He'd be like this." She stopped skating and grabbed the railing and clutched her heart, gave an anguished, grief-stricken look, hunched her back as if she'd fall over and die.

I tried to think of what he'd been missing. Nothing came up.

I heard from a few people much later that in those days my father carried a photo of me in his wallet. He would pull it out and hold it up at dinner parties, showing it around, and say, "It's not my kid. But she doesn't have a father, so I'm trying to be there for her."

"It's his loss," my mother said as we skated home. "His great, great loss. He'll get it someday. He'll come back and it'll rip his heart open, when he sees you, how much you're like him, and how much he's missed."

I sensed it was the right time to make a play for a kitten.

The office of the Humane Society was located on the edge of the Baylands Nature Preserve, in a government-style building.

"They have too many kittens," my mother said on the drive over, as I tried to contain my excitement. "If they don't find homes for them, they put them to sleep."

The main room was open-plan, echoey, with a beamed high ceiling and a stone floor. The animals were in the back, through a door. The woman at the front desk was dressed in an army-green uniform with a matching belt and many stiff pockets. She pulled out a clipboard and asked where we lived and how long we'd been there.

"A house in Menlo Park," my mother said. "For a few months now."

"And before that?" the woman asked.

"We stayed in a friend's house for two months," my mother said, her tone flat. "And in the place before that, four months."

The woman's mouth became fixed as she wrote all this down on her clipboard. I wished my mother would lie, or skip some of the moves, to make us look better; it wasn't until she'd started telling this woman about all our moves that I understood this was something we should have kept hidden. Even though my mother had agreed to come here and get a pet, I began to suspect that she was still ambivalent, and so refused to shade her answers, letting the woman's impression of us sour. Or that she was profoundly dedicated to honesty. Or that she began to derive satisfaction from the dry clarity of an aerial view that this woman's questioning provided, becoming more interested in this unfolding narrative than she was in a cat. Here was the landscape of our lives, seen as a pattern from way high up.

"We have a yard," I said.

The woman addressed my mother. "Do you think you'd be able to care for an animal with so much shifting around?"

"I think so," my mother said. "We've stabilized somewhat."

The woman sat up straight. "I don't think it will be possible for us to give you a kitten at this time."

I didn't expect such decisiveness. We were not even taken in to see the animals. My mother and I walked out of the building into the pungent salt air of the Baylands, not talking to each other, shocked and weary.

A few days later, we stopped at a pet store, where she bought me two white mice and the most expensive cage they had, made of glass.

The bed arrived at some point without my father. It was a loft bed composed of a series of red metal cylinders that twisted into one another, like a circuit, forming a kind of jungle gym. My mother assembled it and flattened the boxes it came in. Beside it, connected with the same metal tubing, was a small white desk made of particleboard and, above the desk, a matching white shelf. I climbed a ladder to the bed at the top, right under the skylight. It was my first bed, and the first gift from my father.

◆

I began going on outings—to the zoo, the park, shopping—with Debbie, the older sister of my mother's ex-boyfriend the rock climber. She taught ESL, worked at the cosmetics counter at Macy's in downtown San Francisco, and cleaned house for a bachelor in a nearby town called Atherton. Debbie was around thirty, like my mother, but without children. She'd offered to take me on outings, inspired by an older girl who had once taken an interest in her when she was young and had difficulties at home, showing her how to apply makeup and wear perfume and accessorize.

My mother and I waited for her near the road on the appointed day. When she got out of the car, she was wearing light pink jeans, white high-heeled mules, a red top with a ruffle. Multiple Bakelite bracelets clacked against one another when she moved; she wore large hoop earrings and a patterned scarf. She was like a tropical bird in a realm of browns.

She drove a red Ford Fiesta stick shift and exuded a blithe optimism that seemed like a high calling, a layer of light that made everything else irrelevant. I was being introduced to the good life. Around her was a haze of scent, of orange blossoms and pleasing chemicals. Her hair was short and coiffed; the color and form gave the impression of soft waves breaking around her head, even though, when I touched it, I was surprised to feel a crust.

"Hair spray," she said.

I hoped to use hair spray, too, when I was older.

On the drives to and from Macy's, the Rinconada pool, the zoo, or her house, on El Camino or on Alameda de las Pulgas or Highway 280, she would talk about finding the Skyway, a road that she said ran way up above us, above the ground, in the clouds.

"If only we could find it," she said. "There's an on-ramp *some-where* around here." We both looked for the on-ramp, though I wasn't sure what such a ramp would look like.

"Darn," she'd eventually say. "I must have missed it. Sometimes they close it. Next time."

The year before, Debbie had been living abroad in Italy with a family in a house on the Adriatic coast, and she'd thought she might stay forever, but her mother flew over and brought her back. Now she was taking the first difficult steps to create a life. I didn't know any of this at the time, only that she seemed unencumbered, a miraculous departure from adult seriousness, delightfully unreal, like the Skyway.

I looked forward to our outings all week and chose my outfits in advance, careful to preserve them, separating them from my other clothing so that I would be sure they were clean on the appointed day. I fell in love with Debbie the way that young girls sometimes fall in love with women who aren't their mothers. With her I was my most pleasing self. Debbie and her airy voice, the oblique angles from which she looked at her life, the percussive sounds of her bracelets, her clothing—a riot of distinct shapes and bright color, chromatically alive—were the counterbalance to my mother, who was slipping into a depression.

"*That's* how it should have been," my mother said after she saw a documentary about whales, who are born already knowing how to swim, drift, float. No diapers, no being stuck, no mind-numbing tasks.

Since she and the stick artist had broken up, my mother didn't want to do much, nor could we afford to do much. She prepared food—brown rice, tofu, vegetables—that neither of us was excited to eat, and she spent long periods in her room, from day into evening, doing I Ching divination with the lights out, the semidarkness scaring me because it spoke of our strangeness, of no formality or separations.

One day she was feeling better and said she would take us to the San Francisco Museum of Modern Art, but first she wanted to stop at an ATM machine. At the museum we would walk through the galleries, the room with huge, silly Claes Oldenburg sculptures, me lounging on the benches or doing headstands while she looked at the art, her whispering into my ear about the artists, a snack at the café at the end.

"Let's not stop at the ATM," I said. "Please." But she stopped anyway, on our way out of town. No money came out of the machine, just a paper slip. She grabbed the slip, walked a few feet, and stopped in the middle of the sidewalk to examine it, stricken. We went home. She did not answer my questions but told me to be quiet, and she went to her room for the rest of the day.

"Go play," she said. "I'm fine. Leave me alone, honey."

Drawing, sorting my clothing, arranging the mice in their cage, doing any ordinary thing at all, seemed risky, like simultaneously being in a little boat out in the middle of a storm. You couldn't take your attention from it or it would tip when you didn't expect.

The next week Debbie took me over to the house where she lived with her parents in Menlo Park on Hobart Street. Her mother, blonde and plump with skin like parchment, was sitting in a breakfast nook wearing an apron, cutting rectangles out of colorful newsprint. The scissors made a pleasing rasp.

I asked her what she was cutting.

"Coupons," she said. "I bring them to the store, and then I pay less." She put each rectangle of paper into a partitioned section of a plastic box.

There was a secret compartment inside one of Debbie's dresser drawers. A drawer inside a drawer. "My family doesn't even know about it," she said, whispering and leaning down so her face was near mine. Inside was a jewelry case, and inside that was a necklace, the fine chain knotted.

"I wonder if you can undo that with your little fingers," she said. "If you can untie it, you can have it." I sat on her bed and worked the filaments away from one another until each knot released.

"Do you have a husband?" I asked her, as she fastened the necklace behind me.

"Not yet," she said. "But I will. I'll be out walking, and bam, there he'll be, around the next corner!"

When we got back, my mother was in her painting clothes.

"Look," she said, gesturing to an almost-finished painting. Debbie went over to see it close up. "It's amazing," Debbie said. "I've never seen more beautiful artwork." (Later Debbie said she wondered why we were poor when my mother had a talent like this. At the very least, she thought, my mother could hawk her artwork on the street. But my mother's artwork didn't make money except for a few illustration projects.)

We all sat at the table, me on Debbie's lap. At some point while they were talking I looked up and said, "Your teeth are white. My mom's are yellow." My mother shifted in her chair; she often complained about the way her teeth looked.

"Debbie has no idea," my mother said, after Debbie had left. "She's phony and judgmental and she has no fucking idea." It was true that Debbie judged her: at some point during the visit, Debbie noticed the dishes in the sink and a stain on our wall, left there by previous renters where a drink must have spilled. Over time the area had darkened like a shadow and Debbie had noticed it and wrinkled her nose.

"She just prances in here and takes you away," my mother went on, "and you're a delight—and she judges *me*. When it's because of all *my* work that you're so great."

"I like her," I said.

"She's not perfect, you know. She's not happy all the time. She's phony."

"You should clip coupons," I told her.

"No way," she said. "It's not the kind of person I am. Or *ever* want to be."

After that day, my mother no longer waited with me near the garage beside the front house by the circle of asphalt in the morning for Debbie's arrival.

♦

One weekend a friend from school named Daniela and her parents took me to a musical concert. I wore heavy-gauge white wool tights. I had to pee in the middle of the performance but it wasn't possible to leave. I held it for as long as I could, and then finally, not able to hold it any longer, I peed in my tights. (I was relieved to notice, when the lights turned on, that you couldn't tell from looking that they were soaked).

In the bathroom at intermission, I tried to flush the tights down the toilet. They gathered near the hole, stuck, a twirl of sodden fabric. When I left the stall, there was a line out of the bathroom; the next person in line, a woman, advanced toward the stall I left. "I don't know if you want to use that one," I said to her, using my best diction, as if she and I were conspirators. "There's a pair of *children's* tights in the toilet." The woman gave me a strange look, and it was only after I walked out that I realized that I'd given myself away.

After the show my mother took Daniela and me for pizza at Applewood, and as we walked back to the car, we took turns swinging her cloth purse by the long handle, making huge and violent circles above the sidewalk. Daniela whipped it around. An X-Acto blade my mother used for art projects must have made its way to the bottom, come uncapped, and poked through the fabric. The bottom of the bag brushed against the top of my wrist and slashed it open. Later, it developed into a scar an inch long, vertical, bisecting my forearm, an "I" shape that was not unattractive and that I have become used to. For a while she felt guilty and could hardly look at the scar. But then years later she would point and exclaim, "I signed you!" like I was her art.

Sometimes my mother remarked how her own mother, Virginia, wouldn't have done this or that: wouldn't have taken her to a café

to get cake, or intervened on her behalf in school, or brought her
snacks in bed when she was hungry—and the summation of these
small comments, as far as I understood, at the very least, was that
her mother had withheld from her the elements of my own childhood that I liked the most.

"When I was little," she said, "my mother noticed I had artistic
talent, and she went out and bought my sister Linda an easel and
an elaborate paint set. Then she said I wasn't allowed to touch it."

I wanted more stories like that one—stories of Virginia's
cruelty—but instead she mostly told me about how her mother was
a great cook and had strung up fat hand-cut noodles around the
kitchen to dry like socks, had insisted on buying feather duvets when
this was not common. Once, on a snowy day, Virginia looked out
the window and saw two bright-red cardinals sitting on a branch
and decided she would buy herself a pair of red shoes, and did.
Through Virginia, we were related to the late Branch Rickey, who
was her great-uncle and the general manager of the Brooklyn Dodg-
ers, the man who helped get Jackie Robinson into Major League
Baseball. It was important to defend Virginia, my mother implied,
even before I knew what we were defending her against.

"My first memory was as a baby in my crib, looking around,
noticing how meager the room was," she said. "As if I'd come from
some other place that was considerably nicer." In her stories of childhood, she was sometimes defenseless and at other times powerful.
She was required to wear skirts and flimsy coats to school in the
freezing Ohio winters; she had the initiative and independence to
save cereal tokens and trade them for binoculars and went wandering
and bird-watching alone at dawn. Now she was looking for something much better than what she'd ever experienced before—she
wanted it for both of us—something exquisite that she could imagine
but that we hadn't seen or tasted yet.

◆

My mother and I went for a hike near Maryknoll Seminary, in a nature preserve of hilly grassland with a residence for retired missionary priests. We walked on a wide dirt path. Around us the grasses and nettles gave off a smell of incense and soap. The insects were loud, then all at once, they'd stop, like a drop in pressure, leaving the air empty, and then they'd start again, building up. This was snake weather. Snakes might sun themselves on paths.

"In India, I saw a baby cobra," she said. "It was blocking the path, rearing its head up." She made an aspirated noise at the back of her throat. "They're the worst. They don't know their power yet; they release the venom all at once." I did not picture my mother in her stories. Instead, I saw her stories from her perspective, as if I had been the one in India with the baby cobra.

On the hill above us was a green cactus with bright red fruit. "Prickly pears," my mother said. "I've been wanting to try one."

She began to climb, setting off little avalanches of dirt with her feet.

"Mom, stop," I said.

"I'm glad you're not *my* mother," she said.

"Let's do it later," I said.

"Come on, Lisa. I've always wanted this."

"There's spines," I said.

"I wasn't born with yesterday's rain," she said, still climbing. She said this when I acted like a know-it-all. Rain was what we needed—we were in a drought, the worst one in a long time. We weren't supposed to flush after we peed. The hillside was yellow, the sound of the grass crackly under her feet.

She made it up to a higher point on the far side of the plant so she was reaching down from above it. The plant didn't look real, but whimsical, jointed like a plastic doll.

"Red is a dangerous color in nature," she said, near the bright-red fruit. "It's a warning color: 'Poison—don't eat me.'"

She covered her hand with the edge of her shirt, sucked in her stomach, reached, and grabbed the top of the fruit and pulled. It did not snap off as she thought it would.

She began to rotate it. "It's fibrous," she grunted. "It won't come off."

I wanted to make her stop; she was acting crazy and I hated her. I knew everything. I was full of premonitions. The grasses hissed.

Finally, she pried it off and brought it down to the path, where I stood.

I said, "Let's take it home and boil it."

"I want it now," she said. "If I can just get the skin off." She used her shirt to guard her hand while she peeled the skin down and then nibbled the flesh at the center, trying to avoid the skin. "Mmm. It's good. Interesting. Want some?"

"No, thanks," I said.

On the drive home, she began to moan.

"My throat," she said. "It hurts to swallow."

At a stoplight she pulled herself up in her seat, looked at her open mouth in the rearview mirror. Despite my resolve not to pity her, I was terrified.

"I told you to wait," I said.

"I know. I can't talk, Lisa, it hurts too much." Small, transparent spines on the skin of the fruit must have lodged themselves along her throat.

When we got home, her throat on fire, she went to get her clothes out of the dryer and found that she had accidentally shrunk her favorite angora sweater.

"Damn," she said. It had a row of mother-of-pearl buttons down the placket. "You can have it."

It fit me exactly, hitting just below my belly button, the sleeves at my wrists, the soft fabric and flower pattern in a sea of pink, as if it were made to be my size.

In the few days leading up to the next excursion with Debbie, I was careful not to wear the shrunken sweater, which seemed to be something I had taken from my mother, part of the tide of good luck that flowed out to me, leaving her behind.

A few days later she sat in her bedroom throwing three pennies at the carpet beside a book, a pen, and a piece of paper, consulting the I Ching. She sat in the corner, the lights off. It was daytime but it was dim in her bedroom. She leaned, her elbow on her knee and her brow in her hand. Strands of hair stuck along her cheek and fell over her ear.

"What's wrong?" I asked.

"I lost my twenties," she said.

She threw the pennies again, looked, jotted down ticks as thin as insect legs in a stack that ran down the page, riffled through a small book.

"But you *did* have them," I said.

"You have it good," she said. "You get to go out with Debbie and have fun. I don't have anyone."

"You can come with us," I said, although I knew this wasn't what she wanted.

"I want my own friends, my own life." On the word *life*, she threw down three pennies. We could not both be happy at once. Her eagerness—for more life, for fun, the prickly pear—felt to me like danger. My happiness had been pulled from the reserve of hers, a limited string we had to share. If she has it, I must not; if I have it, she must wilt. As if the emotional thrift of the world meant there was never enough for both of us at any one time.

"You *have* friends," I said.

This made her sob. "I don't have a man, a husband, a boyfriend, a relationship. Nothing."

The air in the bedroom was stale. "But I love you and *I'm* here for you."

"I try, but nothing works out for me," she went on, as if I hadn't spoken. "I used to have these beautiful, strong hands." She was crying so hard there was spit between her lips and she could hardly get the words out. "And do you know what Faye bought me for Christmas?" she said of her stepmother; it was Jim and Faye whom I called my grandparents because I'd seen Virginia only a couple of times.

"She bought me an *iron*," she said. "And do you know what she bought *Linda*?" Linda was her younger sister, the pretty one who'd gotten the paint set. Now Linda was managing several branches of Supercuts and dating a NASA physicist with a mustache and a hot tub.

"A champagne bucket!" she said.

I knew it was not the utility of the gifts—we used the iron and the ironing board that came with it for years, and later Linda would say it was not a champagne bucket but an ice bucket, and that she'd specifically asked for it, as my mother had asked for the iron—but the symbolism that made this gift so awful. But still I wanted her to tell Faye about the mistake and make Faye take it back and give her what she wanted.

She got up, walked out of her bedroom, grabbed a pair of fabric scissors off her desk in the living room, went to her closet, and began jolting the hangers across the rail, pulling different shirts off hangers and throwing them into a pile.

"Don't do it."

"Don't tell me what to do. I have nothing to wear. Nothing." She snipped the corner of an old gray shirt and then ripped it open, revealing a selvedge edge.

"It's the neckline. It's terrible. I hate my clothes." She sobbed, then growled. She cut a notch in the bottom of a T-shirt and then took it with both hands and ripped it across, bellowing with rage.

She'd done the same with other clothes when she was angry, cut necklines, shortened shirts and sleeves, then never worn them again. Later, she would have to throw these clothes away, reducing further her already small collection.

Around this time, my father threw a large and lavish thirtieth birthday party for himself. He invited my mother, and she planned to go, inviting Debbie to come along, but as the date approached, she began to waver. She couldn't afford to buy a new dress. She would be ashamed to be there in rags, beside people in finery, celebrating him. She canceled at the last minute, leaving Debbie, who had pinned her hopes of finding a husband on the event, in the lurch. I was not aware of the party at the time, only of my mother's shift into melancholy, and her increasing preoccupation with her wardrobe and her feeling of having lost her youth.

I knew the things she didn't like about herself—her thighs, her forehead, her teeth, the wrinkles above her lip—and that she believed these parts and old clothes meant she would not get what she wanted. In fact she was beautiful, her cheekbones high, a delicate nose. She said she, Linda, and Kathy were called the Forehead Sisters in high school, their hairlines starting too high up, but I liked her forehead, bare and smooth like part of an egg. Her figure was like a Rodin sketch I saw later of a woman facing forward looking back, every element feminine and in stunning proportion—back, butt, breasts. A small waist.

That night as she made dinner, she washed the lentils, touching them slowly with the pads of her fingers, looking at them mournfully, as if she were in the process of losing some inestimable thing.

◆ ◆ ◆

When Debbie and I got back to the house one late afternoon, my mother was waiting for us in front of the garage. I could tell by the way she stood that something was wrong—she held her jaw tight and askew. She held her hand over her eyes to block the sun; I could see she'd been crying.

As soon as we got out of the car, she started talking. "You know what, I'm sick of this. How you think you're better than I am."

"Mom," I said. "Stop."

"Stay out of this, honey," she said.

Debbie looked innocent, shocked; she edged her way back toward her car door.

"Don't pretend you don't know what I'm saying," my mother said.

"I don't—I really didn't mean—" Debbie stuttered.

"You wanted to just march into our lives and judge me in front of my daughter. And you think you're perfect, when you're really superficial, silly," my mother said, through her teeth. There was some truth in what my mother said, which made her fury more terrifying.

"You're trying to insinuate yourself into Lisa's life, to be better than her mother. It's disgusting. Who the hell do you think you are? It's like some kind of molestation." She was yelling now. Her brow and her lips wrinkled like tinfoil, she bared her teeth, and Debbie, startled and balanced too high, her heels clicking, retreated, opening her car door.

I was afraid Debbie would think of me as if I was my mother. I imagined others did not see us as separate but as the same person in two bodies.

"Mom," I said.

"Be quiet, Lisa," she said.

It was hard to move or think; shock felt like languor. I was ashamed of my mother. How scary she was when she yelled, snarling and unkempt. The scene unfolded like two ribbons, Debbie pleading, my mother responding, fluttering after her to yell more, Debbie retreating, slipping into her car, turning on the engine, and driving away. I never saw Debbie again.

◆

My mother was supposed to go on a first date with Ron.

He would come to pick her up, meet me, and they would go to an early dinner. The neighbors were home if I needed anything. I was old enough now—seven—to stay alone in the house for two hours, but the details were still a negotiation.

"And afterwards?"

I was supposed to be in bed before she returned.

"I guess we might come back," she said.

I made her promise they wouldn't go into her room, and for some reason she agreed.

Since she'd become interested in Ron, she no longer paid attention to me as astutely, I thought. She no longer consulted the I Ching. She was half-absent with happiness, the same slight smile on her lips as when she ran up the hill to get the prickly pear.

It was between boyfriends—between the loneliness and despair that followed one and the lift that began at the next—where I hoped to stay forever, she and I the only team, the real couple.

On the night of the date, Ron arrived on time. She was leaning over the bathroom sink doing her makeup when he knocked.

I ran to open the door. I saw right away that Ron wasn't a hippie. He was bald, with hair tufted on the sides like a clown's, and had wide bushy eyebrows, glasses rimmed with gold, and large, swollen lips like a fish. He looked clean, and smelled of soap and detergent.

"Hello," I said. "I'm Lisa. My mom's getting ready."

"Nice to meet you," he said, holding out his hand.

He followed me into the living room; I noticed that, as he walked, his feet splayed out dramatically to either side.

My mother called from the bathroom, "I'll be out in a minute."

As we passed the bookshelf, I reached for the album of photographs of my birth—this was unplanned, it surprised even me, one arm jutting out as if I didn't have control of my limbs—and pulled it out of its socket in the shelf.

I'd asked her to get rid of this album many times and she refused, bringing it with us as we moved from house to house. The cover was made of brown woven grasses, and because it was old, the grasses had started to fray at the edges. To me, too, this hinted at the shame of the contents. I suspected other children didn't have shameful books like this around their houses.

He and I sat down on the flowered couch beside each other.

"I want to show you something," I said. "Just some photos of my mother and me."

I opened the book across my lap where he could see it. My mother, younger, lying on a bed with long hair like dark water pooling around her face. These were the pictures of my birth, in black and white, with rounded corners. She had what looked like a man's shirt buttoned around her chest and she was naked from the waist down, with her legs bent and open in the foreground of the photo. I turned the page: there I was, emerging from between her glowing, white legs like a turtle rising up from a pond.

In the following pictures, once I was out, you could see my body wrinkled, my face wax-white, asymmetrical, and squished.

I felt revulsion and disgust and yet I continued to turn the pages. I would not have known how to articulate it: I wanted to disgust him the way I was disgusted, to scare him away. To show him who we were, so that he might leave now, rather than wait.

"And here's more," I said in my sweetest voice.

"Yes," he said. "I see." He made no motion to rise and run. He sat, glancing at the pages and then looking away, as if distracted. When my mother came out of the bathroom and saw us, she snatched the album from my hands and stuck it back in its place on the shelf, giving me a furious look.

Let's Blast

One of the first memories I have of my father is at a birthday party someone threw for him at a house in Russian Hill. He was in his early thirties.

The light was different in San Francisco—we called it The City—slanting and yellow and more watery than it was in Palo Alto. The house, too, was beautiful, tall with soft wool carpets that tucked into the walls and the largest television I'd ever seen. The grass backyard was almost entirely taken up by a trampoline, the large, round kind, high up on metal legs.

My father was on the trampoline, wearing jeans and a flannel shirt.

"Hey there. Wanna come bounce?" he called out to me.

I walked over and someone, not my mother, hoisted me, brought me high enough to lift my leg and grasp the fabric lip, my toes curling like a marsupial's. The surface was the size of a small pool and caught light like an oil slick. I assumed my father and I would bounce the way I'd learned in my gymnastics lessons, but with two people it was different, the cadence irregular and jostling. Despite my efforts to stay on separate but complementary trajectories, we almost hit each other in midair. He wasn't coordinated, didn't have a clear sense of how to fall and rise. Nor did the trampoline have netted walls; we might fly off into the lawn where people were standing, or over the fence. I was lighter, I would be the one to fly. Worse, I might land on top of him. My yellow shorts belled out in the updraft and I worried that he and everyone on the lawn beneath us would see my underwear. But if I held my shorts down I'd lose the small measure of control I had over my movements.

It was not clear when I reached the highest point of up, because inside it was the fall, the pulling feeling of down.

Twice we found ourselves coming down to land at the same moment. I prayed we wouldn't touch; it would be too intimate. I was conscious of scrabbling away from accidental closeness in front of strangers. In midair he looked at me, smiled.

My drop, his bounce; his drop, my bounce. From below, someone took a photograph. We kept bouncing until he said, "All right, kid. Should we call it a day?" I'd never heard the expression before: Call It A Day.

◆

My mother told me a story she'd heard about my father that went something like this:

My father was adopted and at some point in his twenties went to look for his birth parents. The search had been fruitless for a while, but finally he found the doctor who had delivered him. Because he'd been looking for so long, he decided this would be his last attempt; if it didn't work, he wasn't meant to find them.

He went to meet with the doctor and asked for the name of his mother. The doctor said he didn't know, but even if he did, he couldn't tell him, because it would be a breach of confidentiality.

When my father walked out the door of the doctor's office, he decided to stop looking. At the same time, back in the office, the doctor sat down and wrote on a piece of paper: "Upon my death, please tell Steve Jobs I do know his mother, and her name is Joanne." He had her contact information, and wrote it out.

Four hours later the doctor died of a massive coronary attack. My father got the letter, found his mother, and learned that he had a younger sister, Mona.

It was easy to get the timing right when you told a story like this, pausing after he stopped looking, lowering your voice to start in on the doomed doctor writing the fateful note.

Around the time I turned eight we moved again and my father started dropping by our house once or twice a month. By this time he'd been kicked out of his company, Apple, an event I heard later was deeply hurtful to him, but even then I could feel that he was profoundly sad in some way that made him walk funny and act aloof. He was in the process of starting a new company called NeXT that would make computer hardware and software. I knew he also owned a computer animation company called Pixar that made a short film about two lamps, a parent and child, but this seemed minor compared with Apple or NeXT.

Later my mother said that it was the dips in his worldly success that made him come and find us. The pattern she saw was that when he failed at work, when he lost something in the public sphere, he remembered us, started dropping by, wanted a relationship with me. As if in the flurry of work he forgot me and remembered only when the flurry stopped.

When he came over, we all went roller skating around the neighborhood. My mother came along because I hardly knew him and would have felt strange being alone with him. His visits materialized out of ordinary afternoons, an engine shuddered into our driveway to the bottlebrush tree, echoing off our house and the wooden fence on the other side, thickening the air with excitement. He drove a black Porsche convertible. When he stopped, the sound turned into a whine and then was extinguished, leaving the quiet more quiet, the pinpoint sounds of birds.

"Hi, Steve!" I said.

"Hey," he said.

I liked the way he walked on the balls of his toes, tilted forward, falling into each step. His outlines were crisp.

I anticipated his arrival, wondering when it would happen, and thought about him afterward—but in his presence, for the hour or so we were all together, there was a strange blankness like the air after his engine switched off. He didn't talk much. He and my mother talked some, but there were long pauses, the thunk and whirr of roller skates on pavement, the birds and a few cars and leaf blowers.

We skated the neighborhood streets. Trees overhead made patterns of the light. Fuchsia dangled from bushes in yards, stamens below a bell of petals, like women in ball gowns with purple shoes. Some streets wound around huge oak trees. Some had been cracked by roots and earthquakes, the curvy fissures filled in with shiny black tar.

"Look how the tar lines reflect the sky," my mother said to both of us. It was true—they were light blue rivers.

During the skates with my father, I was not voluble the way I was when it was just my mother and me.

Steve had the same skates as my mother, a beige nubuck body with red laces crisscrossed over a double line of metal fasts. I skated behind or ahead. She talked about the college she wanted to attend in San Francisco; he tripped on cracks in the sidewalk and the roads. To me skating was easy, like running or swimming. My mother's back brake pad was worn away, and her front brake, the one that looked like a pencil eraser, was down to a slant. She knit the pavement, ankle over ankle, and slowed to a stop in one long line like Fred Astaire. His brakes looked new.

"Can you use your brakes?" I asked, as we approached a stop sign.

"I don't need brakes," he said. He aimed for the pole, hit it straight on with his chest, hugged it with both arms, and twirled around it, indecorously, stepping and stumbling until he stopped.

As we passed bushes in other people's yards, he pulled clumps of leaves off the stems, then dropped the fragments as we skated, making a line of ripped leaves behind us on the pavement like Hansel and Gretel.

A few times, I felt his eyes on me; when I looked up, he looked away.

After he left, we talked about him.

"Why do his jeans have holes all over?" I asked. He might have sewn them up. I knew he was supposed to have millions of dollars. We didn't just say "millionaire" but "multimillionaire" when we spoke of him, because it was accurate, and because knowing the granular details made us part of it.

"In high school, he sometimes had more hole than jean," she said. "It's just his way. On our first date, when he came to pick me up, my father asked, 'Young man, what are you going to be when you grow up?' And you know what he said?"

"What?"

"*A bum.* Your grandfather was not pleased. He was hoping for an upstanding man to take his daughter out, and instead he got this long-haired hippie, saying he wanted to be a bum."

She said my father had a lisp. "It's something to do with his teeth," she said. She said most people have an underbite or an overbite. "But his teeth hit each other exactly straight on, and over the years they cracked and chipped where they hit, so the top and bottom teeth meet, with no spaces. It looks like a zigzag, or a zipper."

When they were dating in high school, even before they started selling the blue boxes that let you call anywhere in the world for free, he predicted that he would become famous.

"How did he know?"

"He just did," she said. "He also said he'd die young, in his early forties."

I was pretty sure that since the first prediction was right, the second one would be right too. I began to think of him as a kind of prophet, with loneliness and tragedy at the edges. (Only we knew how lonely, how tragic!) All light and dark, nothing in between.

"And he has these strangely flat palms," she said.

Every element about him that was different from others meant some sort of divinity, I thought. I assigned mystical qualities to his slouching, falling walk, his zipper teeth, his tattered jeans, his flat palms, as if these were not only different from other fathers' but better, and now that he was in my life, even if it was only once a month, I had not waited in vain. I would be better off than children who'd had fathers all along.

"He continued to grow through his twenties, when most people have stopped growing," she said. "I saw it."

Of course the parts did not go together. He was rich but had holes in his jeans; he was successful but hardly talked; his figure was graceful, elegant, but he was clumsy and awkward; he was famous but seemed bereft and alone; he invented a computer and named it after me but didn't seem to notice me, and didn't mention it. Still, I could see how all these contrasting qualities could be an attribute, spun in a certain way.

"I heard when it gets a scratch, he buys a new one," I overheard my mother say to Ron.

"A new what?" I asked.

"Porsche."

"Couldn't he just paint over the scratch?" I asked.

"Car paint doesn't work like that," Ron said. "You can't just paint over black with black; it wouldn't blend. There are thousands of different blacks. They'd have to repaint the whole thing."

The next time he came over, I wondered if it was the same car he'd been driving the last time, or if it was a new one that just looked the same.

◆

One day he came over and brought someone with him. She was petite and pretty, wore jeans, had red hair that fell in a line below her jaw, large dark-blue eyes, and a wide mouth that took over her face in a pleasing way when she smiled.

"This is my sister," he said. She was an author, Mona Simpson. After giving my father up for adoption, his biological parents got married, had a daughter a few years later, and kept her. She and my father were soon close, kindred spirits, alike even though they'd just met. She had just published her first novel, *Anywhere but Here*, a book that would be on the bestseller list for many weeks and would become a movie starring Susan Sarandon and Natalie Portman. I read it when I was twelve: it was brilliant. Steve and Mona looked different—tall and petite, dark and light, man and woman—you couldn't tell they were brother and sister until they both smiled and their faces opened and folded in the same way. They had similar lips, and wide teeth.

That my father's sister happened to be named Mona struck me as a great coincidence. What were the chances that she would have a name that went so well with mine as to form, in combination, the name of the most famous painting in the world?

They'd both been successful on their own, neither knowing of the other's existence. They shared an aesthetic sensibility, my father buying expensive lamps, carpets, and books while Mona patrolled flea markets for vintage mercury bulbs, wooden figures, magnolia-patterned plates, glasses with a stripe of silver painted on the rim.

Later, it was Mona who insisted that he rent us a nicer house than our tiny one on Melville; who insisted that he re-carpet and paint the small apartment within the Woodside house where he slept and I slept when I stayed with him, and that he change my bedroom from the one with the red shag rug, which required me to walk through his room to get to the bathroom, to one beside the bathroom. She who bought me a bed, and later argued that he should *buy* my mother and me a house. She was supportive of my mother's artwork and took intense interest in the details of my life in a way that seemed to elevate them. When Mona visited, she brought with her excitement about food, jewelry, clothing. She would find the good restaurants, the places that served the best pie. She wore the same pair of earrings, always, that looked like a long drip of gold on each ear, the front and back sides hitting below her jawline.

Mona had also grown up with a single mother, after her father left. It seemed to me that her mother was unhinged, from stories I insisted she tell me later—one Christmas her mother had bought gifts for her boyfriend's children but not for Mona; once she'd made her order the steak at a restaurant when they didn't have the money for it. Mona's stories gave me a thrill like looking down a steep cliff face, close to danger but safe at the same time. Mona took an interest in me: she noticed and commented on my tastes, judged me wise, gave me a first gift, the *Arabian Nights*.

Mona gazed at me as if she was particularly interested in my face; she watched me sometimes even when she was conversing with the adults. At a restaurant, I doodled on a paper placemat and she pronounced it great, took it, framed it, and put it up in her apartment in New York.

I would grow to be the same height as Mona, and also petite; I would also study English literature in college, and write.

One year she wrote me long letters every week on thick paper in sepia ink. She gave me adult gifts: silver pointed dangly earrings, a set of collected Chekhov stories in pastel-colored paperbacks, a gold Tiffany ring with an amethyst eye.

These gifts were windows into a more sophisticated world to which I hoped I'd belong, later. She had survived her own childhood, and now was successful; the gifts were proof of that.

When I was a senior in high school, she would publish a new book. Before it was published, she sent me the bound galleys and asked me what I thought of the novel, if there was anything I would change. I was honored, but when I started reading I was surprised to find characters like my father, my mother, and myself in the pages. My character was named Jane. I'd had no idea she was writing about us. Mona had collected details of my life and put them into her book—an antique Chinese enameled pillbox she bought for me, with chrysanthemums and multicolored birds painted on a blue background. Other parts were made up—it was fiction—and the combination was confusing. At first I'd felt hurt to find my things on the pages, as if she'd taken the gifts back. Still, when I read Mona's books, they made me want to write my own sentences.

"People write about family in fictional form," she said. "Fiction writers use details from life." We were at Caffe Verona, where we'd gone to talk about it. When she'd learned I was upset after reading the galleys, she flew to Palo Alto the next day from where she lived in Los Angeles to talk with me.

"It's just what writers do. I didn't mean to upset you. Not at all."

Reading her book, I felt there would be nothing left for me to write about. I felt emptied out. Jane didn't like sushi because it felt like a tongue on her tongue. The details she described made me disconsolate, as if, having described them so well, they belonged to her now, not to me.

"Why didn't you tell me right after you read it?" she asked. "I would have changed it, or waited, or even not published at all." But at eighteen, the idea that I could have told her what to do with her work had not felt possible.

Now the book was almost on the shelves.

Also, after reading half the book, I'd stopped. I didn't even know what happened with my character in the end.

"You haven't finished?" she asked. "You'll like it, what happens to Jane."

"Maybe," I said.

"Perhaps you'll mention my book in *your* book someday," she said, surprising me with the idea that one book might refer to another like Russian dolls; and that there might be room for more than one book about the same people, and the same time.

In the end Jane is wearing a school uniform and she rushes into a classroom with the other children. She finally belongs.

◆

Ron thought my private school was elitist and lacked academic rigor, and he managed to convince my mother, too, so we moved house in order to be in the Palo Alto School District so I could attend public school.

Our new place, an apartment in the back of another house, was less than half the size of the small house we'd moved from, but with just as many rooms. It was like a playhouse. The wooden floor, newly sanded and varnished for our arrival, yellow as hay, shone like it was wet. Before this, we'd lived on a series of old wall-to-wall carpets, and my mother's joy about this floor surprised me. She reassembled the tubular bed in my new room.

One night, soon after we moved in, she rented *Desperately Seeking Susan* to watch on our new television. I wasn't allowed to watch it. Before this, we hadn't owned a television. After she put me to bed, I turned myself so my head was where my feet usually were, careful not to jostle the singing springs. From there I could open the door a crack and see the screen over the back of the couch.

In the movie, a woman wore tattered black clothing, her hair in spikes, necklaces layered. The more I watched, the more I knew I wanted to look like this woman.

My mother spun around and caught me watching.

"I thought so," she said. "Get to sleep." She came over and shut the door.

A few days later I found a picture in a magazine—it might have been an ad for Guess or Jordache jeans—in which a woman with short, tousled hair, wet maybe, was leaping. She flew above the dark asphalt, toes pointed: perfect splits in the air. She wore a T-shirt and stonewashed jeans. I wanted to be that girl too.

◆ ◆ ◆

Ron came over while my mother and I were standing in the kitchen. The kitchen alcove was straight across from the front door; when he stepped in, he lifted his camera to his eye.

"Don't move," he said, clicking. "This is really good." We didn't own a camera.

At first the shots were candid, but now he wanted us to pose. *Click click click.* I could feel my smile hardening.

In his interactions with me and my mother he often insisted too much—my mother said he "went too far"—as if only by extreme repetition would he be noticed.

I knew Ron was kind. He'd bought us matching gold necklaces, hers wider and thicker than mine, made of two rows of jointed segments that met like herringbone. It was only because he went on too long and didn't listen that we became infuriated and pushed him away. Now, in the kitchen, it was my mother and me against his frantic urgency. We gave him insolent looks. He turned on the flash.

"Ron, enough," my mother said. "We're done, okay?"

My mother ran into the bathroom; I ducked behind the wall.

"Guys, come back," he said. "Let me take just a few more."

When Ron didn't stay over, I slept with my mother in her bed, which I preferred to sleeping alone.

"Why don't you leave him?" I asked her the next day.

"I just might," she said.

Ron brought over the developed photographs in a paper envelope. As soon as he stepped inside, my mother grabbed the envelope out of his hand and ran to the couch and started looking through the stack. I tried to get at the pictures, and so did he, but her back was curved against us as she flipped through them, yanking out the photos she didn't like and hiding them in a pile beneath her leg.

She had long believed that the essential perspective of the photographer was captured in his or her photographs; flattering or interesting pictures would mean that Ron noticed her beauty and even her soul; ugly pictures would reveal that he did not see, appreciate, or love her.

"Let me see," I said, reaching around her, trying to grab them, but it was too late: she ripped the photographs beneath her leg in half.

She turned and shrugged, tilted her head, lifted her eyebrows—acknowledging our anger and frustration, but smug, the way she always was when she ripped up photographs of herself.

It enraged me when she did this. I became more critical of her. I noticed the way she walked with her toes pointing in, and how her pinkie toes formed yellow calluses sharp as blades that ran vertically along the bottom pad where the toes had been flattened in shoes. She added flakes of brewer's yeast to her salads and they smelled of dusty rooms. Her cakes collapsed with fault lines because she was too impatient to let them cool. Once, I had loved the way the tip of her nose bobbed up and down when she chewed, and sat in her lap to be closer to the sound, like a blade through tall grasses, but now both her nose and her chewing seemed strange and wrong. All these factors, I believed, were why she was only able to date someone like Ron, not my father. I came to believe it was her fault: she wasn't beautiful enough, and was therefore unloved, unloveable—and might make me so, too.

◆

At my new school, the buildings were single-story and Spanish-style with dirty stucco walls, arches, and courtyards. The hallways between classrooms were open to the elements, covered by porticoes, and paved with shiny cement squares. On rainy days, the water poured into the courtyards and over the fenced field at the back of the school. My teacher, Miss Johnson, was young—it was her first year teaching. Her hair fell in a perfect blonde curtain around her face, and her bangs were curled in toward her forehead. When she smiled, cushioned circles formed in her lower cheeks, as if she were holding something delicious in her mouth.

I didn't know the Pledge of Allegiance; the first time the class stood to recite it, I tried to mouth the words. Only one girl stayed seated. She sat as if she meant to sit, not as if she'd forgotten to stand.

"I'm a Jehovah's Witness," she said.

After that, I stayed seated too.

"Why aren't you standing for the Pledge?" Miss Johnson asked.

"I'm a Buddhist," I said. That was the religion my mother said she and my father had practiced.

"Oh," she said, and didn't ask me about it again.

"It's not just parents who decide to have children," my mother said. I was pretty sure this came from Buddhism. "Some say children choose the parents too. Before they're born." I tried to take stock of what I'd chosen: my father far away, glinting like a shard of mirror, my mother so close and urgent. If it was true that I chose my pare I would choose them again, I thought.

At school, I wasn't supposed to mention my father.

"You could be kidnapped," Ron said.

In high school, my mother knew of a girl abducted in a windowless white van, her hands and legs tied up. After they'd driven her outside the town, they'd stopped at a gas station and the girl had managed to open the door and get free. I understood in some vague way that I could be kidnapped because of my father; but because he wasn't part of my life in a daily way, the idea seemed far-fetched and glamorous.

At Ron's urging, my mother and I went to the police station, where they took my fingerprints. A man dipped my finger in thick black liquid, pressed it down on paper from one side of the nail bed to the other, hurting me a little each time as he tried to grip my small fingers and roll them, leaving a pattern of lines on the paper my mother said were unique to me. Whorls, she said they were called. She showed me how hers resolved in a perfect circle, like a topographic map of a hill.

"I have a secret," I said to my new friends at school. I whispered it so that they would see I was reluctant to mention it. The key, I felt, was to underplay. "My father is Steve Jobs."

"Who's that?" one asked.

"He's famous," I said. "He invented the personal computer. He lives in a mansion and drives a Porsche convertible. He buys a new one every time it gets a scratch."

The story had a film of unreality to it as I said it, even to my own ears. I hadn't hung out with him that much, only a few skates and visits. I didn't have the clothes or the bike someone with a father like this would have. My last name was different from his.

"He even named a computer after me," I said to them.

"What computer?" a girl named Elizabeth asked.

"The Lisa," I said.

"A computer called the *Lisa*?" she said. "I never heard of it."

"It was ahead of its time." I used my mother's phrase, although wasn't sure why it was ahead. "He invented the personal computer later. But you can't tell anyone, because if someone finds out, I could get kidnapped."

I brought it up when I felt I needed to, waiting as long as I could and then letting it burst forth. I don't remember feeling at a disadvantage with my friends who had fathers, only that there was at my fingertips another magical identity, an extra thing that started to itch and tingle when I felt small, and it was like pressure building inside me, and then I had to find a way to say it.

At some point I also heard that he'd been named *Playboy*'s "Sexiest Man of the Year." I bragged about it selectively because I wasn't sure whether it was true or exactly what it meant. I had gathered that there was a *Playboy*, and also a *Playgirl*, so I didn't know if he was featured in a magazine of naked women meant for men, or if he was nude himself in a magazine of naked men meant for women. From this I concluded that my father *might* be naked in *Playboy*, and when I thought of it, I got a terrible shiver, and I thought part of growing up would be to take this fact in stride.

One of the girls at school, Kirsten, started following me around outside class, chanting, "Your dad is Steve Jobs, your dad is Steve Jobs."

"Stop it," I said.

She didn't stop. She said it sometimes tauntingly, sometimes in a monotone like a robot. It was annoying, but the advantage to her harassment was that it advertised the very fact I wanted known. She did the brag-work for me, and I seemed innocent, even put-upon, as she did it.

"What's wrong with that girl?" my mother said when I told her. "I bet it's her parents—*they* care. I wonder how she found out?"

I told her I might have been the one to tell her, accidentally.

"*You* told her?"

"It slipped out." I braced for her anger, but instead she was only confused.

"That makes even *less* sense," she said. "You told her, and now she goes around telling you? Tell her to stop. What a strange girl."

◆ ◆ ◆

One afternoon when he came for a skate, my father brought over a stack of six stickers from his company, NeXT. These were beautiful, thick, large, made of a rigid clear plastic, printed with a black cube and brightly colored letters.

"You can give these to your friends at school," he said. I was thrilled: when I gave them out, they would know I hadn't made him up.

This was the same time I guessed the number of corn kernels in a jar as part of an activity Miss Johnson called Guesstimation. It was the second time in a row I'd guessed the number within a few kernels, even though I'd just written a series of numbers I couldn't have put into words because I didn't understand place order. When my mother came to pick me up, both she and Miss Johnson looked at me curiously, as if I was a secret prodigy. A week later, a poem I wrote was selected for publication in the weekly school newsletter: *The pilgrims are so pretty, the pilgrims are so grand, they sailed here on the Mayflower, and walked upon our land.* Everything was finally coming together: I was becoming the girl I wanted to be, famous like my father, and lucky.

Soon after that my father brought over a Macintosh computer. He pulled the box out of the back seat and carried it into my room and put it on the floor. "Let's see," he said. "How do we open it?" As if he didn't know. This made me doubt he was the inventor.

The room had only the loft bed on the bright wooden floor. Parallelograms of light shone in from the window, lit dust twirling like sparks in midair.

He pulled the computer out of the box by a handle on the top and set it on the floor near the outlet on the wall.

"I guess we plug this in." He held the cord loose like it was unfamiliar.

He sat on the floor in front of it with his legs crossed; I sat on my knees beside him. He looked for the on switch, found it, and the machine came alive to reveal a picture of itself in the center, smiling. He showed me how I could draw with it and save my drawings on the desktop once I was finished with them, and then he left.

He didn't mention the other one, the Lisa. I worried that he had not really named a computer after me, that it was a mistake.

"You want to make the kids like you? Tell them you went to NASA and played with the flight simulators. That's what'll make them jealous," Ron said. He worked as an engineer for NASA's Ames Research Center, so he could get us in. On the day we finally went, after he'd talked about it for months, the sun was blazingly hot, and the white rocks outside the tinted glass door radiated heat. He took my picture beside the NASA sign, and then inside at the reception desk, and then again outside the door to the simulators. I'd recently had my hair cut straight across my chin at Supercuts, where we got a discount because my aunt Linda was a manager.

Inside, the simulator wasn't working. "Damn," he said. "The one day we come. What are the chances?" It didn't look like an airplane, but like an office. There were yellow and blue levers embedded in the desks near the keyboards. The screens remained black.

"These simulators are so incredible—it's just like flying," he'd said. When he talked about it, I wondered, would it really feel like flying, with wind, and if I crashed the flight simulator, would I feel as if I were falling?

"Look at the screen and pretend you're really concentrating," he said, the camera against his eye, taking picture after picture. "And pull down the lever at the same time—that's it. You can tell your friends at school that the screens didn't show up because of the flash."

He took me to lunch at a place with white tablecloths and water poured from silver pitchers into wineglasses. He apologized for how disappointing it was that the simulation hadn't worked. I told him it was okay.

He took more pictures of me elbowing the table and taking sips of water and smiling until the food arrived and we ate.

That night I wrote in my journal that I loved my dad.

Then I clarified: not Ron. Steve Jobs.

Underneath the name Steve Jobs, I wrote, "I love him! I love him! I love him!" I felt it there inside my chest like my heart would rip apart with it.

♦

My mother was admitted into California College of Arts and Crafts in San Francisco, where she would work toward her bachelor's degree. My father offered to take me on Wednesday nights, the only night of the week she had class. I would be alone with him for the first time. We would sleep at his mansion, with its glowing white face and seven acres.

It gave me a shiver of excitement and disbelief, sitting in school that first Wednesday. My new fourth-grade teacher, Mrs. Keatsman, sat at the front of the class and twisted a snug gold ring around and around her finger when she was upset with us for being unruly, the flesh tugging near the band. At the end of the day I ran outside at the bell, the first one, and looked for the white Honda Civic I'd been told to watch for—Barbara, my father's secretary, would pick me up.

She was parked against the curb in front of the school. She leaned over and rolled down the window.

"Lisa?"

"Barbara?"

"That's me," she said, opening the latch of the passenger side door.

She drove us to my father's office. Her fingernails on the stick shift were painted red and she wore a long skirt and a blouse with two sections of cloth at the collar that tied in a bow. Her brown hair fell straight in a glossy line that almost hit her shoulders. She wore glasses. I liked being near her; I realized later this was true of the people I knew who worked with my father during the years I was growing up. They were kind and gentle; often I felt more at home with them than I did with my father. They seemed soulful and modest—I think he must have admired these qualities and chosen them, even though he was not always like that himself. Barbara had a matronly presence, calm and mature, although she couldn't have been much older than my mother.

I sat on the carpeted floor in the middle of a huge room with a few low couches, large cement pillars painted white, a plant, and offices around the outside windowed wall of the building. The room smelled like new paint and carpet. Barbara brought me paper and an assortment of pens. From the place where I sat, I could see my father's office across the expanse of floor, the same size as all the offices around him, the door open. I could hear him talking on the phone. People would walk into his office, talk with him for a while, and then stop and say hello to me and ask if I was all set and look at my drawings. I couldn't see him behind his desk because there was a venetian blind, mostly closed, on the window that faced into the central room, but I could hear him, and sometimes he would walk out of his office, waving and smiling at me, and I'd think that maybe we were leaving, but then he'd return to his office again. All the offices had whiteboards. When he was speaking with someone else, he spoke very fast and loud. His office began to glow brightly along with several other offices along the same wall, lighter as it grew dark outside.

"I wanna show you something," he said at some point, walking up to me. "Leave your backpack." I followed him down the stairs, into another set of closed rooms. We passed a wall with a whiteboard with names and photographs with numbers beside them.

"At other companies they try to hide what people are earning and it's this big secret," he said. "We just write it here and everyone can see it. It stops all the stupid gossip."

I followed him down into a basement office with bunch of desks, a low ceiling, lots of computers, and a few men standing around. Most of the people must have already gone home. He introduced me as his daughter, and then they started talking to each other rapidly, and I couldn't understand what they were talking about.

"Look at this," he said to me, pointing at a computer with a large screen. "And this and this. It's like they have a blind midget on the assembly line." He was pointing to Sun Microsystems logos on big monitors, each attached at a different place along the panel at the bottom of the screen.

His voice was so sharp that I wondered why they bought them at all.

"We need them to make ours," he said. So computers make computers, I thought.

After that we said goodbye to the men and walked back up the stairs.

I figured we'd head out now, but he left me near my backpack and went back to his office. Soon he was back on the phone.

"Ready to go, champ?"

By this time it was night. Barbara had already left; before saying goodbye, she held her purse against her lap and squatted down to ask me about my drawings. I was woozy with Fanta from the stocked refrigerator.

The thought of going with my father to his big house, alone in the dark, was unsettling. I hadn't considered the possibility that we'd still be far away from his house—not inside it—when darkness fell.

The town of Woodside, a twenty-minute drive from Palo Alto, was a place with forests and people who owned horses. His house was a mansion built on seven acres of land.

This phrase, *seven acres*, seemed vast and grand, more grand than anything I knew.

The house was Spanish-style, white stucco, with an old metal gate at the front with a lock strung through that had to be opened by hand, and a flagpole with no flag. The rooms were large and dark and empty, with huge windows on both sides that nevertheless did not let much light in. I knew this from the time I'd been there with him and my mother years before, in the daytime, soon after he'd bought it.

This time he'd said to bring along my bathing suit, just in case, but remembering that dark pool in the middle of the ragged field from years before terrified me now. Would it be filled with dead bugs and dead animals?

Along with the fear was something else, a kind of ecstatic expectation: for on this night, at some moment I couldn't predict, he'd say, "Let's blast," and we'd walk down that wide staircase through the chemical smell of new textiles and out into the sweet-smelling night air, we'd get into his car and it would wheeze and rumble the way it did, and for the first time there would be no one but the two of us, heading for his mansion on the seven acres of land.

We drove with the top down, the heat blasting through the front vents. As we set off I thought: Here I am, with my father, at the beginning. I am Lisa and I have a father and we are driving between the outlines of dark hills, inside a strong wind perfumed with dry grasses. I told the story of myself *to* myself. I didn't know what the story would become, but I knew it would be something, maybe something big.

I was too scared to talk. It was almost pitch-black inside the car except for the dashboard lights, the trembling needles and round instruments that were nicer than those in other cars I'd seen. Their movements were precise, and they gave off a whiter glow. His kind of driving felt heavy and light at the same time: the car solid, fastened to the road, but accelerating quickly, with no resistance.

He turned on music, loud: "A Hard Day's Night." Ribbons of cool night air slipped in from the outside and mingled with the heat from the vents. I used the lever on the side of the seat to bring it up and forward as far as possible. My butt and thighs grew hot. The leather had small puncture holes like tiny dots—that must be where the heat came through.

We drove over Highway 280 on Sand Hill Road, then into the dark hills where there was only the smell of the grasses and far away the jagged ridge of redwood trees that met the bright night sky. My father didn't speak or look at me. It was hard to keep thinking of things to talk about. I wanted to be close with him all at once—to feel the way I imagined other children felt with their fathers; I wanted a conflagration of talk, of questions, of noticing. I'd been waiting for so long and now that we were here it felt too late.

Near his busy silence I felt a new kind of dissolution. I was starting to disappear. I noticed details about him with exact focus, but had difficulty locating myself.

I watched his hands on the steering wheel; he had smart fingers with fine black hair that grew straight on the first joint after the knuckle. His thumbs had wide fingernails. Like me, he bit his nails, and the skin on the sides. His jaw clenched on and off, making a rippling pattern in his skin, like a fish beneath the surface of a pond.

I swallowed air, worried that when my voice came out, it would squeak, or about the very real possibility that he would not respond. I was filled with what I might say, if he asked me a question: how I didn't do the Pledge of Allegiance at school because I said I was Buddhist; how Mrs. Keatsman twisted her ring; how my mother let me steer on the steep hills of Portola Valley when I was six; how I'd guessed the number of corn kernels in the jar; how I was practicing to do the leap like the girl in the magazine; how, when I was younger, to pass time while my mother was waiting in line at the bank, or looking at a painting at the art museum, I'd done headstands on the hard ground, painless, popping up to vertical in one motion. The moment was too fragile for these stories. I didn't want to break it.

"How was your day?" I finally asked, my fingers shaking, in my stomach a nausea creeping up toward my throat. (What would we have for dinner? What did he eat?)

"Okay, thanks," he said. It didn't make him look. He lapsed back into silence and didn't look at me for the rest of the drive.

It was not enough.

It was not enough!

The canopy of gnarled oak branches over the road flared into view and then went dark as we passed.

A single car came toward us, moving down the hill. My father toggled a rod beside the steering wheel and it gave a satisfying click; the headlights dimmed. Once we passed, he did it again, this time restoring the forest to light. I'd never noticed anyone dim lights for an oncoming car, and I felt a burst of affection for him, seized with an idea of his *fineness*. (When I told my mother about it the next day, she said everyone did that, everyone dimmed the brights for oncoming traffic.)

We turned onto Mountain Home Road, then onto a road with white pillars on either side, cracked and leaning, silvery in the darkness. And then we were approaching it, the face of the house: the flagpole, the gate, the house glowing white.

In the open courtyard two crates the size of small cars held giant trees shaped like bonsai, with clouds of spongy-looking foliage suspended off trunks that grew at an angle. I followed him to the front door under a high curving arch made of other rooms and suites that connected to more of the house on the other side. The front door was made of a rough wood that would give me a splinter if I ran my palm along its surface, much larger and heavier than I remembered from when I'd visited before.

Inside he flicked on a switch; the flick sound echoed against the tile floor. In the dim light I saw the grand staircase with its twisting banister disappearing upward and a motorcycle leaning against the wall in the huge entryway, the body black leather and bright chrome, double-lobed, like a wasp.

"Is that yours?" I asked. It hinted at a different life.

"Yeah," he said. "But I stopped riding it. Wanna take a hot tub later?"

So that's what the suit was for. When I asked, he showed me to a high-ceilinged bathroom I'd never seen before that would, in future years, come to define my idea of luxury: a disconnected cistern mounted far above the toilet; a hanging lamp in the shape of a three-dimensional star; Moorish tiles around the sink patterned in thick and colorful geometries, and bronze faucet handles shaped like wings. The room was dim and echoey, the ceiling so high you could hardly see it. I looked around for the flush and found a chain with a white ceramic knob, and when I pulled, the water came rushing down fiercely into the toilet.

I followed him into the ballroom, the ceiling ribbed with dark beams. In the center of the room was a glossy black piano with its lid lifted, a lamp, and a black leather couch. The furniture was large but looked small in this room. In the next room was a fireplace with a high arch, beneath which I could walk without stooping; beyond that, a pantry with empty white shelves that went all the way to the ceiling. Through a swinging door, we stepped into the huge white kitchen. I remembered the progression of vast rooms, the smell of mold and decay, from the time I'd visited before, but that time there had been no motorcycle or piano.

My father reached into the fridge and pulled out two wooden bowls containing salads and a bottle of juice murky with brown silt. There was nothing else inside but clean white shelves. He poured us each a glass to the brim, far more than I could drink, then filled a huge plate with the salads, piling them side by side, one shredded carrots with currants, the other bulgur wheat with parsley.

"I'm going to give you some of both, all right?" I nodded. No one had ever put so much food in front of me. Did he expect me to eat all of it?

"Now this," he said, holding up a rectangular bottle of green glass, "is the best olive oil in the world." I didn't usually like olive oil, but I let him draw a green line on the salads.

He handed me an enormous fork. The salads were cold and tasted of nothing, just their own rough textures. We sat side by side on stools at the island, facing the stove; he read a newspaper while he ate. After a while he asked if I was done, and when I said yes, he took my plate and glass—both still mostly full—and put them in the sink. He didn't say anything about how much I'd eaten.

"Let's change into our swimsuits," he said.

We went through a different door to a hallway and another whole set of empty rooms and a staircase with steps painted white, the paint wearing off in places.

"We're going to have to make a run for it," he said. There was no way to turn off the light from the top of the stairs. He flicked off the switch and we were plunged into darkness. The stairs creaked. I hugged the wall, feeling my way up. "Boo!" my father said. Then, ghostlike, "Woooooh, oooooooooooh!"

At the top I followed him to a door that led to a spindly covered wooden balcony that overlooked the courtyard with the boxed trees. The balcony trembled with the weight of our steps. "This thing's falling apart," he said. We walked along it to a screen door that creaked when he opened it. "The in-law suite," he said.

"What's an in-law?" I asked.

"A person you want to put somewhere far away." It was a whole apartment.

It smelled like the rest of the house—old carpet and mold and wood and paint. I followed him up some steps and down a small hallway into a big, empty room, his room. There was a mattress on the floor and a huge television on a metal rack.

"And this is your bed," he said, showing me to a room off his. There was a red shag carpet, and a futon on the floor made up with sheets tucked into its sides, and a pillow.

The small, somewhat furnished apartment somewhere inside the cavernous, echoing, and empty house gave the feeling of camping.

He left me alone to change. When I came out, he was waiting, barefoot, in shorts and a T-shirt. He handed me a big black towel—much bigger and plusher than other towels. Everything he owned was big: the trees in their crates, the front door, the fireplace, refrigerator, forks, and television.

Near the stairwell I noticed the same elevator I'd seen before. It looked like a plain doorway, except for the two black buttons beside it. I asked him if we could take it; he said yes, we could. It wouldn't move until the outer door was closed and the latch was closed on the inner accordion door, the diamond-shaped bars traveling with us, a buzzing sound coming from somewhere inside the cage. The wall slipped by, as if it were the thing moving and not us. It was like a little prison that held you and released you somewhere else. When it stopped and he reached over to unfasten the metal latch, his arm brushed mine. I pushed open the door and leapt out into the hallway.

Past the asphalt, down the hill to the pool, the sharp, stiff curls of dry oak leaves dug into my feet. The wind ruffled the leaves of huge trees around us. The path on the lawn sloped down to the pool and, beside it, the hot tub. In the moonlight I could see the hot tub was clean but the pool was filled with leaves.

My father took off his T-shirt and slipped into the hot tub. "Ah," he said, closing his eyes.

I got in and said it too: "Ah." I was sitting on the bench across from him. I leaned my head back: above me the whole vast sky was covered in stars. They ripped at my heart. I felt the cold wind on my face and listened to the crickets, the creaking of the trees. It was like being in the car with the top down and the heater on—the cold air, the hot water—two temperatures at once.

We sat in silence, the bubbles and mist on the surface of the water. I dipped my head underwater. I thought about doing a handstand, but with the current from the jets and the cement benches and the possibility of hitting his legs, I decided not to.

"All right, champ," he said. "Ready to get out?"

"Okay," I said. My fingers were wrinkled into hills. We wrapped our towels around us and walked back on the prickly ground. I felt that I was with him and also alone. On the asphalt where the car was parked, he pointed up to the second floor on the corner. "We should build a slide from the bedroom to the pool. What do you think?"

"Yes. I think we should, definitely," I said. I wondered if it was just a joke. I hoped it was real.

His house was crumbling in places and tended to in others, a configuration of attention and neglect I didn't understand. The toilets had rust-colored rings in the basins, and water dripped into the corner of a distant wing, while outside raspberries were trellised meticulously in the garden. He left the whole place empty, as if he didn't own it but was a visitor or a squatter. When I asked him how many rooms there were, he said he didn't know, he hadn't set foot in most of them.

Later, I explored. Rooms and suites and dusty doors swung open to more empty dusty rooms, more tiled sinks and showers. Toward the back of the property was a huge building that looked to me like a church. It was meant to house a water tower, but inside it was missing the cistern, had only circles cut out of wood at every story, empty in the center where the tank would have been. These outlines of circles were covered in leaves and bird poop and cobwebs, silvering with age, like the abandoned bones of a huge animal. The whole time he lived there I don't think I visited every last room—a kind of magic, to have unconquered space, to be past a frontier. I found a tennis court beyond the pool, with vines clogging the surrounding fence. Roots warped and cracked through the court's green surface; in places the color had faded or worn away. The net was dirty and sagged between the poles all the way to the ground.

"Is the tennis court yours?" I asked him.

"I don't know," he said.

"Do you know how to play?" I asked.

"Nope," he said.

"I don't know how either," I said.

After the hot tub, we watched *The Red Balloon* and then we watched *Harold and Maude*, lying on our sides in his bed, him closer to the screen. I didn't like *The Red Balloon*, because it seemed too young and immature for me; also, I had a feeling I was supposed to like it because he'd chosen it beforehand, the First Movie, and this made me self-conscious. *Harold and Maude* I loved. He paused the movie when I got up to pee. "That's the church in Palo Alto," he said, about the church where they meet.

Both movies were on laser discs, which looked like bright silver records. He held the disc from the center and edge, not touching the surface, and when the player closed, it made a series of mechanical sounds: four notes.

The laser disc insertion, the hydraulic thump of the car doors, the click of the lever that controlled the headlights—the noises surrounding him were different. Beside his bed was a lamp with a cloth shade and gold-colored base. You only had to touch the base to turn the lamp on and off. I tried it a few times. Ingenious. Why didn't everyone have one? Why did we bother with switches and serrated knobs?

"Time to go to bed," he said after the movie ended.

Was it late? I couldn't tell. We existed outside regular time. The mornings with him, too, would have a timeless quality, more empty space and white light and silence—unlike the mornings with my mother, when we raced to dress in front of the heaters and ate toast in the car on the way to school, the windshield mostly white, waiting for the heat to work. Here there was no rush, no breathlessness.

At night the crickets made a roar I hadn't noticed before lying in the bed. The sound would advance toward me over the dark land, the dark lawn, the big dark house, and press against my ears, but just when I thought I'd be swallowed up, it would stop, empty. It was terrible and lonely, I felt then, to be in this cavernous house with this man I hardly knew.

My mother had a string of lentil-sized bells on a ribbon she'd brought back from India, meant to be tied around the ankles of Indian dancers, and the crickets sounded like these bells—thousands of dancers moving vigorously almost in unison faster and faster until they all stopped at once.

"Why don't you wear a watch?" I asked the next morning. I was already dressed for school. Fancy men wore watches.

"I don't want to be bound by time," he said.

"What's that?" I was looking out the kitchen window, pointing to a tall structure that looked like a booth for a ticket collector, with a screen in the front so you could see in, topped by a minaret.

"It's an aviary. For birds."

"Are there birds inside?"

"No. A friend gave me a peacock once, but it wandered off."

"Will you get some birds to put in?" I asked.

"Nope."

I could tell he was getting annoyed by my questions. How big was seven acres, I wondered. If you stood on the huge lawn and looked toward the gathered hills with your back to the tennis court and the pool, and looked past the aviary, past a huge copper beech tree, the raspberries, more oaks, the building where the water tower would have been—maybe *that* was where the property ended, where the hills rose up and the forest began. "There," he'd said once, pointing, but I wasn't sure where he meant.

He put two apples and a handful of almonds in a paper bag, a grocery bag, not a lunch bag, and rolled up the top. "Here's your lunch," he said, handing it over. The almonds rattled around at the bottom of the bag.

I walked out ahead of him, through the pantry, the dining room, and into the huge room with the piano. On a small table in front of the couch was a coffee-table book called *The Red Couch*. The pictures inside were of a worn red velvet couch, upon which sat various famous people in different locations around the world. I flipped a page, and there he was. In the picture he looked dreamy, his eyes like vellum. Unlike the others in the book, he steepled his hands, the fingertips meeting, index to index, middle to middle, and so on, the wrists held out from each other like the rib cage of a small animal. Over the next few months I tried to incorporate the steepled hands into my own repertoire—on top of my desk in class, or on the table before my mother and I ate dinner, or on my lap sitting outside with friends at lunchtime. I could never make it look natural; in that position, ballooned out, my hands felt huge and foolish.

We walked out the door. "You don't lock it?" I asked.

"There's nothing to take," he said.

"You could get more furniture," I said. I imagined how grand the house could be if he'd just get some furniture. I wanted him to be attached to it so substantially that he wanted to decorate it and keep it. At school, we played a game called MASH: mansion, apartment, shack, house, writing down options about cars, husbands, and houses and then counting out our futures based on a random number. I had firsthand knowledge of all four categories—even a shack, if you counted the studio on Oak Grove. My father had a mansion. I didn't know anyone else who could say that. Everyone wanted a mansion, and also the best kind of car—Porsche, Ferrari, Lamborghini.

At the curve that led over Highway 280, my father said, "If you look where you're going, your hands naturally know how to steer toward that point. It's really amazing."

He had no idea that I'd driven, too, sitting on my mother's lap when I was six. For him, maybe I had no past; I was simply here now beside him.

At the top of Sand Hill Road, he pointed to Hoover Tower sticking up past the rooflines.

"Look," he said. "It's a penis."

I wasn't sure what he meant.

"The Penis of Palo Alto," he said. "Just look at it, with that red top."

The tower was glowing in the morning sun, and the dome at the top matched the red terracotta of the university rooftops. I'd been up there with my mother, near the bells and the pigeons and the wind. There was a net surrounding the bells so that the pigeons wouldn't roost inside them.

"Oh," I said, laughing a little, trying to make the connection between this structure and the very few penises I'd seen, skin-colored cylinders that dangled down.

"It looks like a penis," he said again, defiantly.

♦

"I'm going to die in my early forties," my father said to me around this time. He'd come to pick me up at a friend's house for the first time. His delivery was dramatic, as if to stir some action, but there was no action I could see to take. Forty seemed pretty old from my vantage point of eight. I was secretly happy he'd confided in me, pleased by the implication that we'd have more time together—four to nine years! I already knew he'd predicted both his fame and his early demise. My mother had told me about it. Did he think we didn't talk about him in his absence? The serious way he spoke suggested he thought that for all those years he'd been gone we didn't think of him, or talk about him; as if when he left a room, the room ceased to exist.

Anyway, his pronouncement didn't seem tragic, but uplifting. I'd take a few years over none at all.

He was great, and great people, like JFK, like Lennon, died young. I didn't know about that but he did.

On the drive to his house that night he said, "It used to be orchards, all of this." Now the land was roads and low huddled buildings that looked like they'd always been there.

"When I die, bury me under an apple tree," he said.

I remembered to remember later.

He repeated this often when we were alone, and I figured I would have the responsibility to make it happen. Unboxed, he meant. So the roots could drink him up.

The next two Wednesdays were similar: the drive to his house with the top down and the heater on, an assortment of cold salads and juice, a hot tub, a movie on laser disc—*North by Northwest, Modern*

Times, City Lights. Before we watched one, he would ask me if I'd ever seen the movie before. When I said no, he'd shake his head, seriously, in silence, like it was some big mistake. Each time I had to pee during a movie, he paused it. The night of the third visit I wet the bed and woke up mortified that the people who made the beds would tell him about it. A couple lived in a small house on the land, made the salads, and washed the sheets. I was almost nine; I hadn't wet a bed for many years. But the next week the bed was made again and he didn't mention it.

Before dinner we played "Heart and Soul" on the piano, alternating parts. I think it was the only song either of us knew how to play. The notes rang out in the large, empty room.

After I was in bed, I waited as many minutes as possible, building up my courage in the cricket-jangling darkness, then emerged from my bedroom and walked to the end of his bed, fake-crying. Maybe I got the idea from *Annie*, a girl ingratiating herself with a gruff man. Standing over my father in my sleep T-shirt, looking down at him in his bed on the floor, I was aware of being small and using what I had, as a girl. Inspiring love, I thought, had to do with being defenseless. For him to be close with me, like other fathers with their daughters, he needed to love me. Also, his bed was more comfortable than mine.

He removed his headphones and looked at me. He watched movies with a big pair of headphones after I went to bed.

"I had a nightmare," I said. "Can I sleep in your bed?"

"I guess so," he said, and pointed to the side farther away from the television. I jumped in and the pillow dissolved under the weight of my head, as if it were made of nothing.

My request seemed to annoy, rather than charm him. I hoped this might change over time. He was not the father I'd imagined from the skeleton of facts I'd known. Yes, there was an elevator and a piano and an organ, he was rich and famous and handsome, but none of this satisfied completely; it was tempered by an unmistakable emptiness I felt near him, a feeling of a vast loneliness—the stair behind the kitchen with no light, the wind coming through from the rickety balcony. It was supposed to be what I wanted, but it was not possible to enjoy as I'd hoped, as if it were a sumptuous feast frozen solid.

He woke me up in the morning by shaking my shoulder very quickly like a pulse. "Rise and shine," he said.

I pulled on my clothes, and as he was getting ready I explored, opening a door off his bedroom and peering into what turned out to be a closet with a row of suits hung on matching hangers, the sleeves in a perfect horizontal row. Unlike the rest of this house, these suits had been chosen and collected. You could tell they were new, and expensive. Not one sleeve lower or higher than another. I ran my hand along the rounds of fabric where the sleeves ended, each of them so soft and light it felt like I was brushing my hand over ridges of water in a stream.

"Ingrid Bergman's incredibly beautiful," he said the next week while we watched *Casablanca*. "Did you know she didn't wear any makeup? She was *that* beautiful."

I liked her lips, how they were flat and full and formed a ledge where they met her cheeks; I liked her accent, and the way she swayed gently as she walked. It seemed my father's idea of beauty demanded no artifice, it simply *was*, although, looking back, I think she must have been wearing mascara, at least.

I liked women who wore lipstick and makeup and fancy clothing and long painted fingernails and hair spray; those, to me, were beautiful.

It gave me a strange feeling when he talked of the beauty of other women, the longing in his voice when he talked of blonde hair or of breasts, gesturing weights in his cupped hands. When he talked about them, they were all details, no movement, exempt from the mess of life.

I would be truly loved by him only if I was tall, blonde, and large-breasted, I would gather later. I had a fantastic notion that it might happen, despite the evidence.

"You know, I heard this great story about Ingrid Bergman once," he said. "But it's kind of a secret, so you can't tell."

We'd finished watching the movie and he was putting the laser disc into its case.

"I won't tell, I promise," I said.

"I have this friend," he said, "his father was a movie producer, and when he was a boy, Ingrid Bergman came to stay at his house. They had a pool, and she was lying on a chair beside it."

My father was crouched on the side of the bed, near the television. When he told gossip and secrets, he used better diction and spoke more rapidly.

"Well," he continued, "it turns out Ingrid Bergman liked to sunbathe in the nude, and my friend, who was a boy then, whose bedroom looked out over the pool, was watching her. And then she was, well, she was . . ."

He trailed off. I had absolutely no idea what he was talking about.

"Anyway," he said, "the moment it happened, the climax, she looked up at him. *Right at him.*"

"Oh," I said. What had she done? What did he watch? Why was she naked? "I mean, the friend is my age now," as if to clarify. "Anyway, for him it must have been incredible," he said, shaking his head and looking down, smiling to himself.

He repeated this story several times over many years, each time telling me he'd heard a great story, and a huge secret, forgetting he'd told me before.

At some point around that time, with my new allowance (five dollars per week), I bought a navy blue eyeliner pencil and brought it over to his house. In the morning before we left for school, while he waited for me, I went into the bathroom and leaned against the sink so I was close to the mirror and tried to apply it to an eyelid.

"Come on," he said holding the screen, standing out on the balcony.

"One minute," I said. The liner was waxy and didn't set down like pencil on paper. I was afraid of making it too dark, so I drew it on very lightly, almost imperceptibly. I'd heard my mother say that makeup was good when it was not obvious. I was giddy with the idea that he would realize how sophisticated I was; my hand shook. At the door I asked if he noticed anything on my eyes.

He leaned down. "Nope," he said.

"Good," I said. "You're not supposed to see it."

"See what?"

"Eyeliner," I said. "I put some on."

"Go wash it off," he said, angry. "Now."

"Look at the sky," my mother said. She was driving us home. "Isn't it incredible?" Out of the corner of my eye, I saw a stripe of hot-pink clouds running over the telephone wires, and glowing gold leaves on the sycamore trees beside the road.

"I guess," I said.

My mother felt color acutely; it was one of the ways we communicated, her driving around the town, pointing out colors. She'd broken up with Ron, and although I was initially relieved to be rid of him and have my mother to myself again, now I wasn't so sure. I'd found him annoying, but once he was gone I missed him. Ron had been variety, someone else besides my mother and me. When he walked into our house, he disturbed the air. Men brought life. You couldn't take the measure of it until they were gone and left everything flat, without zest or surprise. We couldn't afford to go out for dinner or to the museum in San Francisco.

Now, in the car, she wanted me to look at the sky.

"Look up," she said. "What's wrong with you?"

I slouched in my seat like the flare of color was the most boring thing in the world. It seemed to me it would take too much energy to appreciate every phenomenon she pointed out. It was just a sunset. We'd seen a lot of them already; already, life had begun to repeat.

Kirsten invited me to her house to spend the night. She was the girl who'd followed me around announcing my father's name. Since then, she'd stopped doing that, and we were part of the same group of friends at school. We had permission to walk from school to her dad's house, which was north past University Avenue, the opposite side of Palo Alto from where I lived. It was a privilege to be able to walk that far alone, without an adult.

Her house was a Victorian with a cement path leading up to the wooden steps. Tree roots snaked and strained through the dirt yard like neck tendons. Her bedroom was under the eaves at the top of the house, the ceiling tucked into the floor. She had her own small television. I sat down on the bed and it shifted around me like Jell-O, a surprise.

"It's a water bed," she said, stretching out.

There was something exotic about her, and slippery, that made me feel conservative and ordinary. I also got sleepy around her, the way I would get sleepy around people who cared about my father being famous. We went downstairs, where I followed her into the kitchen.

She pulled a big carrot out of the fridge.

"You know what some women do with these, right?" she said. "Put it *inside* them. Instead of having sex."

"That's gross," I said. The world contained disgusting, revolting elements—like sex, which I knew about, and which still felt unsettling, how people might be doing it and yet continuing to exist in an ordinary fashion on the surface, like an infestation of bugs under a clean, white wall.

"Look," she said, pulling out a black gauzy string from her chest of drawers. It was a bra made of elasticized lace, two triangles bound by black strips of Lycra. It looked like a woman's bra—sexy for a grown-up—yet small, made for a child. I'd had no idea something this perfect existed in the world, in these proportions. It was tantalizing for being a perfect miniature, the way dollhouse furniture, food, and cutlery had been thrilling to me before. I wanted all of what she had—the remote, the television, the water bed, the lacy bra.

"Hey, you want to watch *The Texas Chainsaw Massacre?*"

"Okay," I said. I wasn't sure what it was. She took a tape out of a worn paper case, pushed it into the VHS player under her television. The film was grainy like a sweater woven out of too many

colors of yarn. I could make out only the figure of a man walking
up a path in dry grasses, toward a house.

"I watch this a lot," she said. "Before I go to sleep."

Before we turned off the light, her father came in to check
on us.

"Dad?" Kristen said.

He sat down on the edge of the bed facing her.

"I'm feeling insecure," she said, in a baby voice. "You told me
to tell you when I was feeling like that, and I'm telling you now."

"Oh, honey," he said. He hugged her close.

I'd had no idea she was feeling insecure. I was impressed she
knew that word, and jealous that she could say something like this
to her father. It was an adult word. I wouldn't have thought to say
it, ever.

"Sorry, dear," he said and then stood up and looked at both of
us. "Well, goodnight, you two. Sleep tight." The stairs creaked on his
way down.

In the morning, just before my mother came to pick me up,
after Kirsten had gone down to the kitchen, I found the bra in the
thicket of rumpled cotton in the top drawer and stuffed it into my
backpack.

By the fifth visit to his house I was impatient. For a long time I
hoped that if I played one role, my father would take the corresponding role. I would be the beloved daughter; he would be the indulgent
father. I decided that if I acted like other daughters, he would join
in the lark. We'd pretend together, and in pretending we'd make it
real. But if I had observed him as he was, or admitted to myself
what I saw, I would have known that he would not do this, and that
a game of pretend would disgust him.

Now we were together in his car driving to the Woodside house
in the dark. Tonight he wore a leather jacket with black fabric at

the cuffs that matched the color of his hair and gave him a rakish look. He was still quiet. But I felt bolder.

"Can I have it, when you're done?" I asked him, as we took a left at the leaning, crumbling white pillars that flanked the thin, bumpy road that ended at his gate. I'd been thinking about it for a while but only just built up the courage to ask.

"Can you have what?" he said.

"This car. Your Porsche." I wondered where he put the extras. I pictured them in a shiny black line at the back of his land.

"Absolutely not," he said in such a sour, biting way that I knew I'd made a mistake. I understood that perhaps it wasn't true, the myth of the scratch: maybe he didn't buy a new one with abandon, maybe the idea that he was profligate was false. He was not generous with money, food, or words; the idea of the Porsches had seemed like one glorious exception.

I wished I could take it back. We pulled up to the house and he turned off the engine. Blue hydrangeas with flowers bigger than my head billowed out from both sides of the gate to the courtyard.

(Many years later he would quiz me. "What do you think is the best kind of hydrangea?"

"The blue ones. The bright blue ones."

"I used to think so, too, when I was young," he said. "But it turns out the white ones, the cone-shaped ones, are actually much nicer.")

Before I made a move to get out he turned to face me.

"You're not getting anything," he said. "You understand? Nothing. You're getting nothing." Did he mean about the car, something else, bigger? I didn't know. His voice hurt—sharp, in my chest.

The light was cool in the car, a white light on the roof had lit up when the engine turned off. Around us was dark. I had made a terrible mistake and he'd recoiled.

By then the idea that he'd named the failed computer after me was woven in with my sense of self, even if he did not confirm it, and I used this story to bolster myself when, near him, I felt like nothing. I didn't care about computers—they were made of fixed metal parts and chips with glinting lines inside plastic cases. They mesmerized you when you sat in front of them, but were otherwise boring to look at, not beautiful—but I liked the idea that I was connected to him in this way. It would mean I'd been chosen and had a place, despite the fact that he was aloof or absent. It meant I was fastened to the earth and its machines. He was famous, he drove a Porsche; if the Lisa was named after me, I was a part of all that.

I see now that we were at cross-purposes. For him, I was a blot on a spectacular ascent, as our story did not fit with the narrative of greatness and virtue he might have wanted for himself. My existence ruined his streak. For me, it was the opposite: the closer I was to him, the less I would feel ashamed; he was part of the world, and he would accelerate me into the light.

It might all have been a big misunderstanding, a missed connection: he'd simply forgotten to mention the computer was named after me. I was shaking with the need to set it right all at once, as if waiting for a person to arrive for a surprise party—to switch on the lights and yell out what I'd held in. Once he'd admitted it—yes, I named a computer after you—everything would click into place. He would patch the holes, get furniture, say he'd been thinking of me the whole time but had been unable to get to me. Yet I also sensed that if I tried too hard to set it right, it might tip some delicate balance, and he would be gone again. And so I waited in this suspended state, in order to keep him.

I followed him from the car into the house. We didn't take a hot tub. We ate salads as he read the paper, we watched *Flashdance*. I didn't try to sleep in his bed. At some point I awoke in the dark because I had to pee, the darkness pressing on my eyes, nothing visible. It was silent; the crickets had stopped. I wouldn't be able to find the bathroom in the pitch-black. I couldn't even tell what direction I was facing, or whether I was upright. I waited with my eyes open in the darkness and nothing emerged; it was as if the darkness were pressing back at my efforts to penetrate it.

To get to the bathroom I would have to walk through his room, down a few more steps in a hallway that led to another empty room and, off that, the bathroom.

I crawled out of the bed and found the door frame, also chalky, half-there, but now shapes emerged with more clarity, and I saw that in his bed across the room was someone with bright blond hair.

It was a man who had come to kill my father—he'd killed him already and was now sleeping in his bed! I already knew what this new man was like with his shining white hair: phony and full of blandishments. He'd say he was my new father, but he would be nothing like my father. I couldn't see his face, but I was terrified; the blond hair glowed in the dark. I could hear my breath. I worried for my real father. After I crept to the bathroom, I crept back through the room and the blond man was still there, in the bed. He moved in his sleep, diving down under the covers as if plunging underwater. I returned to my bed and spent what felt like hours terrified, wondering what to do, dreading the morning when it would be clear that my life would be different forever and my father would be gone. I was too afraid to get up again and confront the blond man. I decided to wait until morning, and at some point I must have fallen asleep.

In the morning, there was no blond man and my father was alive. I thought I must have imagined it—I didn't ask him about it. I was embarrassed for the terror I'd felt, and the protectiveness.

The next Wednesday night, my mother drove over to visit us when her class was unexpectedly canceled. We didn't know she was coming. She found us in the kitchen, having knocked and called out and then entered through the unlocked front door, walking through

the dark house into the bright and cold kitchen where we were sitting, eating. She sat with us as he teased me in the usual ways.

"How about that guy for your boyfriend," he said pointing to
a picture of an old man in the paper he was reading while we ate. I
looked, then sneezed, and a few grains of the salad flew onto the
picture. "The boys'll love that. You'll have that bed warmed up in no
time at all," he said, about a new bed Mona was planning to buy for
me. "Who you gonna invite over?" The jokes were profoundly awkward. He was refined in other ways, but seemed unsure about how
you were supposed to talk with children. I wanted to be close with
him, but the jokes confused me. I didn't know how to respond. That
might have been the look she saw on my face.

Later she said his jokes that night, his avuncular manner, and
my obvious discomfort in the kitchen had surprised her. I had a look
of being lost, she said, not confident the way I usually was. She
arranged for me to stay at a friend's house on those Wednesday
nights, telling me that he planned to come and take me skating
instead. I thought that sounded okay.

Small Fry

Our next house would be the place we'd live the longest during my childhood, seven years, a Craftsman bungalow on Rinconada Avenue in Palo Alto—the only house on the lot, with three bedrooms, two bathrooms, and a separate garage my mother would later transform into an art studio. It was a real house, painted light yellow with royal blue trim, a blue door. It was symmetrical from the front, with a cement path that bisected the lawn, and dirt patches under two front windows where my mother would plant multicolored impatiens. An arbutus tree grew on one side of the driveway, with scaly twisting bark and fruits we did not yet know would ripen and fall onto the lawn in the autumn rains and burst open, leaving a slimy orange jelly we would be forever wiping off our shoes. The side door opened to a thick bower of wisteria that smelled of soap and candy when it bloomed, and attracted bees.

Before we moved in, a man who worked for my father at NeXT as facilities manager helped renovate the rental house. He was a kind, beanpole-tall man who stooped down to talk to me, telling me that I was allowed to pick out the shape of the bathroom sink and the linoleum for the floor. He had a high laugh and a large, sharp Adam's apple that bobbed alarmingly up and down his neck. Under his direction, the house was repainted on the inside, the wood floors were refinished and stained blond, linoleum was laid in the bathrooms and kitchen, metal venetian blinds were attached to the windows. In the bathroom, the sink I'd chosen belled out, regally, at the top.

My mother bought a set of encyclopedias with pictures of a gold thistle on the spines, and when there was a question about something, she would rush over and pull one off the bookshelf, dividing the gold-painted seal across the pages to read the relevant section aloud.

She had a walk-in closet. It wasn't big, and maybe it wasn't big enough to fit the definition of the phrase "walk-in closet," but because it was large enough to get inside, and turn around, that's what we called it. There were bars for hangers and wire shelves for clothes. She also had her own small bathroom, with a skylight.

One day, standing in her bathroom, she showed me her new wallet.

"It's from Neiman Marcus," she said. I examined it under the skylight: shades of taupe skin made of strips sewn together vertically, darker in the middle than at the edge, wrinkled at the center of each strip as if a thread was yanked to form tucks. It was the softest leather I'd felt, and waxy.

"It's eel skin," she said. "Isn't that terrible? Eels!"

"It's like silk," I said. "Or butter."

"I know. And look at this." She showed me the metal snap, the size of a dime. I could feel it was a magnet: it found itself, and pulled shut.

As far as I knew, she'd never owned a wallet before. These luxuries—the wallet, skylight, closet; a new microwave that spun the food as it cooked; a cordless phone—suggested that some great change was brewing, that we were entering a new, more exquisite realm. It turned out that my father had increased the child-support payments to include a larger amount of rent and maintenance. Soon, he would also agree to pay for her therapy once per week. She couldn't afford to replace the couch, but she got it re-covered in more muted flowers.

My father stopped by a few times, just after the renovations. He and my mother seemed easy with each other, joking and admiring the house, both of them liking the shade of paint inside, the new industrial light fixtures, two white metal bars over a ridged frosted-glass shade, fixtures that were meant for outdoors but looked good inside too. When my parents were together, I felt something inside me click into place, like the magnet clasp.

A few times, during that first year in the house, when it was still new and perfect around us, she would walk in the front door and stop and gasp, putting her hand on her heart, at the beauty of a gold parallelogram made of light glowing on the wall above the heater vent.

Over the years in that house my mother told stories about my father and her family when they occurred to her, or I asked about them. She said my father was so shy and awkward in high school that when he would talk or tell a joke, no one would listen. He had made my mother a kite and a pair of sandals. When they lived together that summer at the end of Stevens Canyon Road in the house with the goats, they slept under quilts my mother's grandmother from Ohio had made, and for a treat, they ate those cheap, miniature hot dogs out of jars.

At some point that summer, my mother said, they were down to their last three dollars, and they drove to the beach, where my father threw the money into the ocean.

"I was terrified," she said. "But then he sold more of the blue boxes, and we had money again."

The story of my parents is not complete without a picture of my mother's disintegrating family life, of how, after the family arrived in California when she was twelve, her mother became mentally ill. Her parents, Jim and Virginia, had moved the family west when my grandfather's employer, the Department of Defense, transferred him from Dayton, Ohio, where she was born and both her grandmothers lived, to Colorado Springs, then to Omaha, Nebraska, and finally to California. In California, Virginia was diagnosed with paranoid schizophrenia and my mother's parents divorced.

My mother spoke of Ohio like a lost paradise: in Ohio her grandmothers had made quilts and doted on her, let her play with the skin on the back of their hands. One of them had a farm and a chicken coop, where my mother ran to collect eggs in the morning. The time before her mother went crazy. Anytime my mother pointed out some beauty around us that looked established and grand—gold

dusk light stretched across brick buildings with pillars, great trees—
she named the beauty Ohio.

In California, Virginia would sit in the darkened living room
drunk, smoking, the only visible thing the lit tip of her cigarette,
waiting for her daughters to get home from school. My mother was
only a little older then than I was now when Virginia aimed much
of her spite and contempt at her—maybe because my mother, sensitive, artistic, and bright, reminded her most of herself. When my
mother was twelve, Virginia accused her of playing the recorder only
because it reminded her of a penis, and Virginia told the neighbors
that my mother had sex with dogs.

When my mother met my father in high school, what impressed
her most were his kind eyes, compared with her own mother's eyes,
which by then were hateful, dark sparks.

"The third time I visited Steve's house in high school, his mother
took me aside. She told me that in his first six months she was afraid
she might lose him because his birth mother wanted him back, and
she couldn't allow herself to get close to him. At the time, I had no
idea why she was telling me this," my mother said. "I was just a high
school student. It wasn't like I thought I'd know him that long."

She told the story as if it meant something, but I wasn't sure
what it meant.

They fell in love. My father wrote long notes to Virginia and
left them on her front door, telling Virginia she was cruel, imploring
her to stop being cruel to my mother. My father was my mother's
savior then, noticing her talent, beauty, and sensitivity, caring for her
when her own mother was violent and insane. "You're the most
creative person I've ever met," he told her.

My parents took LSD together. His first time, not hers. The
drug took a while to kick in, she said, so you just waited around and
then at some point you realized the world wasn't normal anymore
and the trip had started. The idea of my mother doing drugs made
me squirm, but she said, "Don't worry, Lisa. It was just a time—a

different era." She said he was terrified of making a fool of himself on drugs, and made her promise to tell him to snap out of it, in case he got weird. That was around the time my father told my mother he'd get famous and rich one day and lose himself in the world.

"What do you mean, 'lose himself'?" I asked her. I pictured him confused in the middle of a crowd.

"I mean, lose his moral compass," she said. "Trade his character, his soul, for power, for money, for worldly gain. Contort himself. Lose the connection to his soul."

Beside the house where they lived together over the summer before he left for college was another bungalow with a couple of kids in their twenties from a rich family. They did a lot of drugs and sat around waiting for their parents to die so they could get their inheritance. This left a big impression on both of my parents, how people could waste their lives.

Years later she would tell me this story as a way to explain why my father wouldn't help me with money, repeating the story of those lazy, lost children he'd seen and didn't want me to become.

"When were your parents divorced?" other kids would ask me.

"They were never married," I said. I liked saying it: it was usually a surprise, disarming the questioner. It gave me distinction. Instead of a dad who was around and then left, mine was a story in reverse: parents who spent more time together now than they'd spent when I was born.

♦

Now on weekends when he was around, my father came over to take me skating on my own, my mother staying home to paint, waving goodbye to us as we set off. He called me Small Fry. "Hey, Small Fry, let's blast. We're livin' on borrowed time."

I assumed small fry meant the kind of french fries left at the bottom of the bag, cold and crusty; I thought he was calling me a runt, or misbegotten. Later, I learned fry is an old word for young fishes sometimes thrown back into the sea to give them more time to grow.

"Okay, Fat Fry, let's go," I said, once my skates were on. Sometimes he worried he was getting too thin. "They say I need to gain weight," he said. "Who?" I asked. "People at work," he said, standing in the middle of the room with his skates on. "What do you guys think?" Other times he worried he was getting a paunch, and asked us about that too.

We would head for Stanford University. On this day the pavement was still wet from rain.

The palm trees that gave Palm Drive its name grew in the dirt between the sidewalk and the road, their roots winding beneath the old cement path so the cement was ridged severely, and layered over several times in messy uneven layers, but these hadn't worked to hold down the roots, each layer buckling up. We bounced our knees to absorb the shock. Fronds had fallen from the trees, sometimes blocking the path, so we had to step around them into the dirt on our skates. The missing fronds left a pattern on the trunks like fishes, stacked.

"I wish I'd been a Native American Indian," he said, looking up at the hills beyond the university—from far away they appeared smooth and unblemished. The neon-green blades shot up through

the dirt clods two or three days after the first heavy rain and remained
through winter.

"They walked barefoot, you know," he said. "On those hills.
Before all this was even here." I knew from school they left traces
where they had ground acorns into flour on slabs of rock. "I love the
green hills," he said, "but I like them best when they're yellow, dry."

"I like them green," I said, not understanding how anyone could
like them when they were dead.

We reached the Oval and then the Stanford quadrangle with
its covered, shaded pathways made of diamonds of cement in alternating earth-toned colors like a faded harlequin costume.

"Want to get on my shoulders?"

He leaned down and grasped me under my armpits—I was
nine and small for my age—and hoisted me up. His weight tilted
and bobbed. We did a loop around the square, under the arches, past
the gold numbers on the glass doors. He held my shins in his hands,
but let go when he started to lose his balance. He tripped, tripped
again, struggling to stay upright—I swayed, terrifyingly high up.
And then he fell. On the way down I worried for myself, for my
face and my knees, the parts of me that might hit the pavement.
Over time I learned he would always fall. Still, I let him carry me
because it seemed important to him. I felt this like a change of
pressure in the air: this was part of his notion of what it meant to
be a father and daughter. If I said no, he would retract.

We got up and brushed ourselves off—he wound up with a
bruise on his butt and a scrape on his hand; I got a skinned knee—
and headed for the drinking fountain at the side of the quadrangle.
It was built into a wall of patterned tiles. From there I could see the
green leaves in another, smaller courtyard beyond us, like stained
glass. I liked looking at sunlight from the shade, the way it didn't
wash all around and blind you, but was a separate, glowing thing.

We skated farther into the university. The asphalt was rough,
full of rocks; skating over it tickled my throat and my thighs, made

a tune play in my bones. We skated uphill past the fountain and the clock, to the metal tables in the courtyard of a Tresidder café, where we sat for a moment and drank apple juice. I strummed my legs with the weight of the skates and poked my fingers through the cool metal lattice of the chair. There was an oak above us on a raised part of the courtyard with silver ridges twisting up the trunk and deep grooves with black at their centers.

On the way back through the campus, on the sloping downhill on the rough cement, I was a tuning fork for the road, flying out ahead of him. "Ah AH!" I sang, my throat vibrating with the stones.

"You're all right, kid," he said. "But don't let it go to your head."

"I won't," I said. I'd never heard the phrase before: Let It Go To Your Head.

He pointed out the stained glass and golden tiles, the way the masons had used local sandstone, from the pillars to the big rocks that made up the exterior walls. The stone had thick granules of sand in it; the light gave it dimension, made it look faceted and rough; some areas had carvings, like the stone was embroidered.

"Do you think these stonemasons came from other countries to do this?" he asked, touching one of the big rectangles tufted out like a pillow.

I saw the building the way he did then, just a pile of stones that human hands had carved and placed. I began to see how inside my father there were two competing qualities: one sensitive and specific as a nerve in a tooth, the other unaware, blunt, and bland. Because he noticed the details and care of the craftsmen who built this place, the way they'd chipped at every block and arranged it, I knew he must be capable of noticing other people too. Of noticing me.

"You know, I didn't go to college," he said. "Maybe you won't go either. Better just to go out and get into the world."

If I didn't go to college, I would be like him. At that moment, I felt like we were the center of the world. He carried it with him, this feeling of center.

"They teach you how other people think, during your most productive years," he said. "It kills creativity. Makes people into bozos."

It made sense to me. Still, I wondered why he always wanted to skate around Stanford, why he seemed to love it, if he didn't believe in it.

"He's just got a chip on his shoulder," my mother said, when I told her we thought college was a waste of time.

When we crossed the street, he grabbed my hand.

"Do you know why we hold hands?" he asked.

"Because we're supposed to?" I hoped he'd reply, Because I'm your father. Other than these crossings, we didn't hold hands, and I looked forward to it.

"Nope," he said. "It's so, if a car is about to hit you, I can throw you out of the street."

On University Avenue he pointed to a bum crouched in a nook with a cardboard sign. "That's me in two years," he said.

A few minutes later, as we got into the residential streets farther away from the main street of the town and closer to my house, he farted, the sound loud and high like a balloon opening, interrupting the silence. He kept skating like nothing happened. When he did it again, I looked away. After the third time, he muttered, "Sorry."

"It's okay," I said, mortified for him.

When my father and I got back to my block, kids were out playing in the yards and on the sidewalks. Straight across from our house lived a tall, short-haired woman named Jan, whose husband worked at NeXT. Farther down the long driveway that ran beside Jan's house was the dark wooden house of a woman who'd dated my father when my mother was pregnant with me, and who was now married and had a baby boy. It was a strange coincidence to move here and find ourselves living on a line with two people connected to my father; my mother said he attracted coincidences in an uncanny way.

We stopped on the sidewalk across from our house, and a few men who lived nearby gathered around my father—three fathers holding three babies. They wanted his opinions, wanted to know what he thought about this or that. The mothers chased after the toddlers to give the fathers a chance to talk. I stood nearby, proud that it was my father they wanted to talk with. They discussed people I'd never heard of and companies I didn't know.

Soon, the babies began to fuss, squirming, letting out little cries and yelps.

My father continued to talk—hardware, software—the same discussions that seemed to come up over and over with all the men we saw in Palo Alto those days. All three babies began to wail. My father talked as if nothing had changed, and the men tried to listen, bouncing the babies, who wailed louder. He talked louder, faster, so his words got through the noise. His voice was high, loud, and nasal, with sharp points at the end of his phrases that hurt my ears and knifed into my sternum, and I wondered if that's what it was like for the babies who were bawling. The fathers had to stop talking and take them away.

Back inside, he and I stood by the radiator and took off our skates and my mother joined us. My parents liked each other, you could tell. I leaned over to make folds in the legs of my jeans, pulling the extra fabric over itself and rolling it up. This gave the impression of a thinner leg. With my jeans pegged, my proportions were right: I favored a big T-shirt that bagged around my upper body, my legs like sticks poking out.

"What are you doing?" he asked.

"Pegging my jeans," I said.

"Do you think that's cool?" he asked.

"Yes. I do."

"Oh," he said. Then, in a mocking tone, he said, "Oh, Biff! Oh, Blaine! I hope you like my *jeans*."

"Steve," my mother said. She was smiling but I could tell she didn't like it.

"Maybe she'll marry Thaaad," he said.

Dirk, Blaine, Trent, Trav—these were his names for my imaginary future boyfriends and husbands. I was nine, the thought of marriage irrelevant to my life. I laughed, to show I knew it was a joke, but I wondered if he picked ugly, truncated names and fretted about my marriage prospects because he thought I was ugly or without promise.

"Or maybe you'll marry Christian," he said.

Christian lived across the street and was around my age, with blond hair and gold-rimmed glasses and a trace of an accent from Georgia, where he was from. He wore plaid shorts and T-shirts, and he was skinny, and he did his homework in a tiny scrawl with a mechanical pencil. He also had a single mother. I liked him, but I knew I didn't want him to be my boyfriend. Once a month or so, another boy, named Kai, with dark hair, petal-light skin, and red lips, would visit his father, who lived in the house beside us. He poked his head up at the window that looked into my bedroom window, a surprise. He was shy and didn't want to play, but his presence gave me such a thrill I thought I might pick him, if I was required to choose a husband, but I didn't say it.

"Let me see your teeth," I said, to change the subject. "Show me how they come together like a zipper."

"No way," he said, as if I might be trying to mock him, when I felt only admiration and curiosity.

"Please," I said.

He leaned down and opened his mouth. No overbite, no underbite, no spaces in between: a mountain range and sky.

"They're amazing," my mother said, "how they come together like that." He closed his mouth.

"Let me see yours, Lis," he said. I showed him.

"Interesting. And yours?"

He looked into my mother's mouth. Her bottom teeth were fine, but crowded, like too many guests mingling in a small room.

"They don't look so great. Might want to see about that," he said, even though he'd been kind just a moment before. She winced and closed her mouth. It was as if the magnet changed direction suddenly and now they repulsed each other; it was not possible to know in advance when the switch would occur.

"Maybe she'll look like Brooke Shields," he said, about me.

"Who's Brooke Shields?" I asked.

"A model," my mother said.

"With these really great eyebrows," my father said.

After that, he left, saying something like *may-be you wi-ll* in a trailing voice across the lawn. He was in stocking feet, carrying his skates over his shoulder. When he left, it was like stepping into a dark room after being in the bright sunlight. It was dim and uniform, washed out with the afterimage of light. I played the flute, my mother ordered new tropical fish–patterned sheets for my bed, my cousin Sarah was coming to visit in a couple months. Before he'd arrived, these things were exciting, but for days after his visits they didn't seem so important anymore. It would take time to build it all back up again.

I saw, now, in my eyebrows, promise.

This was around the time, my mother would say later, that my father fell in love with me. "He was in awe of you," she said, but I don't remember it. I noticed he was around more and grabbed me and tried to pick me up even when I didn't want to be picked up. He had opinions about my clothes and teased me more about whom I would marry. "I wish you'd been *my* mother," my father said to her,

strangely, one afternoon, as she was preparing lunch and I was playing. Another time he said, "You know she's more than half me, more
than half my genetic material." The announcement caught my mother
off guard. She didn't know how to respond. Maybe he said it because
he'd started feeling close to me and wanted a greater share.

I remember an abundance of crisp sunlight, shadows like blotches
swaying inside the light, as if there was more sunlight in those days
than there is now.

We looked for houses we wanted while we skated around. He
liked dark wood-shingled ones, vines twisting up the dark brown or
grayish face. Wood so old it silvered. Mullioned windows, small
panes of glass. Gardens with plants that looked blown into heaps.
If you looked in the windows of those houses, you could tell they'd
be dark inside. I liked the houses that were painted white, symmetrical, with columns and plain lawns, heavy and sturdy on the land,
like banks.

"You gotta stop and smell the roses," he said. He said it urgently,
then stopped and put his nose deep in a rose and sighed. I didn't
have the heart to tell him it was only an expression. But soon I got
into it anyway, and we looked for the best rosebushes in the neighborhood, crisscrossing the streets. Roses were plentiful in the yards.
I noticed good ones he'd missed behind fences, and we trespassed
across lawns on the toes of our skates to get to them.

Since Ron was out of the picture and my mom and I were on our own again, I figured it was clear to both of us by now that we didn't want anyone else. We didn't need boyfriends. We were doing pretty great: the new house, my father dropping by. So it had surprised and infuriated me when she told me about a new man named Ilan. Ilan would be the one who stuck around the longest—seven years—and change my life for the better, but first I would ignore him for six months, and smirk at him, trying to get him to leave us alone.

He had black hair that formed tight ringlet curls around his head, a long face with a large nose, and intelligent brown eyes. He had a PhD in chemistry and founded and ran a small science toy company.

I was interested in his stories—he had traveled around the world as a boy because his father was a world-renowned Hungarian opera tenor, and he'd played clever pranks in school—but as I listened, I still noticed with condescension how unglamorous, how nerdy, he was compared with my father. He drove an old white VW Rabbit and sometimes pretended he had a car phone, mocking the Silicon Valley types who'd recently bought car phones the size of bricks, miming at stop signs as if he were receiving an important phone call.

He had two children: a younger son and a daughter around my age named Allegra, with whom I danced to Madonna's "Lucky Star" at her house one afternoon when I still thought he and my mother were only friends.

He'd had an open marriage, but had fallen in love with my mother against the rules and had separated from his wife. I didn't like the idea. I taunted my mother, but I couldn't irritate her much when she was in love.

"He's *married*," I reminded her.

"Oh, honey," she said, like I was a fool.

When I was with Ilan and my mother together, I felt the grumpy rage I'd felt when she started dating her last two boyfriends. "Are you all right, sweetie?" she asked. Being in love made her seem as if she was far above me, looking down, separate. She was unable to keep a slight smile off her lips.

With the others, I had still believed my mother and I were a team against them. With Ilan, I sensed she might let go of me, not him, if she had to choose, and I was going to make her choose. I hunkered down for a long campaign.

One weekend morning several months after they'd started dating, we walked to breakfast.

I complained but went along. We dashed across busy Alma Street to the curb on the other side, through a hole in the fence through the bushes and onto the elevated mound of white rocks where the train tracks ran. From there, it was a straight walk north for twenty minutes along the rocks and the tracks, balancing on one iron track or stepping between wood planks.

We watched for trains.

"Look," Ilan said, as a train came toward us. He placed a penny on the rail before we ran to the side and the train thundered past. Afterward, the penny was hot and had become a shiny copper disc, an uneven oval. It was an object I would have liked to keep.

"Whatever," I muttered when he showed me.

It took a lot of energy to despise Ilan and my mother continuously, the way I did for months. Around them I was lethargic, smirked, and was pointedly silent when either of them made a joke. When we had dinner with others, I noticed how Ilan would find a way to bend the conversation toward his father without quite mentioning him, so that someone else would become curious and ask, Who *was* your father? My cruelty and unhappiness around him felt like a fierce tamping down of myself. It was exhausting and hadn't worked so far to break them up, although it had made them both cautious around me. If I broke out of character for a moment with one thread of happiness, I knew my mother would take it as permission. I refused to give her that. It was as if she'd forgotten what we went through during each breakup, and I hated her for how she was misty-eyed and foolish.

The restaurant, MacArthur Park, was in a converted barn and served a fancy buffet brunch with bowls of strawberries, bowls of fresh whipped cream, waffles and eggs in nickel domes, and fresh juice. Usually we went to simpler places.

That morning something changed as I stood at the buffet and looked back at my mother and Ilan, who were sitting at a round table facing me, smiling. Looking at them, past the piles of fruit and the billows of cream, I felt too weary, and too content, to stay enraged. And they looked like parents. I surrendered. I felt safe here under the vaulted ceiling, with the clinks of silver-plated serving implements. However awful I had been, they would take me even now, and I could let them if I wished to, and it wasn't too late to have it—a family.

When I talked with him much later, when I was an adult, Ilan told me how he'd taken several walks with my father when they happened to see each other at the Rinconada house, encouraging him to spend more time with me, framing parenthood and time spent in terms of personal advantage—it's for *you*, Steve, he'd said. Think of it that way. He'd noticed my father was opportunistic. He went for whatever was most appealing in the moment, ignoring me if someone else arrived. Ilan encouraged my father, praising him for even small gestures toward fatherhood. He praised him, for example, when my father took me for a skate. Ilan's work, too, was entrepreneurial and consuming, but my mother said he had the ability to transition from work mode to family mode with ease and speed, so that when he was with us, or with me, having dinner with us as he did most nights before going back to the office, he was focused, not halfway listening, the way a lot of businessmen were.

It was Ilan who, after staying home several nights to help me with my math and science homework, sitting beside me on the couch, patient, even though he had planned to go back to work in the evening because his company was struggling, gave me the first taste of what it felt like to arrive prepared for class, to understand the lesson and have a homework sheet filled out right. After several nights of his help, I wanted to arrive prepared, and to feel the calm and get the attention that came with it, and so it would be Ilan, later, who was part of the reason I would start to do well in school.

That summer, Ilan's daughter, Allegra, and I went to my father's house in Woodside to go swimming, and afterward we explored the house. She found a room I'd never seen before near the front door, empty bookshelves covering the walls up to the ceiling, a couple of books and magazines here and there. In the middle of the room was a crude model of the property, with the land made of the crumbly green material used to hold stems in flower arrangements.

"Do you think he's ever been in this room?" she asked.

"Probably not," I said. We rummaged through the things, which I thought looked as though they might have been left by the people who'd lived here before.

High up on a shelf, I found several copies of a *Playboy* magazine.

"Look."

We flipped through it sitting on the floor. That rumor about my father in *Playboy* might not have been true—but there, on the next page, was his face. A postage stamp–sized black-and-white photo above some text. He looked innocent in a white shirt and a bow tie. Fully dressed.

"I knew it!" I said. "I've heard about this." I was so relieved he
was not nude or leering, and I wanted Allegra to notice him.

I felt lucky to have a father like that. We turned the page. A
naked woman was sprawled out across two pages, a brunette with
big hair, bedroom eyes, red lipstick.

On one of our skating outings that year, my father and I stopped at a low building nestled in trees near downtown. We each had one mildly skinned knee from another fall.

"I know some people here," he said. "It's a design company." We didn't remove our skates; inside it was carpeted, so we could walk almost normally.

We went down the hallway and into a room with a large table lit up with fluorescent lights, with pages of white paper fanned out on top, messy.

"Do you know what a serif is?" he asked.

"No," I said. I wished he'd give me the context. I wanted to impress him; maybe he wanted to impress me by teaching me something. He pointed to a page with black letters.

"Look," he said.

"An *S*?"

"No," he said. He pointed to a *T*, the top right side, where the letter curved down. "See the lines around the letter?" he asked. "There's a small line at the end of the long one—that's a serif. Some people think you can read better with them."

His voice was urgent. I gathered that serifs were very important.

"Look, here," he said, pointing at others. "Here, and here, and here."

The serifs became visible, separated from the letters. Caps and tails, flips you might make with your pen at the end of the word if you didn't lift it off the paper. Serifs had always been there, but now I could name them. Feet are like serifs of the legs, I thought later. Toes are serifs of the feet.

Of all the details on the planet, he wanted to show me this.

He pointed to other fonts. The serifs were different between fonts, longer, shorter, thicker, thinner. They reminded me of notched branches in the spring, tendrils that might grow out and later become letters themselves.

"Bauer Bodoni," he said, "and Times New Roman, and Garamond."

He pointed to a blunt-edged font and asked me what that was called.

"Not . . . serifs?"

"There's a word in Latin that means 'without,'" he said. He paused. Was I supposed to know Latin?

"It's *sans*," he said.

"So they're called *sans*?" I said.

"Sans serif. Like these," he said, pointing: another S, but: S. Letters without serifs looked naked now.

My mother liked letters plain and fine. She liked them thin; he liked them thick. In my adult life I would work at a science lab, a bank, a study-abroad office, a restaurant, a cosmetics company, a design company. There are codes and marks for each; different languages to describe beauty and importance. I could not be a full member of every group; I would have to pick.

"So, have you kissed anybody yet?" he asked me on the skate home. He meant French.

"No. Yuck. When did you have your first kiss?"

"I was around your age," he said.

"Who'd you kiss?"

"Her name was Deirdre Loupaletti." Like loopy, spaghetti, confetti. It was too perfect. "She had brown hair down to here," he said, motioning to his butt. "We kissed in the basement at her parents' house. Actually, she was the one who kissed me."

I wished for his story, not mine, and for his confidence. A story with a name like that. I was already behind—if he'd kissed by my age, I should have kissed too.

◆ ◆ ◆

My cousin Sarah came to visit. She was my mother's older sister Kathy's daughter, and our only relative around my age. Soon after I was born, we'd lived with her and her parents for a few months in Idyllwild, California.

Now, Sarah was tall but stooped; she spoke sharply and sometimes too loud and piercingly for indoor spaces. She was the only child I knew who could be wry, as if she was already life-weary. There was something else about her, maybe wit or irony, that she possessed despite her too-bold voice and jolting movements and her seeming unawareness of her surroundings, a mature perception that meant she was both a child and, at the same time, watching from a distance.

I'd been looking forward to the visit for months. She'd never met my father, and tonight we would all have dinner together at Bravo Fono in Stanford Shopping Center. When we'd played together as children, neither of us had a father around. Now I did, and I wanted her to see what it was like.

He'd picked the place. He was late. He was always late. When he walked in, I could sense he was not happy—it hadn't been a good day at work maybe. His angles were wrong; he didn't want to be here. His mood was like black soot in the air.

My mother ordered the Bibb lettuce salad; I ordered the linguini with shrimp. We were careful about what we ordered around him—he disapproved of meat. His dietary code didn't have to do with animal welfare, but with aesthetics and bodily purity. Later when he looked at people with his particular disdain, I could see what made them foolish, in his eyes: their complete unconsciousness of how ignorant they were, picking at their dead food.

There was a thin line between civility and cruelty in him, between what did and did not set him off. I knew he wouldn't like the idea of the shrimp; I also knew it would pass. But we'd forgotten to warn Sarah. "I'll have the hamburger," she said, too loud. I wanted to muffle her to protect her, and to protect myself. The trick, I learned later, was to give him less surface area to knife, so he would stab someone else. Always someone, if not me.

The food arrived. I hoped Sarah wouldn't feel the tense static in the air, or notice that my father hadn't said a word to her yet, and glanced at her dish with disgust. She talked too loud for the echoing, semi-empty restaurant with its wall of windows, glass bricks, and stone floor. I didn't know how to tell her to talk more softly.

After we'd taken a few bites, my father's face shifted and tightened.

"What's wrong with you?" he asked Sarah.

"What?" she said. She was chewing on a bite of meat.

"No," he said. "Really."

At first it seemed that he was asking her to answer him. What *was* wrong with her? Why did she miss social cues? Why did she have such a biting, high voice at the top of the register, always calling for attention, as acute as a baby crying?

His voice became high-pitched and piercing.

"You can't even talk," he said. "You can't even eat. You're eating shit."

She looked at him; I could tell she was trying not to cry.

"Have you ever thought about how awful your voice is?" he continued. "Please stop talking in that awful voice."

I couldn't believe it was happening even as it was happening.

"Steve, stop it right now," my mother said.

I could see him through Sarah's eyes, or I thought I could: if having a father around was like this, it wasn't so great.

"I wish I wasn't here with you," he said. "I don't want to spend another moment of my life with you. Get yourself together. Pull yourself together."

He talked loud enough so the people at other tables could hear him. Sarah slouched in her chair and looked at the table and began to cry.

"Steve," my mother said. "Stop."

"You should really consider what's wrong with yourself and try to fix it," he said.

He got up and walked toward the bathroom.

We leaned in and flanked Sarah so that no one else could watch. I was aware of the tables beside us and what they could hear and what they thought and how people sat beside violence and were not really a part of it. Sarah was sobbing messily, with snot and tears, wiping her nose on the back of her sleeve and telling us she was fine. I was smaller than she was, shorter, slighter. But she was small too.

"He's a mean person," I said in the parking lot on the way to the car. "It has nothing to do with you." My mother had told me that last part before when he'd hurt me.

"I know," she said. I couldn't tell if she did know or she was just saying it so I would stop comforting her. But she looked at me and said it again: "I know."

♦

My father's girlfriend Tina's hair was long and light blonde, the color of the hottest part of the flame: the same hair, the same person, I realized later, who was in his bed the night I thought the blond man had kidnapped and killed him.

I don't remember when I met Tina, but maybe it was one day in the kitchen at my father's Woodside house, where my mother and I had come for lunch. The people my father hired to make the beds and make his salads had made fresh whole wheat pasta, the machine still attached to the side of the kitchen counter, the pasta ribbons floured and long on a tray.

My father and a few others were playing with a toy, rolling it across the kitchen island. A small silver-painted plastic robot figure with a red helmet that rolled with one wheel between its fused legs and, as it rolled, from a dark round hole in the chest cavity where its heart might have been, sparks shot out. I wanted to try it.

Tina noticed me watching and called out to them, "Why don't you let Lisa have it?" Her thick bangs were feathered on both sides. She had a smooth, low voice and a kind face.

My father kept rolling it, swiping his finger in front of the sparks. But then he handed it to me and said, ceremoniously, "A gift. You have it."

Tina and my father had met several years before, when she was working at the philanthropic wing of Apple and my father was still living at the house in Monte Sereno where we'd taken the couch. She was a software engineer, warm, an introvert. Her beauty was something she shied away from, as if she didn't want it, or care for it, and so it wasn't notable to me, even years later, because she didn't foster it or nudge it forward with affectations, makeup, or fancy clothing. She was just Tina.

There was a group of good people that hung around Tina, family and friends, artists and scientists, who, like her, took an interest in me and my mother, so that during the years that she and my father were together, I felt there was an extra layer of protection around my mother, my father, and me.

She told me years later that my father insisted, persuasively, when they first met, that I wasn't really his kid. When she saw me, it was obvious that I was, but when she brought it up, he refused to discuss it.

My father invited me to come on a vacation to Hawaii with the two of them. I was in the fourth grade, almost ten. My mother and I didn't go on vacations, so I wasn't sure what to expect. When we arrived on the tarmac, the sky was bright white, the airport buildings were not enclosed but outside with wide brown roofs, humidity blurring the line between my skin and the air. A man wearing a polo shirt gave us each a long necklace made of many sweet-smelling hot pink blossoms with yellow centers, and we followed him to a white van. On the drive, there were only miles of charred black land, and I worried he was taking us to a moonscape only he thought was beautiful, but then we took a left toward the ocean and a circle of green.

The grass at the resort was mown short as baize and dotted with shade from palm trees with long, thin trunks, like strings. At breakfast, brown birds the size of my fist chirped in the high rafters and dropped down onto each just-vacant table, messy with napkins, syrup, and bitten pieces of toast. They hopped and picked at crumbs and squabbled until a waiter came to clear and they rose back up in unison to wait for another. Beside the pool I watched a peacock fan out, quivering, cawing. It stood still for a while and then strode away, still fanned out, in slow, methodical steps that made the whole semi-circle of plumage sway.

That week I walked barefoot along the sand paths, the warmth rising up through my calves to my knees. After a few days, the dark hairs on my arms became blond to the roots. In the ocean the grains of sand and the yellow fish that were strummed up in the shallow waves were bright and clear, magnified by the water. Before this trip I'd never heard of virgin piña coladas; now I had at least three a day.

I made a friend around my age named Lauren, who also lived in California, and together we ran between lawns, meals, pools, beaches; the black-lipped fish, the one black swan, the birds and geckos. In the gift shop were cuff bracelets an inch wide, each made of a single piece of koa wood polished to a glow.

"Let's pick one out for your mother and Tina," my father said. They clacked against each other on the rail.

I wanted a bracelet too, but my hands and wrists were too small.

He bought me a bikini made of red cotton with a flower pattern. I'd never worn a bikini before. My new friend Lauren had a similar one, also from the gift shop, but in blue.

Tina wore jeans and T-shirts and china flats. She had wide wrists and large breasts and crouched down on her heels when she was speaking with me so we were closer to the same height. She laughed in a full way, and it made her whole face pretty. Her nose was like my mother's, straight and small, with a pointed end that veered slightly to one side. She cut her own bangs.

Tina had a happy-sad quality and dry, self-deprecating humor. She was delighted by me, she liked me, I could tell. To me, she seemed like she was a woman but also a little girl, or could remember so clearly what it was like to be my age that there wasn't such a distance between us. When we were back in Palo Alto and we went somewhere all together in my father's Porsche, she would squeeze her tall body in the back so I could sit up front with him. She was a strange combination with my father, I could tell even then; he would often become grandiose about himself, leaving behind the part of him that matched with her.

"She could wear a sack, a brown sack," I heard my father say. As if beauty was measured by how strong an obstacle it had to overcome. It was the same way he spoke about Ingrid Bergman. I watched for it, in Tina, because I didn't think of her as particularly beautiful. Her eyelashes were as blonde as her hair. She didn't try, and the trying *was* beauty to me then. But a few times when she tossed her bangs out of her face, her eyes shone in the sunlight, the color of the swimming pool, and her face opened up, beautiful, until she looked down and adjusted her bangs and looked ordinary to me again.

On the way to dinner on the white sand path that wound through the forest, Tina and I flanking him, he put an arm around us both. A hand around my ribs, under my armpit. "These Are the Women of My Life." He said it in a slow, measured, nasal voice, like he was announcing a new act at a show. He looked up and out as he said it, addressing the statement to the forest.

I was one of his women! It filled me up with such a surge of joy I had to look away, look down at the path, at my bare feet, so he wouldn't see I was smiling.

He leaned toward Tina to kiss her, and the arm he had around me yanked up as he leaned, so that he clawed under my armpit, fingers jerking with his steps. I wanted to stay within his grasp, to be one of his women.

"Isn't she beautiful?" he said at dinner, when Tina got up to go to the bathroom. Whenever he and I were alone for a moment, he talked to me about her beauty, sighing as if she were far away, or it was out of reach.

When she returned, he leaned forward and kissed her, murmuring and whispering in her ear. She demurred; he grabbed the back of her head, his chair balanced on one leg. As they kissed, he pressed his palm against her breast, wrinkling the fabric of her T-shirt. "Mmm," he said.

I was simultaneously repulsed and intrigued. I guessed my role was to watch and note how much he adored her, even though it gave me a strange feeling to be near them when they did this.

The act was exaggerated like a performance; it did not seem natural or real.

Why didn't she stop him? Maybe because she was very young, and in love.

"Why did you two make out in front of me?" I asked Tina at some point much later.

"It's what he did when he was uncomfortable," she said. "He was uncomfortable around you because he didn't know how to relate to you," she said. "The charm that worked on adults didn't work on you, a child. You saw through it. So he would lunge toward me to ease his own discomfort." The idea that my presence was the very thing that made him seem to be unaware of me was almost inconceivable, because in those moments I felt like nothing, a speck, not worth a look. It was so extreme, Tina said, that when we returned from Hawaii, she decided not to come over when I was around so that he might learn how to be with me on his own.

Mona and my mother had also noticed the way my father made out with Tina, sometimes for minutes at a time, moaning—it wasn't just me, he did it in front of adults too. But I was a child, and this behavior was inappropriate. My mother and Mona were concerned about his jokes and public displays, and this had been, in part, the impetus for Mona's insistence, not long after we returned from Hawaii, that as the child of a single mother without a continuous fatherly presence, it would be a good idea if I saw a male psychiatrist, in order to have the experience of forming a close relationship with a good and stable man.

My mother agreed it was a good idea, and my father agreed to pay. My mother drove me to meet Dr. Lake, a therapist, recommended by Mona's in New York, whom I would continue to see once per week, starting at age nine, for many years. My memory became clearer after I started seeing him, perhaps because I was older, or because during our weekly sessions I tried to put my life into words.

When he was done kissing Tina, my father righted his chair, sighed, and ate.

"You know," he said, "Tina was on television once. In a commercial. When she was a girl. Younger than you."

I was impressed. Later my father played it for me, a blonde girl standing beside a boy who opens his fist onto the counter of a beach shop, releasing pocket change and a marble to pay for a box of Cracker Jack.

After dessert, he took Tina's hand and looked at her palm.

"I don't know what the lines are supposed to mean," he said.

"I'm not sure either," Tina said. "If only we could tell our futures."

"I know how to read them," I said to my father, "Give me your right hand."

"How about the left," he said, because it was closer.

"No. That's the destiny you were *given*. I want to see the right one: what you will *make* of it."

"Okay," he said, and stretched it across his body.

His palms were flat, without the knuckle hills that poked up around the finger joints, a quality my mother and I had talked about along with others, like the zipper teeth. The inside of his palms glowed pale yellow, the lines deep orange; he ate and drank carrot salad and carrot juice the color of wet clay on the hillsides in such great quantities they tinted him from the inside out.

"So this one's your lifeline," I said. "And this one's your mind. This one's your marriage, and this one's your heart. See?"

"Okay, so what does it mean?" he said.

The line curved from below his index finger to his wrist. "It's a pretty long life," I said. "But your mind line isn't long. See, it's here. It cracks, splits open."

I was predicting what I knew he'd like the least—to live a long and intellectually middling life. It would puncture his arrogance, the way he seemed magnanimous but disconnected, his feeling of his own tragic greatness so strong he had less energy to notice others. I knew

he wouldn't be aware that I already knew this about him, because
every time he told me a story about himself and what he wanted, he'd
forget he'd told me before. He wouldn't know that I understood he
was sad to die young, but he also found it glamorous.

"All right," he said, and pulled back his hand.

Tina sat still while my friend Lauren and I French-braided her hair
beside the pool. Lauren showed me how to save hair as we wove
down to the nape of her neck.

After we were done, my father pulled me onto his lap. He was
sitting on a lounge chair and Tina was sitting beside us on another.
He told Lauren he wanted some time alone with us, and she left to
find her family. I wanted to play but he held me.

"Look how we both have eyebrows that come together in the
middle," he said. "And how we have the same nose."

He ran his index finger down the bridge of my nose.

"No, we don't," I said. "Mine's smaller. Mine doesn't point down
like that." "Just wait," he said, "it will." Like he knew the future. He
grabbed my ankle and held it in his hand, inspecting my foot.

"Looks like your second toe might become longer than your
big toe," he said. "It's a sign of intelligence," he said, to have the
longer second toe. "Maybe yours will grow if you're lucky."

"Ha," I said, as if I didn't care.

"Uh-oh," Tina said, looking at her foot on the ground. I could
tell she was joking.

"Did you know I've got narrow feet?" he said. "It looks like you
do too. And look at your fingers—they're like mine too. Our nails
are shaped the same."

We held out our hands. I couldn't tell about the nails; mine
were so much smaller that it seemed impossible to compare. My
heart beat like a bird's heart, quick and light in my chest: it was
what I wanted, all his attention focused on me, all at once.

"You're my kid, you know," he said, holding me even though he'd stopped looking.

"I know," I said. I wasn't sure why he said it. He stopped speaking but kept his hold. I was hoping the moment would end, the heavy, oppressive feeling of being held like that.

"Let's just sit here," he said. "Let's all just be quiet for a minute and sit here."

His arm was like a seat belt around my waist. "Lis, you're gonna remember this," he said, full of feeling. I sat still, hardly breathing, hoping it would be enough and he'd let me go. Lunch was being laid out, vats of fresh salads and fish, avocado, grapefruit, crab claws on ice. A separate table just for cakes.

Finally he said, "Let's get lunch," and released me. I took a huge breath and a running leap. They lingered behind, walking slowly toward me and lunch.

After dinner that night, we walked back to our thatched huts, called *hales*, on the white-sand path. The tiki lanterns along the path flickered and cast patterns of light and, in pockets, the sour kerosene burned my nostrils. Geckos chirped like metal birds, wound around the poles of black lights stuck in the ground, and spun away when I tried to touch them. The forest was thick with veined, waxy leaves wrapped around leaves wrapped around other leaves. The fragrance was stronger at night, sweet and cool, as if the flowers were exhaling. The air smelled of flowers, decay, and salt.

◆

"Steve's taking us out to breakfast at Late for the Train," my mother said. It was almost the end of my fourth-grade year.

"Just us three?" It was unusual, now that Tina and Ilan were around, for the three of us to eat together.

"Yup."

The restaurant was nestled up against the train tracks at the Menlo Park station. When a train came through every half hour, it was hard to hear anyone speaking, even those at the same table, but the clanking, deafening noise was part of the experience. The owners were a husband and wife. The curtains were lace, and the place smelled of the buttery whole wheat scones they delivered to tables in baskets inside patterned napkins.

Before the food arrived, after we'd received our goblets of fresh-squeezed orange juice, my father raised his glass.

"A toast," he said. "You're going to a new school. You got in."

My mother smiled—she was in on it, I realized. I burst into tears. I would have to leave my friends, again?

Nueva was a private school in an old Crocker mansion on thirty-three acres of land in Hillsborough that I'd visited for three days a few months before. The school was founded for young musicians and allowed students to leave class for private music lessons. It was meant to be a school for the gifted. I'd visited the classroom of a teacher named Bryna, who played the guitar and ended the days in a group rendition of a song about a man named Charlie who couldn't get off the subway and never returned home.

The school was made of gray stone, with balustrades and huge trees. During my three-day application visit, I went each day to the schoolwide thirty-minute morning sing in a room called the ballroom with high curved windows looking out to lawns and forests. I didn't know any of the songs, but I let them wash over me, including one called "Russian Picnic" with multiple parts. All the students in every grade sat on the floor and sang.

I learned later that Ilan had resisted the idea of private school. Like Ron, he believed private school was elitist and advised my mother not to send me. But my mother decided not to follow his advice. A few months before, my father had asked my mother, angrily, "What happened to her?" He'd noticed I wasn't able to do my Current Events homework. She said, "See? I told you so." She said my eyes had become duller. Before this she'd asked him to pay for private school, but he'd said no, not wanting me to move schools again. Now he made her promise that if he paid the tuition and they moved me to Nueva, she wouldn't change schools again.

My mother had pulled me out of speech therapy lessons a month or two before.

"Why should she take speech therapy?" my mother asked, when the lessons had been proposed at the start of fourth grade.

"For her lisp. So it doesn't bother other people," the woman answered.

My mother didn't like the answer—she liked my lisp, anyway— but she thought I might enjoy the one-on-one instruction.

She came to pick me up one day and looked at the textbooks meant to teach the *s* and *th* sounds. They were inaccurate and uninspired, she said.

"Lisa's applying to Nueva," she'd told the tutor, a woman I seemed to like. "Would you be willing to write her a recommendation?"

"She's not smart enough," the tutor said.

At school, when they did the homework check, calling out our names to verify if we'd put our homework in the basket, I learned I could just say yes, even though I hadn't and, so far, no one had bothered me.

We'd applied to Nueva in the middle of that year and I understood I wasn't admitted because there wasn't space. Later I learned it was not only space but also my IQ, which was much lower than it had been when I was tested in kindergarten. My mother said that the principal of the school had lectured them, asking them what schools they had been putting me in, and why they'd let me move schools so many times. Mona wrote a recommendation letter. My father asked, uncharacteristically, if he could contribute money to get me in. I didn't know this then. But the principal said no. It was school policy, in any case, to allow all applicants to do a three-day visit.

After the visit to her classroom, Bryna, one of the most respected teachers at the school, wrote a five-page letter to recommend me, my mother said, and another girl dropped out, and I was admitted. I don't know what I'd done to impress her, and I never saw the letter. They wanted me to start soon, right away, at the end of fourth grade.

For the long drive to Nueva, my father bought us a new car: an Audi Quattro. My mother and I went to the lot and chose the maroon model, with a light-gray leather interior. Under the emergency brake was a stitched leather skirt that bagged loose, like elephant skin; on the dash in front of the passenger seat was a glossy panel of wood.

"Now I can knock on wood when I'm driving," my mother said. She knocked to un-jinx. She would knock when she saw an odd number of ravens or a black cat wander across our path. She noticed signs and premonitions and would sometimes become despondent if she saw the wrong number of birds—until she saw another bird that changed the count.

In the mornings, we drove north down Highway 280, past the reservoir. The drive to Nueva was about forty minutes. There were birds in the rumpled hills around the freeway, turkey vultures, sometimes eagles and hawks.

"How fast do you think we're going?" she asked, covering the speedometer with her hand.

"Fifty?" In the old Honda we would have had to yell to be heard; inside the Audi, it seemed like we were hardly moving. Nothing vibrated or rasped.

She removed her hand. "Eighty!" she said, "my God," and braked.

My mother learned about a new kind of braces made of a bone-colored polymer to blend in more effectively with the color of teeth. She asked my father to pay for them, and he'd agreed. But the coffee she drank every day discolored the clear bands that surrounded the bone-colored cabooses, browning the bands after just a few sips, making her teeth look yellow.

"I'm going to quit coffee," she said. The next day, she had espresso breath, the bands were stained, and she was despondent as she cooked dinner.

"Quitting is harder than it seems," she said when I asked her about it.

When she smiled, her lips got caught and bunched above them. At a shop, a woman said, "I can't believe you're willing to wear braces at your age." She came home, moved around the house in a jerky, angry way, dislodging papers from her desk.

Soon she learned how to change the bands herself. She ordered bags of extra bands and did it every day, crouching with a knee up on the toilet seat, cutting the old ones out with a silver X-Acto knife into which she'd inserted a new, sharp blade. It made a sound like *flick flick flick* as the old bands were spliced and flew across the bathroom. She pulled the fresh bands open with her index fingers, releasing them over each brace.

Mona stopped by one day, and she and my mother stood talking in the kitchen near the microwave. My mother was worried the house was too small for a studio. "Just paint," Mona said. "Bedroom be damned. Make it into a studio and sleep in it." Mona had just returned from a residency at an artists' colony called Djerassi.

After that, my mother taped up black-and-white photocopies of the etchings and lithographs of Picasso, Kirchner, Cézanne, Chagall, and Kandinsky from the 1920s and '30s until her bedroom wall was completely covered in overlapping pages taped at the tops, free at the bottom like tiles or scales, that lifted and fell in the breezes. Soon, she also converted the garage into a studio, adding Sheetrock to the walls.

In my mother's final semester at school, in addition to creating lithograph prints, she started making stencils. She hand-cut the patterns in vellum paper, but later she planned to have them laser-cut for mass production and to sell them as a part of a kit.

"This is going to work," she said. "How could it not?" She'd seen a stencil of flowers around someone's living room that struck her as twee. "If a person can make money doing something like that, I can certainly make money doing something much more beautiful."

She'd created birds for children's rooms based on Audubon's drawings, using multiple anatomically correct stencils in overlapping layers.

Around this time we became friends with a family that moved in across the street. The mother was named Lisa, her husband was a podiatrist, and I played with their daughter.

When I turned ten, Lisa insisted that we do a ceremony with a hula hoop in our living room. My mother was there, and my friend and her little brother too, all of us sitting around on the rug near the couch. Lisa wanted me to undress outside the hoop, then step inside the hoop and put on the new dress that was my mother's birthday gift to me.

I was skeptical. I didn't want to undress in front of them.

"Think of it as a symbolic gesture," Lisa said. "A new age—double digits! You're coming into your own, becoming this full, new, beautiful Lisa.

"And the hoop is like the zero in the number ten," she added.

It was a hippie thing.

I took off my clothes and stepped into the hoop wearing just my underwear. My mother lowered the venetian blind on the front window. All of them were watching me, including the little brother, whom we called the Noodle, or the Naked Noodle, when he was naked. Inside the hoop, I put on the new velvet dress from my mother, turned around, and crouched down for her to zip it up the back.

While I did this, Lisa began to speak about me in the third person: "Lisa is moving from her childhood into a new kind of maturity. She is stepping into the circle of her life and becoming fully herself. All these wonderful changes are happening in Lisa's life as she moves from age nine to age ten." I had to admit, it felt good to be the center of attention, to have a ceremony focused on me. When she said the words, I believed them: my life was special and something new was afoot.

On the night of my tenth birthday there was a dinner at a big table at a restaurant called Greens in San Francisco, including Mona, Tina and Tina's brother and her cousin Finn, my mother, my father, and me. At the end, we all walked out into the night together, and I walked between my parents, holding their hands. It was ecstasy. My arms were like the hyphen that would be added to my name later, joining the two sides.

"We're going to play hooky," my father said when he came over the next time.

"What does it mean? Hooky?" I asked my mother when he left.

"He's going to skip work, you're going to skip school, and you'll have a day together."

We drove to the city on a Tuesday morning, first stopping at a tailor's shop overlooking Union Square with bolts of fabric strewn over a table. "Just one second, kiddo," he said.

"Versace really does have the best fabrics," he said to the tailor, running his thumb over a plaid made of grays. "Better than Armani."

He said this with a mournful note, as if there was something sad about how good it was. Versace made two lisps. He handed me each fabric sample after he'd felt it and I felt it after him.

We drove to the Golden Gate Bridge and parked at the start of it and got out to walk across, as he'd planned for us. In the city, looking at the fabrics, he'd been voluble and confident, but with no one else around, wearing a backpack, he seemed less sure, and younger.

"People jump," he said, looking toward the Marin side. "That's what the nets are for."

"Really?" I figured they were there for the workmen who repaired and painted the bridge. The bay below us was the waxy, opaque green of a diorama, and from so high up it seemed as still and fixed as resin, the white edges unmoving and permanent.

"If you jumped from here, the water would hit you like a brick wall." He slammed the flat of his hand onto the other one.

The walk across the bridge was long and windy, with neither of us speaking much, and we'd forgotten to bring any water, so by the time we walked into Sausalito, past a thin stretch of sidewalk over the hill with the cars and buses passing close beside us, we were ragged and thirsty. We took a taxi back to the car.

I figured we'd have many other days like this, playing hooky, but we never did it again.

A few weeks later it was the night before my mother's final project for an art class was due, and she was frantic, still not having a piece to show. At some point late at night after I was asleep, she enlisted the help of a neighbor who was also an artist; he said he had a good idea, and he brought over a trash bin and shook it, emptying its contents on the floor of our house. Crumpled papers, a nest of brown hair from a brush, boxes, plastic bags. She'd thought he had a good idea, but all he had was this. But then she started to stuff his trash inside a garbage bag, the thin kind made of semitransparent black plastic, adding in a string of small white Christmas lights held in cardboard as a kind of spine. These lights glimmered from its depths, shining through the blackish-green plastic like a flash of a fish belly in a murky pond. She arranged the object in a heap on the floor, smaller at the top and wider at the bottom.

"It's a Trash Buddha!" she told me in the morning. There it huddled, bright and wrinkled against a wall on the living room floor. It was two feet tall, squat, lumpen, its lights plugged in. The plastic skin flickered slightly in the currents. It seemed to breathe. It made me uncomfortable that she would bring it to school and show others, as if it would expose us. What would they think? Maybe it was her idea of herself, or of us: holy refuse.

The configuration and shape changed every time she picked it up and placed it somewhere else, but it still had the same quality of being not quite trash.

The next afternoon, my father stopped by. "Come in!" my mother called out. "Look," she said, taking him over to where she'd resurrected the Trash Buddha against the wall. "What do you think?" In art school, she said, she'd turned off the overhead lights and the object had seemed alive.

He glanced at it but said nothing. You could tell by the way he was walking and standing that he was suffering. I'd seen him approach the house hunched over, too thin. He had a stricken look.

"Tina and I broke up," he said. "It's over," and then he collapsed on the flowered chair in front of the window. Or he sat at a chair at our table and didn't speak and leaned back, tipping the chair back until he was almost horizontal so that I could not focus on anything else. Over the next six months, they broke up and got together again at least ten times. When he and Tina broke up, he could hardly walk or talk for grief; he had trouble lifting his feet in between steps and became yellow and wan, fasting on carrots. When they were together

again, he bounced when he walked, he crowed, forgetting how he'd
been before. Each time they broke up, we were supposed to believe
this time it was *it*.

He seemed to need us, and this was flattering. Even though in
his sadness he was remote and hardly spoke, we were the ones he
came to when life was dire—when Tina was gone. Sometimes he
came over and took a nap on our couch. This feeling of being needed
was what I missed when he and Tina got back together a week or
two later.

He did not want to be our protector, but he dabbled in it. The
more he approached and pulled away, the more I wanted him to
spread a vast, fine net below us.

I don't remember seeing Tina much during this time. It became
harder for me to muster joy at the reunions, knowing that a crash
would follow soon. I overheard my mother and Ilan talking about
how NeXT wasn't going well either, and I knew that if NeXT failed
and he and Tina really broke up, he might collapse with grief. I was
terrified for him.

"I wrote a song for Tina," he said, one night when my mother had
a date with Ilan and I went to stay with him at the Woodside house.
"You wanna hear it?"

I sat on the couch to listen. He didn't turn on the lights but
there was some moonlight from the windows. I didn't know he could
play anything but "Heart and Soul."

He sat down at the piano in the semidark, cavernous ballroom.
I don't remember much of the song anymore, his voice and his notes
were very loud and clear and rang through the room. I couldn't
believe he could play so well, and sing so well. Afterward he wanted
to know what I thought, and I had a hard time convincing him of
the truth—he kept asking again and again—that it was beautiful,
and sad. At some point he gave Tina a tape, but then he took the
tape back.

◆ ◆ ◆

When he and I were in the car together a week later, he said, "I don't know what's wrong with me. Any other guy would snatch her up in a second."

It wasn't just him but other adults, too, who sometimes treated me as if I were another adult, asking me for advice, telling me about their feelings and wishes, confiding in me about their relationships in ways they must have known I couldn't understand. Their *love lives*, they called them. None was married yet; not my father, my mother, Mona, or Tina, and I was often the only other person around; it was natural that they sometimes talked to me. I listened and thought, if it were me, I'd live life better, avoid the mistakes, the drama. I listened closely and dispensed advice and figured I'd have an advantage when I was older myself.

"Maybe you should figure out if *you* like her," I said to him.

A couple of weeks later Steve and Tina were back together and we three walked down University Avenue on Saturday afternoon, Tina and I flanking him, on the way to lunch at the Good Earth. Inside the door came a blast of air that smelled of the proprietary tea blend—cinnamon, cloves, orange, ginger. The tables, chairs, benches, and uniforms were all in dreary shades of brown to communicate health food. A line of vinyl-upholstered chairs ran the length of the bar.

"Lis, you're gonna remember this," my father said loudly and with solemnity, as if I was the designated record-keeper. NeXT was fine, Tina was here, I was here. The sunlight was so bright it erased the spots it hit. He said this phrase a lot when he and Tina were back together, confusing his swell of emotion for mine. I wondered if I would.

These days I alternated between pitying him and being in his thrall. He was tiny and weak, then vast and impenetrable, big and out of scale. These two impressions flipped back and forth in me, not touching.

A homeless man walked toward us on the sidewalk. He had long segments of brown-gray hair falling against the sides of his face, but the top of his head was bald. A red T-shirt hugged a large, round gut. As he walked, his mouth gaped open and snapped shut, like a fish's. He had only a few teeth left.

"That's me in two years," my father whispered to us.

He said this often, pointing to a variety of old men who lived in the town and sat on curbs with dirty hair and dirty, weather-beaten faces. Some looked like they were wearing diapers. He couldn't look like these men in two years if he tried. It was as if his comparison was also to say, Look how far I am from *him*. Or: Not *really*.

Or else he said it to try to remind himself that he was no different from anyone else, no better.

"Yeah, right," I said, to make him laugh.

My mother and I went for a few days to a place called Tassajara, a Zen Buddhist retreat with natural hot springs, where she would be what was called a guest student and do work during the day in exchange for a small, less luxurious cabin than the other guests stayed in. Our cabin was up a long series of small steps made of wooden blocks inserted into the hillside. When it rained one day, the dirt and wood on the path up to our cabin became slippery, and there was nothing to hold on to, and we scrambled up, complaining and laughing.

During the days, she swept and peeled vegetables in the kitchen while I roamed around, making friends, swimming, and making concoctions with the free coffee, ice, and milk in glass mugs at the beverage bar brought out in the afternoons. Around the pool's concrete lip, thirsty bees alighted to drink the wet spots that formed when people got out, and I was careful not to step on them.

"Are you allergic?" a woman asked.

"It swells up and I can't walk."

"And where's your mother?" she asked.

"She's working." I burned with the desire to let this woman know that I wasn't just any girl staying in an inferior cabin far away but someone who mattered.

"And your father?"

"He's not here. He's—he—runs a company," I said.

"What company does he run?" she asked.

"It's called NeXT."

She looked at me more carefully, studying my face, and I knew she'd understood that I wasn't just a girl by the pool avoiding bees, I was a kind of princess in disguise. "I know who your father is," she said. "But I heard his company failed."

"When did you hear that?"

"I read it in the paper a couple days ago," the woman said. "NeXT failed."

We'd left him; he'd failed. He would perish.

He'd been talking about a NeXT presentation that was coming up in a month or so and how the "demo" wasn't working. "If it doesn't work, the presentation's gonna tank," he'd said.

"I have to go," I said. We needed to get home right away. I had to convince my mother to take us; I had to convince her without letting her know that I'd told someone who my father was. If she knew I was advertising his name, she'd worry I'd endanger myself, worry while she worked.

I ran along the tree-shrouded dirt path to the place my mother said I should go, to the building that housed the kitchens.

"We need to leave," I said when I found her. "I want to get home. I'm worried about Steve."

"Why, honey?"

"I heard NeXT failed."

"How did you hear that?"

"A woman said it was in the papers."

"What woman?"

"A woman here." I imagined him crumpled over, needing us as we blithely passed our days where he couldn't reach us. We were all he had—I was all he had—and I'd left him. Remorse felt like suction in my stomach. I hoped she wouldn't ask me how the conversation went.

"Let's call him first," she said.

A pay phone was attached to the wall of a building. She dug out a quarter and found his work number. I dialed, worried the line would be defunct, my heart in my throat.

He picked up.

"Hi," I said. "Are you okay?"

"Yup," he said.

"Is work okay?"

"Yeah," he said. "Why?"

"No reason," I said.

And then he had to get off the phone and we said goodbye, my throat still aching with what felt like desperate love.

A few months later we were going to see his NeXT presentation at Davies Symphony Hall. He'd been preparing for months and I knew he was nervous, especially about the demo, where he'd show how the computer worked in real time.

I wore a dark blue corduroy dress with a red ribbon sash that my mother and Mona said they preferred, even though I would have liked to wear something cooler. The pink light and cold wind in San Francisco that morning whipped at my face and blazed on the glass surfaces of buildings.

We were directed down the curving drive where other cars could not go. A woman in black stockings gave us laminated tags with clips and walked us to our seats near the front in the huge theater. Huge banners on the sides of the stage rippled and caught light, a NeXT logo in the center of each. In the middle of the huge stage was a desk, a computer, a bottle of water, and a chair. When I thought of how he'd feel if he failed in front of all these people, it felt like acid in my stomach. People were filing into the seats behind me, expectant, their sounds more muffled and pointed than sounds in the world, the acoustic properties of the cavernous room softened by thousands of thick velvet seats.

Barbara came over, carrying a clipboard. "Do you want to go backstage and see your dad?" My mother nodded yes. I felt as if I was about to view a great secret. People in the theater would probably notice I was walking alone toward the stage. I could feel eyes on my back; it made me walk straight, and step carefully.

Barbara held open a thick velvet curtain, the dark space inside subdivided into velvet rooms. In one was my father, standing, surrounded by other people. He was wearing a suit and looked more polished than usual. He did not seem particularly anxious. He noticed me and smiled.

"Good luck, Steve," I said.

"Thanks, champ," he said, and then walked back into the velvet darkness of the rooms. I followed Barbara back out through the curtain. I was terrified the demo would fail and wanted him to know it was okay with me if he failed. Aaron Copland's "Fanfare for the Common Man" filled the huge room. The uneven horns set my nerves on edge. Toward the front, waiting for me, were my mother, Tina, Mona, my father's father Paul, and my father's sister Patty. It was the only time I saw Tina wearing makeup or a dress. She seemed uncomfortable, too tall, rustling, striking. I sat beside my mother.

Our part darkened, his lit up. He walked out, seeming more at home and natural than he'd been a moment before, as if being on stage was easier than being in life. When he sat down at the desk, his small screen projected on a huge screen above, I knew it was the moment he might fail and the computer might freeze and humiliate him.

He announced that there was a whole dictionary, and the complete works of Shakespeare, inside each computer. He looked up a quote about books and brooks from *As You Like It*. I'd never heard him talk about dictionaries or Shakespeare before. After that he created a three-dimensional shape in a window on the screen, a cylinder or tube with a bouncing molecule inside. Below it, he added a virtual button that compressed the container to make the molecule bounce faster. He made another button that added heat. It moved faster still. All the shapes moved in a smooth way; they did not catch and stutter the way moving images did on my computer when I dragged them from one side of the screen to the other. Whatever pixels made up the image were much finer than I'd seen on a computer before; they did not granulate with motion. And then, unexpectedly, he made another button, clicked it, it was sound, and the rhythm of the dancing molecule was all around us resounding through the hall, miraculous.

"See? Look what we can do here," he said, moving the window around the desktop that contained the tube that held the molecule that continued to bounce, and affecting nonchalance, as his voice was drowned out by thunderous applause. People stood up to clap behind me. I clapped with relief. It had worked. Soon, we were all on our feet.

He was smiling, as if he both hoped and didn't hope the applause would stop—and stood there on the stage before us, everyone's man.

♦

At the start of fifth grade at my new school, I had planned to become popular. At my old school I'd noticed a few popular girls; at my new school I wanted to be one. The summer before, at the bead shop, I discovered a pair of large plastic loops that could be attached to metal hooks, making cheap, sexy earrings that would later be the cause of bitter fights between me and my mother, who found them too provocative.

In the mornings before school my new friends and I congregated in the girls' bathroom off the hallway, leaning over Silly Putty–colored sinks to get close to the mirror, sharing mascara, hair spray, and lip gloss. With hair spray and water I sculpted my bangs into a glossy wave.

I slipped into a miniskirt meant to be a neck cowl from a shop called Units, the happy accident of repurposing I'd discovered in the changing room, and, finally, I put on the pair of dangly earrings I wasn't allowed to wear. They swayed with alternating rhythms, reflecting light from the smooth plastic surface, elongating my round face into a more womanly shape. I snuck them to school in my backpack, along with everything else I wasn't allowed to wear.

The part that kept me wearing clothing my mother didn't allow and adults didn't like was related to the smell of lipstick and hair spray and the pendant quality of earrings. It was sex—not the act, but the awareness and excitement of something new I felt around me like a force. It was a switch that had flipped, unexpected and powerful.

Adults seemed to think academic work was most important, but I figured that was because they didn't understand the greater satisfaction of being popular, perhaps because they were too old or ugly to be popular themselves, and were jealous. I felt this way about my mother too, so her rules about clothing and earrings seemed like a bitter wish to stop me from having what she could not have.

I dressed provocatively on purpose, but when I was with any adults I admired who disapproved of me, I felt that they had seen into my soul and that there was something lascivious and wanton about me, impossible to mend. A wickedness my friends would never possess. Once I'd stayed for a night with my aunt Linda at her condo in Fremont.

"Do you have a boyfriend?" she asked.

"I'd like to," I said. She played me her favorite song: "Get Outta My Dreams, Get into My Car."

"What's your favorite?" she asked.

"I don't know if I can tell you," I said. "It's by George Michael."

"Which song?"

"'I Want Your Sex,'" I said. She scowled and looked away.

At Nueva we sometimes had class in the library. The library was an open room at the end of two parallel hallways, a series of low shelves with books on both sides. In the middle were three couches around a chair where we sat while Debbie, the librarian, read to us from a book about the components of toothpaste, which turned out to be mostly chalk, the chalk itself made from the bones of marine creatures that lived thousands of years ago, died, sank to the bottom of oceans, and were compressed, then ground up. Debbie was tall and handsome with short, brown pixie-cut hair and thick gold-rimmed glasses. She wore long corduroy skirts. Her skin was a waxy layer of white on top of red, and when she became angry, the red bloomed through to the surface.

When she finished reading out loud, we were supposed to read quietly to ourselves.

I was not interested in books; I wanted to talk with Catie and Kate and Elena, who followed the rules and didn't talk, unless I was with them. I was an indifferent student and lured my friends into fooling around with me. For this reason Debbie singled me out for censure.

I put a book on my lap as a prop and whispered to Catie and Kate. We sat at the farthest area from Debbie, with our backs to the shelves and our legs out, elbow to elbow, whispering the in-breaths, making consonants with a light clicking sound.

It seemed impossible that Debbie could hear us from that distance, but there she was, towering above us, blooming red.

"Lisa," she said, pointing to a new patch of carpet, too far to talk. "You sit there."

In the library, now isolated from my friends, I picked a book at random from the shelf and opened it up to find pictures of naked women, drawn in exacting detail, down to the patches of hair and the bumps on the nipples.

I moved farther away to another corner, holding the book against my side so that if Debbie looked up, she would see it only in profile. I sat on the floor, opened it up, and leaned over to look. My heart raced: in the middle of the book across the two center pages were five drawings of the same woman moving through the stages of physical maturation.

In the pictures her breasts swelled and her nipples became larger. As the hair on her body took on a definite shape, the wavy hair on her head went from long to short. She began without glasses but acquired them in the fourth picture, kept them in the fifth. One of her feet was angled to the right in the same way in all the pictures. She smiled unself-consciously, as if unaware she was naked, like a paper doll poised for a business meeting before the clothes are cut out and attached.

The sequence was like the charts I'd seen of the evolution of man, from the chimpanzee to the profile of *Homo sapiens* in final form, heading off the page, bound for civilization. He began hirsute but ended almost hairless; this woman's progression was in reverse. She ended with hair but started putty-colored, chromatically unified except the nipples and the hair on her head, like me. And while the final man seemed to look out at possibilities beyond the page, the final woman was planted, hips wide and square, smiling like she wanted to stay where she was.

I knew that grown women had pubic hair, breasts, and hips. But I didn't know the stages in between, and it was this *becoming*, more than the first or last version, that gave me a feeling of disgust and excitement. I wanted to mock it, but also to keep on looking.

"Elena, look!" I whispered when she walked by.

"Oh, wow," she said, sitting down beside me.

"Shhh," I said, and looked over the bookshelf at Debbie, who was talking with another teacher.

"I'm like that one," Elena said, pointing at the pubic hair of the second one. Little hairs I could see skin through.

I was surprised by her earnestness. I thought we were making fun of it, a zillion miles from these stages—so her tone caught me off guard. I went from being an insider because I found the book to an outsider because I didn't have breasts or hair yet.

"Me too," I lied. Reading this book gave me the same thrill, the same fear and gathering warmth in my abdomen, as looking at the naked woman in *Playboy* magazine.

"But I'm more like this one in my chest." She pointed to the third picture, where the breasts were small yet might cast shadows. I'd assumed the parts in each phase evolved in synchronicity; was it possible to mix and match?

"I'm like the first one for those," I said.

She turned the page to a close-up of several configurations of pubic hair. "Pubic hair," the book said, "comes in different shapes for different women." One shape curved up in a half circle toward the stomach, one was straight across, forming a triangle, and one had a sharp V in the middle, a reverse widow's peak. "Some women have pubic hair in the shape of a heart," it said, with an arrow to the V-shaped one. I had no idea such a thing was possible. I fervently hoped that mine would be shaped like a heart.

I didn't notice Debbie until she was so close her skirt blocked light. This book was proof she was right about me.

She leaned down from her waist, not smiling. I thought she would deliver the damning speech about my character, or move me, again, into isolation. Instead, she held out another book about sex and changing bodies, with pictures of naked people. When we were close to having finished that one, she walked over and handed us yet another, smiling. Her smile was kind, but her eyes glinted, as if this might be a trick. She continued to feed us books; there were at least six of these books in the library, although I had never seen them before. We pored over them the next few days, sanctioned by her, as if this subject was plain and right and necessary, like history or math.

The school didn't give grades. Teachers wrote evaluations in long handwritten notes for the parent-teacher conferences. Since I'd started at the new school, all my focus had been concentrated in the social realm, so my evaluations were poor.

I dreaded these parent-teacher conferences, the solidarity between my mother and the teacher, two women disapproving of my ideal look, my lack of studiousness. My mother wore nice clothes to these meetings, and she was solicitous and formal, as if we were formal and deferential with each other at home too, when in fact she was becoming increasingly frustrated with me.

My teacher Lee told my mother I should get a hobby. "If she develops a passion outside school, she'll start doing better *in* school."

"Anything that interests you," Lee said, looking at me. "Something you think might be fun you can apply yourself to. Nothing to do with school."

Was this supposed to be a punishment? It sounded like a gift! A month before, my mother had taken me to a dance recital at a studio called Zohar on California Avenue behind Printers Inc. bookstore, where women in leotards jumped to music inside colored lights in a white tent. Arms out, fingers splayed, shimmying fast back and forth like birds shaking in puddles.

"I'd like to dance," I said. "Jazz."

"Okay," Lee said. "We have a plan."

I started to dance twice per week, but my mother and I still fought about my clothes and my lack of studiousness. Every element I needed for my style was the exact element she forbade me to wear, and so I found myself perpetually lying and sneaking, terrified she'd come to the school one day without warning or a teacher would call and she'd find out.

And then it happened. Usually I took the bus home and wiped off makeup and changed before my stop, but one day my mother spontaneously came to pick me up and found me wearing makeup, dangly earrings, and a short skirt pulled over ripped stockings. We walked in silence back to the car.

"They're just earrings," I said in the car. "Why do you care so much?" These earrings were the very linchpins of my appeal. They hinted at sex.

"They're not appropriate," she said. "Take them off."

"But other kids wear them," I said, aware both that this statement was true, they were nothing, and also that they were something, that she was partially right, although I wasn't sure exactly why.

"I don't give a damn what other kids wear." She reached toward me as if she would rip them out of my lobes. I dodged.

"You're grounded for a month," she said. I'd already been grounded for two months for sneaking a miniskirt and black nylons to school in my bag. "You're also grounded from using the phone, young lady," she said, her jaw clenched. "You sneak, and you lie."

It was true. I snuck clothing. I snuck into her shower when she was out and shaved my legs for the way it made my calves reflect a line of light, and then I lied about using her razor.

"And no allowance this month."

My allowance was five dollars per week, but I'd been in trouble for long enough for the clothing, my poor evaluations at school, and not doing my homework when I said I would that I had not received it for at least three months. Any money I had was from Kate Willenborg's father, who would give us each a twenty-dollar bill and drop us off at the mall. I believed money should be used, transformed into objects as quickly as possible before it disappeared.

Back at the house, she screamed. I worried the neighbors would hear us. Some strange power was moving through her veins and her extremities, the voltage almost too high for the instrument it ran through. She waggled an index finger right up close to my face and her cheeks got pink.

"You're wasting your life," she said. "If you don't study now, you won't find what you love to do, and then you won't get to work with intelligent people later."

"But I'm only in fifth grade," I said.

"You don't understand," she said, starting to cry. "The work you do now will lead to the work you do later. It will inform who are the people you spend your life with, how interesting they are. Your colleagues."

"I don't care about *them*," I said. I pictured people in an airless room who thought they were enjoying themselves, but who were not. I believed my mother was lying to me, wanting me to become just like her. This made no sense—she didn't have colleagues—but her insistence that I abandon my own sensibility and adopt hers made me assume the story would end with me as her. Were I to abandon joy for study and long-term gratifications, I was sure I would be rewarded with a situation as tepid and flavorless as the studying itself. It didn't occur to me until years later that she had been referring to her own loss, having a child so young when she might have continued at school, at work. Working alone now, when she might have liked to work with a team of people. That she had been fighting so hard for me to apply myself to my studies to help me have a good life, the closest she could come to describing the eminence she felt she had lost for herself.

"You *will* care, you little shit," she said, kicking my bedroom door hard, and leaving a hole in the white paint that looked like a mouth dropped open in surprise.

A few days later I found my mother leaning over her bathroom sink again, yanking her braces off with needle-nose pliers.

"What are you doing?"

"The orthodontist said one more year," she said, "but I don't think so." The sound of something crackling.

"Mom, go to the orthodontist. Let *him* do it."

"I can't wait. I can't live like this anymore." I'd noticed she'd been complaining about them more than usual lately: they were painful, food got caught, she was sick of changing the bands. She wanted them off for good. The adjustment had moved faster given how often she'd changed the bands; her teeth were straight enough, she said.

"Please, don't," I said. I stood next to her in the small bathroom. The wires stuck out like silver whiskers.

"I'm not stopping," she said. "Get out. Go do something else."

◆

Some nights Toby called. He was a popular sixth grader with white-blond hair, a long neck, and ears that stuck out like delicate shells. His voice was a low, rich scratch with the higher notes still inside. At school, I flirted with him, glancing and looking away, giggling with friends.

"Do you want to go steady?" he asked one day.

"Sure," I said. *Sure* was the word I'd decided to say if he asked—it was positive, but held something back.

We planned to French-kiss. Kate and Craig would escort us to the Stumps at lunchtime. The Stumps was an area down at the bottom of school property, a level clearing named after a collection of logs sawed into pieces near a bend in a fire road along a dry creek bed. Lunch was only forty minutes—with travel time factored in, we wouldn't have long.

We followed a path below the middle school, over a small bridge in the shade of the trees that reminded me of *Bridge to Terabithia*, a book that had made me feel the great importance and weight of life and love. There were cool ribbons of wind inside the warm, dry air. The leaves cracked under my feet; the trees above covered the paths in cool shadows, with dots of light like white paint flicked all over the forest.

"*So kiss a little longer, longer with Big Red,*" Kate sang.

The path became steep and less determinate after the bridge, and I almost slipped on my butt, but scrambled up, grabbing at branches, being careful not to snag my earrings.

When we arrived, Toby said, "I guess you guys should go away now."

"Yeah," I said. "Thanks for bringing us!"

At school, I lied and said I'd kissed before, ashamed to be later than my father had been at kissing, and thinking it would make me more attractive if it got around that I'd done it before. I felt woozy. I stood on a low stump to be level with his face.

"Well—I guess," he said.

He smelled of soap and detergent. A thrill moved through my back, heat moving up. I wasn't sure how long to keep going, how frenetically to maneuver my tongue. It was warm and good and electric, the temperature lower in his mouth by a degree or two, and less salt. Was I moving my tongue in the right way? How much was my tongue to be entertained, versus entertainment for his tongue?

My heart fluttered; his tongue seemed to be searching, avid, pointed at the tip and forcing his way through the cavity. An excess of saliva made my chin wet, and in the midst of it I worried about what I would do when it was over, to dry off. He ran his tongue over the back of my top front teeth, a hollow ring in my jaw.

My neck got sore and so I took a risk, detached and tilted my head to the other side, flipping my hair along with it. At the reattachment, we knocked teeth. We both laughed, nervously, then continued. Later, I would teach myself to twist my tongue both ways to reveal the soft underside.

It was unclear when to stop, but we'd have to get back to class, and now we'd done the kiss on both sides.

"We'd better go back," I said. I jumped off the stump, looser in my limbs. His lips were red around the edges. He wiped his mouth with the back of his hand.

I did, too, when he looked away.

The following summer, after more kisses in movie theaters, at the Baylands, the beach, and in the back of his mother's station wagon, and letters exchanged back and forth, Toby called to end it with me. I talked on the now paint-spattered cordless phone my mother had purchased when we moved into the Rinconada house, the phone that was, like the microwave, a sign of moving up in the world.

"I think we should break up," he said.

I felt a stab of guilt I couldn't place. "I'm sorry for what I did wrong," I said, choking up.

"What? It's okay," he said.

I put the phone down and fished through my mother's small red leather pouch that held her jewelry, where I'd once found my baby teeth. Beside it on the tile shelf were a necklace and two bangle bracelets I coveted but was not allowed to wear. I put them on. It was Sunday morning, and my mother was doing errands and would be gone for a few hours. Holding my arm so the bracelets wouldn't fall off my wrist, I went to her closet and rummaged through her clothing and took from her dirty clothes pile a peach silk shirt with buttons down the front, short sleeves, and a collar. I wasn't allowed to wear it. I slipped it over my head so I didn't have to unbutton the buttons. Already I felt different—stronger.

I grabbed the phone again and went to sit on her bed. I would call him to communicate my confidence, my new independent spirit, set him at ease.

"Hello?"

"Hi, it's me again. I just wanted to call and say not to worry. I'm fine." As I said it, the stupidity of the idea became obvious: he wasn't worried. "I just wanted you to know I'm okay, you know. After I got off the phone so fast, and everything."

"Thanks." There was a long pause.

I hung up, shaking. At least it had been quick. I grabbed my mother's hairbrush and walked across the house to my room, wearing her bracelets, her shirt, and my pajama pants.

I brushed my hair as I walked, flipped it up and down a couple of times so that it would fluff and feather. I put on jeans from the dirty clothes pile in my room, grabbed my journal from the shelf, and lowered the scraping venetian blinds over the window that looked out on the street.

I opened my closet door so the mirror that attached on the inside faced the room—but I resisted looking. I sat in front of the mirror on the floor and began to write. I could see a fuzzy silhouette of myself in my peripheral vision, and I wrote in a slanted, adult style, as if this first painful breakup experience had already made me older and more mature. I sat on my knees and bent forward, my hair falling to one side, as if for a camera or another person watching—all of this mattered as a record of who I was.

I adjusted my arm to get the bangles to clack. I looked down and noticed my shirt, how the peach went with the cream bangle, how the cream went with the wood. Adults mentioned forgetting parts of childhood and memories of others, and it was not clear to me which moments would create memories and which would fade away; the moments did not indicate which type they were.

I wrote that I'd broken up with Toby—well, he'd broken up with me, I wrote—and I was sad about it. But, even so, I wrote, I was doing just fine. I described what I was wearing in detail, in case my older self would want to know and picture my younger self at this moment. I implied that the shirt and the bangles were mine, not my mother's.

I flipped my hair and looked up. In the mirror my hair did not hang or cascade but fluffed, thin and foolish. The items I described did not look the way I imagined them: the shirt fell wrong from the creases formed in the dirty clothes pile; the short sleeves hit my arms below the elbows; I didn't have breasts to fill out the front, which hung down hollow. The color was dingy, almost like skin. The bracelets were not glamorous, just big and foolish.

Runaway

I started up in the darkness, my heart pounding. Dread sat like a weight on my chest, the taste of tin in my mouth. A roar in the distance had displaced the air, a heaviness still tremored in the earth below my futon. This was the end, a nuclear bomb on its way to NASA.

I knew what to do. I'd planned for this moment, the short interval after I knew the bomb was coming but before it hit: I would run through the dark center of the house and wake my mother, tell her the bomb was on its way and we had only a few minutes. We would hold each other and cry before we dissolved into the awful radiation and light.

I was up on my feet when I understood the sound was only a freight train. The heavy trains came through at night, longer than the passenger trains. I'd never woken up to the sound of them before.

Before this, when I was eleven, I'd started getting migraines. I knew one was coming when I looked down at my hand and part of it was invisible, or when I looked into the mirror and half my face was gone, replaced by a gray cloud with a shimmering stitch. Within twenty minutes, the first silvery, electric saw would slip down from my forehead, move through my eye and into the center of my brain.

The migraines and the fear of an impending nuclear holocaust became intertwined. A woman on NPR explained that once bombs were launched, it would not be possible to un-launch them. Our missiles were pointed at Russia; theirs were pointed at us. The Russians would have bombs trained on NASA, I thought, because it was strategically important. NASA was only a few miles from us.

That fall I became certain there would be a nuclear attack at Christmas. I also felt it was up to me to stop it, to get the adults to believe me, even though I was only eleven. One day, another migraine starting, my mother called Ron, who still worked at NASA. I hadn't seen him for a few years. I was lying on my bed with the blinds drawn, dreading the start of the pain. My nerve endings spread out to touch every worry on the planet—each individual suffering, actual or potential.

"How you doing, kid?" Ron asked, walking into my room, where I was lying in bed, the curtains drawn.

"I'm worried about a bomb," I said. "They'd want to hit NASA, right?"

"Maybe," he said. "But *if* it happened—and I'm not saying it would, because it won't—you wouldn't feel anything. Not a *thing*. It would be like, poof. Over."

"But in Hiroshima—"

"The bombs are a thousand times more powerful now," he said.

"You mean, faster?" I asked. "Or covering more space?"

"Both," he said.

"But what about just before it hits? Those minutes after we know it's on the way but before it explodes?"

"You'd be vaporized before you had any idea. You'd be dead"—he snapped his fingers—"like that."

"Thanks for coming by," I said weakly. I didn't believe anything he said. There would be at least a second when I knew it was coming, when the world still existed and I was still material. I could catch that moment if I was vigilant.

A few days later my father came over, biting triangles off an oversize Toblerone bar. He didn't usually eat chocolate. A gift, he said, from a woman he'd just started dating.

"It's mine," he said, when I asked for a piece. "You know, she's really smart," he said. "She's pretty too. She looks like that model, Claudia Schiffer." Who was Claudia Schiffer?

It had been only a month or two since the last break with Tina. I figured the attraction would blow over, so I wasn't very interested. It was too much to keep track of. But I'd never heard him talk about smart before. I hadn't known to want both: pretty, smart. I felt as if I'd been duped, trying for pretty when pretty was not enough.

"You know, at the end of things, you forget how easy and great the beginnings are," he said.

When the bomb didn't come on Christmas, I became sure it would come just past midnight on New Year's Eve. My migraines continued. My father and Mona had reserved a long table upstairs at Chez Panisse in Berkeley on New Year's Eve, and my mother and I were invited to come along. At least she and I would be vaporized together.

My father invited his new girlfriend, Laurene, who brought a friend and arrived separately. After the party, my father would drive Mona, my mother, and me back home. I didn't notice Laurene or her friend, and I don't remember him introducing them, but there were many people I didn't know and it didn't matter. We were all about to perish.

Mona's friends were there too, including a petite woman with short hair.

"Hello, sweetheart," she said, leaning down to look into my eyes. "What's your name?"

"I'm Lisa. Mona's niece."

"Ah," she said. "That's right. I'm so happy to meet you. And how old are you?"

"Eleven."

"And that's—what grade?"

"Sixth."

"Well isn't that wonderful," she said. "And are you having fun?"

Every sound startled me. I looked around for my mother, so I could beg to go home. But she loved parties; we didn't go to many, and when she would finally agree to leave, she had to say goodbye to everyone she'd spoken with, initiating a new round of conversations, so that the leaving was sometimes longer than the party that came before.

As I walked through the clot of mingling adults, the same petite woman found me again and asked me all the same questions. I'd never encountered a drunken adult before and didn't understand what it was that made her forget me so soon—unless it was proof that the fabric of the world was in decay, that any minute the bomb would hit.

At midnight there was a cacophony of noise—honking horns, paper whistles like lizard tongues—and my heart flew around in the cavity of my chest. When the noise quieted, however, the dark world was still there, intact. I shook all over but felt grateful for our survival, proud, as if my worry had held the world together.

On the drive back, my father yelled at us. He said that we hadn't paid attention to his new girlfriend. It was pouring rain. He put the wiper on full blast—his kind of car had only one thick wiper, bending and whipping back and forth like a reed in high wind.

"I didn't see her," I said, meekly. He had been told I was anxious about a nuclear bomb, watching for the end of the world. He knew I had migraines, in an abstract way, but he was not one of the people who knew more or soothed me. He was not involved, and now that the world had not exploded I felt relieved but also foolish.

"We were talking with everyone else, Steve," Mona said. "We had friends there too, you know."

"For Christ sakes," he said. "You guys are so damn selfish. Think about how embarrassing this is for me. I told her I had this great family. But why would she want to be with me with a family like this?"

We didn't look like a family; I hadn't thought of us that way except for the few times I'd been together with my two parents, but I was surprised he'd admit it. It was nice to hear him say it, even in anger. He seemed to think of himself as undesirable, as if he didn't notice his own allure, how people hung around him.

As if a woman would leave him because *we* hadn't noticed her at a party!

That night I stayed over at his house, as we'd originally planned. He shook me awake several times throughout the night, crouching beside my bed in the dark and shivering my shoulder. By that time I slept in a different room, in a woven-frame bed Mona had bought for me after he painted and carpeted these rooms. "I can't get hold of her on the phone," he said. "Maybe she's mad. Maybe it's over." He was on the verge of tears. At first he seemed distant and moody with me, as if insinuating I was to blame while also wanting me to reassure him, but then he sat on the side of my bed and put his head in his hands.

"She's probably at a friend's house," I said. "I'm sure it's okay. You can talk to her in the morning."

"I'm so worried she's gone. She's never coming back." It had been only a few hours since we'd seen her; it was the beginning of morning by now, a frail light in the sky.

"She'll call tomorrow. You should sleep."

"I'll try," he said, and walked back to his room.

For my twelfth birthday, Mona gave me a CD by Patsy Cline, with a sad song about a weeping willow and walking all alone at night. Soon after, she came to visit, and after she'd come into the house to see my mother, I followed her outside. She and I stood on the lawn. It was evening, the light was yellow, the air quiet without the lawn mowers, leaf blowers, and prop planes. Gnats bounced like the surface of carbonated water where the grass met the air.

Mona was small, five feet two, but stood as if she belonged, as if wherever she stood became her plot of land. Her small stomach poked out like a girl's. I thought of her as both a woman and a girl. I believed she understood me and I trusted her to help me in the future. I knew her father had also left, that she and her mother had struggled with money. Unlike my parents, she'd been to college and graduate school. When she walked, she ticked her hips back and forth. She taught at a college called Bard and used words I had to look up like "amortize" and "salubrious." She didn't repeat the good words but said new ones each time, in a clipped way, folded into sentences, as if she expected I knew the meanings.

Now we stood in front of my house together, tips of grass catching the slanting light and becoming translucent, like backlit straw.

"If Steve doesn't pay for your college, I will," Mona said, apropos of nothing. College was a long way off, but it worried me in a way I had not been able to articulate to anyone, and I wondered how she knew. When he talked about college, it was often with contempt; he didn't need it, so why would I? Also, sometimes he decided not to pay for things at the very last minute, walking out of restaurants without paying the bill, refusing to buy things other people bought as a matter of course, like furniture. Everyone in his life had been treated to his whimsy about money, offering and rescinding payments for small and large things.

Once Mona, my father, and I went shopping at a vintage clothing store in Palo Alto. Mona and I found hats and jackets we liked, and he watched us try them on. "They don't look as good as you think. When you're shopping in vintage stores, you start to think the things look good when they don't," he said too loudly, and walked off down the street, when it had seemed only a moment before that he might treat us to a hat each, at least.

"Thank you," I said to Mona.

She walked to her car parked under the magnolia tree, waving before she drove off. I ran inside to tell my mother. My mother said, "Did she?" as if she was pondering the significance, or didn't believe it.

At the end of sixth grade, my homeroom teacher, Joan, called me to her desk. I walked to where she was standing and braced for criticism. I'd been reprimanded often for how I dressed.

"This," Joan said, holding one of my papers, a paragraph about Harriet Tubman. "You did something quite *good* here." Joan's glasses magnified her eyes, which were already big and watery. She spoke in an earnest voice, her lips sticking to one another.

I felt a rush of joy. It was the first time I'd been singled out for good schoolwork. I remembered how the night before, while I was writing the assignment, the words had come easily, even delightfully, as if they were greased; they slid out right, and I simply wrote them down.

So I might become smart too. And writing the paragraph had not been boring. The satisfaction I got from Joan's praise was greater than whatever pleasure I seemed to be getting from the tattered jeans that I alternated with the miniskirts and on which I'd now written the names of all the boys I'd kissed, whose names, coincidentally, all began with a *T*: Toby, Tom, Trip, Taylor.

The summer before the start of seventh grade, my mother and Ilan took me to a production of *A Winter's Tale* at UC Berkeley, the actors wearing modern suits. I liked Hermione, who fooled the king into thinking she was a statue. The king walked around her, speaking about her, wishing he'd been better to her. She didn't budge until she'd heard her fill.

For the first time, I wanted the kind of clothes my mother would not object to: simple, matter-of-fact clothes that were easy to pick out in the morning, like a uniform. I resolved that in middle school I would change completely from the girl I was into a new studious, smart girl. I needed a wardrobe that didn't distract me with choice. Jeans and button-down shirts.

The middle school was separate from the elementary school, housed near the upper field on a hill far above the mansion. Steve Smuin and Lee Shult, who had been my teacher in fifth grade, were the main teachers, and were rumored to be very strict.

Seventh grade included a geography class in which we were supposed to learn every country, ocean, sea, and landmark in the world. The assignment was to create a map, with every geographical element included. We worked continent by continent and we'd just arrived at Europe. I would spend ten hours creating this map, even though it would not be graded and was only a tool to learn the placement of the countries we would later be tested on. I spent the hours because I knew that if I made it splendid, it would be praised and pinned on the wall. I didn't care how long it took—the anticipation of praise kept me afloat.

I was coloring in the Ionian Islands with a sea-foam green called Empire. My mother was wearing her tennis shoes, wrinkled at the toes, paint-stained cotton trousers that bagged, a sweatshirt turned inside out. Her head was cocked to one side, watching me. "You need light," she said, and took a lamp from the painting studio she'd made by adding Sheetrock to the garage, plugged it in, and bent it over where I sat.

I finished the map that night, turned it in the next day, and Lee pinned it up facing the classroom—the only one pinned up.

At night, in addition to homework, I copied my notes into a large spiral notebook, sometimes ripping out pages and recopying if my handwriting was not neat enough. I stopped dotting my *i*'s with circles, and added a sophisticated slant so my words drove forward toward the edge of the page.

Mornings, we were quizzed on the information from the day before, and then we announced our scores in front of the class to

Steve, who sat at a computer and entered them without looking up,
unless someone scored low enough that he gave a sarcastic look. The
room would grow silent. It was as if a low score was not just academically wrong, but morally depraved; as if the low score announced
one's unwillingness to participate in the grand experiment of the
school. Almost every day, someone cried.

I was afraid of Steve and this motivated me to work harder.
Our poor diction and our selfishness in all its forms were what set
him off. His lips were thin, his mouth was small and not fully visible
through his short beard. A flash of contempt from those thin, bearded
lips was enough to deflate me, sometimes for an entire day. Away
from school, whenever I saw a car that looked like Steve's blue
Honda, my heart leapt into my throat, I was self-conscious and
careful; I walked with a straighter spine, spoke with clearer diction,
for the chance he might be watching. This continued for years, even
after I'd left the school.

The work I did was not just for grades or to become smart or
to go on the much-anticipated monthlong trip the eighth-graders
took to Japan, but to avoid his contempt; to feel myself, never clearly
but at least possibly, in his good graces. We were quizzed one morning on the Components of Culture, and I'd memorized them with
a friend and a mnemonic device we invented the night before. For
the first time, I got a ten out of ten on a quiz—I'd never scored well
before—and Steve did not grunt with incredulity but nodded his
head in approval.

For the first parent-teacher conference, a few weeks later, my parents arrived separately. The sight of my father walking into the
classroom—bouncing on his toes, vibrant and young—gave me
a pleasant jangle. The conferences would take place twice per year.
At the time, I didn't think about the similar effect the two Steves
had on me.

We sat, the five of us: Steve, Lee, my mother, my father, me. Lee spoke, her triangle eyes winking and sparkling when she blinked. "She's doing very well. She's challenged herself." They commented on the map. They commented on how I'd liked the book *The Forest People*, how I was prepared for quizzes and early morning tai chi. I kept silent and let them talk about me. They talked about the dramatic change from the previous year's miniskirts and makeup. Lee's eyes flicked between me and my mother and father. Mostly my father, who seemed to carbonate the meeting with his presence, both teachers becoming giddy near him. I worried they looked at him too much, ignoring my mother. As if he and I were the show, my mother just the shadow.

"If we expected the student we saw in sixth grade, with her emphasis on boys and clothing, we were mistaken."

"That's great," my father said. "In general, I think middle school is so awful it would be better if kids just sailed around the world instead. Just put them all on a boat. But this place is an exception."

"Yes," Steve said. "We've been very pleased with Lisa's progress here." I tried to hide a smile. "As long as she keeps it up," he said, before stepping out.

"We're impressed with her dedication," Lee continued.

I would get to go to Japan, she said, as long as I kept working at the same level.

"I'm having some trouble getting her to do the dishes," my mother said, sinking down in her chair. "Just because she's doing well at school doesn't mean she should be ignoring her chores."

"I agree," Lee said. "At our house, the girls help do dishes; sometimes they make dinner. They also do laundry and some light cleaning."

Lee looked at me. "Lisa, if your mom comes up with a schedule for chores, would you do your best to do them?"

"Okay," I said. I could tell my mother was relieved. But I wanted to tell Lee that our fights weren't really about the chores, but about the way my mother didn't feel she had enough moral and emotional support. Even though my father was sitting there, she addressed Lee with her concerns.

My mother had already asked my father for help—not the financial kind, but for his time and energy. She said she had begged. She'd never asked him for this kind of help before, but allowed him to come and go, watch me or not watch me, as it suited him. Now, I was becoming an adolescent, and the middle school, which was an hour away by car, began at seven, which meant she had to wake up at five. She wasn't getting enough sleep. There were other troubles too: my father's accountant called one day to tell her my father had decided not to pay for her therapy anymore (after paying for a year); she and Ilan were fighting; I was receiving the accolades she'd worked so hard to help me earn, and yet she felt she was being treated by the school as the inferior half of my parentage.

My father refused, saying that if she wanted more help, I'd have to live with him full-time. Later, he said it was the school that had insisted that it would be better if I lived with him, because of our fights and her increasingly violent temper. She believed that if he'd helped more, it wouldn't have come to that.

After the conference, I hoped my parents would linger. I stood in the classroom for a minute, gathering papers into my backpack; they walked out of the room into the covered walkway, my mother wearing a long skirt, boots, and a blouse, my father in a crisp white shirt and wool suit trousers. It was the kind of day with mist from the ocean hanging in the air; my mother's hair formed ringlets, my father's was newly cut and fell like black lacquer. From where I stood near the glass door, I could see them facing each other, talking. I didn't care what they talked about, only that they kept talking, for the feeling of peace it gave me. I came outside to be near them, but they said they had to get back to work and, parked in different places on the school property, they left separately.

When my mother and I got home after grocery shopping, it was almost dusk; the lowering sun made a wide gold line across the street. We got out of the car and our neighbor Margaret, an older woman who sometimes watched me after school, walked over to us.

Around this time my father had offered to buy us the house we lived in, but the landlord refused to sell. I worried my mother wouldn't own a house by the time I left for college. I thought we should convince the landlord, or find another house of equal value before my father changed his mind, but my mother did not seem to feel the same urgency. She must have told the neighbor Margaret that we were looking.

"There's a house for sale," Margaret said. "The brick one that looks like a fairy-tale house, at the corner of Waverley and Santa Rita?" It was only four blocks away.

"I know that house," my mother said. "Across from the Nancy's Quiche house?" A woman named Nancy Mueller had made a lot of money, enough to buy a huge Italian-style house, selling frozen quiche with flaky crusts we sometimes ate.

"That's the one. It's not on the market yet. I thought I should tell you in case you want to check it out." She winked.

My mother thought we should drive over to take a look before it got dark. Up to the top of our street, past the dip, over a block, and then up again a block to the corner: a brick house built in a fanciful style, with a roof composed of overlapping slate tiles. The windows were paned, leaded glass; on the rooftop, the tip of a small spire twisted up in a corkscrew, like a pig's tail. At one side of the house rose a high wall made out of the same weathered brick as the house, shaped in a curving pattern, surrounding a courtyard. At the part of the wall farthest from the house was a small built-in wooden door with a curved top and an iron latch, as in a storybook.

We peered through the gate. "Wow," my mother said. Her face opened up and flushed, her eyes got sparkly, as if she were letting herself believe it might already be ours, the way when she had just a few sips of wine she let herself feel a little tipsy.

"He's not going to buy it for us," I said, to mute her excitement. "It's too nice."

"He might," she said. "He'd finally have done something really good, really generous. I wish he'd just do it. Just buy it for us."

I'd liked the feeling when he'd bought us the Audi—a miraculous improvement bestowed upon us as if from nowhere.

"He won't," I said. Still I hoped. How would it be if I already thought of it as mine? In this house, my mother would be happy. "Anyway, how would we afford furniture?"

"We'd figure it out," she said.

Peering into other people's windows made me think of the story of the match girl who stood out in the snow, lighting matches and imagining scenes in the flames, found dead the morning after the last one went out. I felt a sentimental attachment to that story ever since I'd heard it as a girl.

A few nights later my father stopped by. My mother was in the kitchen, making squash soup. She'd already told him about the house on the phone, saying she wanted it. He said he was planning to take a look with a realtor.

"You know what I told Laurene?" my father said.

"What?" my mother asked.

"I told her I come as a package." He meant that we—my mother and I—came with him.

"She's really smart," he said to me, again. "Did I tell you she looks like Claudia Schiffer?" He was repeating himself again. This was frustrating, less because stories and lines twice told are boring, and more because the way he'd told it the first time, with intensity and excitement, gave me a notion the story was specifically meant for me. Sometimes he told me a secret and swore me to secrecy and later I found out he'd done the same with everyone else.

He dipped into the soup with a metal spoon, slurped. "Mmm," he said, closing his eyes. And then, with his mouth full, "Is there butter in this?"

"A little," my mother said absently.

At that, he spit the soup out into his hand making a gagging sound, then washed his mouth in the sink.

My father bought the house on Waverley Street for himself. Before moving in he did a few renovations. Walking around with him, as he pointed out what he would change—the floorboards, the high triangle of yellow glass, the light-blocking trellis of a wisteria vine in the courtyard—I felt embarrassed that my mother and I had wished it for ourselves. It had cost three million dollars, after he negotiated the price down. The widow who was selling it became so desperate with his slow pace, he recounted to my mother after he'd bought it, that she had been willing to sell it, finally, for less than she wanted to. He would keep the house in Woodside, which he hoped to tear down anyway in favor of the trees and the land. My mother thought his haggling with the owner was wrong, and was hurt that he'd bought for himself the very thing she'd wanted. It was sad, but it was not unexpected, perhaps, and it was also a compliment: she had good taste; she found the best things first.

◆

Laurene moved into the house on Waverley. One weekend day a few weeks later, I walked over to see them and found her upstairs putting on exercise clothes. She was wearing a new ring. "We got engaged," she said, and held out her hand. The ring was an emerald-cut pink diamond. "I've been proposed to twice before this," she said. My father was at the grocery store, but I ran out to him when he returned. "I've seen the ring," I said, when he came in through the gate. "Congratulations."

"She could buy a *house* with it," he said, "but don't tell her," as if he worried that she might leave, knowing how much the ring was worth. He brushed past me to go into the house and put the juice into the refrigerator.

Sometimes after that I'd walk over to the house on Waverley when Steve and Laurene were out in the midafternoon. They always left the doors unlocked. I went in through the door that opened into a small entrance room and then the kitchen. Continent-shaped blots of sun shone on the wall. It was calm here. A mourning dove trilled high low, high low, the second note seeming to sway the patch of light.

There was a box of Medjool dates on the counter. Beside it was a wooden box of bing cherries from a farm nearby that were allegedly also sent to kings, shahs, and sheikhs, the stems tucked under the fruits, arranged in perfect rows beneath a layer of waxed tissue paper, as shiny and black as beetles.

There was a bowl of ripe, flushed mangoes. When my mother and I bought mangoes, we bought only one because they were so expensive. Here mangoes were unlimited.

I roamed the house. The widow who'd owned it before had left cans of paint in the pantry along with bags of brushes, empty cans of nails, bottles of oil, and instructions written on scraps of lined paper in a fine, tilted cursive.

The house felt alive to me. I walked into the hallway that looked out into the courtyard. It was basically *my* house, I told myself. It was my father's house and I was his daughter. I was pretty sure I was allowed to be here, but I still didn't want to be caught snooping.

The Rinconada house would rattle with the many small earthquakes and the heavy trains, the window glass singing. Here, it was still. It was a few more blocks away from the trains, out of sight of Alma and the tracks. The walls were thick and dense, the doorways and hallways rounded and wide, like Spanish mission buildings.

I walked up the stone steps to the second floor, holding on to the thin iron railing beneath a long paper lantern that twirled slightly in the breeze, feeling as if a string at my sternum pulled me up to Laurene's closet and her chest of drawers, the pressure inside me growing. I longed to understand her—to see if I could be more like her.

A couple of weeks before, I'd asked her, "If you had to choose one, would you buy clothing or underwear?" I'd gotten the idea from a Shel Silverstein poem—you were supposed to ask people to determine their predilections for the inner or outer life, the soul or the skin.

"I'm not sure," she said. "Do you mean, would I rather have nice clothing or nice underwear?"

"Yes," I said, losing my conviction that whatever she said would mean something about her character.

"Nice clothing," she said.

She showed me how she could still do the splits, dropping down to the floor. I observed everything about her, including how, when she talked, she used a group of words I'd never heard people use in speech before—*gratify, garner, providence, interim, pillage, marauding*—slipping the words into her sentences like jewels. When she said *marauding*, she elongated the vowels in a way that made it sound like adulthood and self-sufficiency. Her eyes were icy blue, flat, and small. Sometimes it hurt me to look into them; I wasn't sure why. She said she was legally blind without glasses or contact lenses, the world reduced to shapes.

Her friend Kat lived nearby and sometimes came over when I was there. Both of them were in their late twenties. When she and Kat talked about losers, which they did sometimes, Laurene made an L shape with her thumb and index finger and moved it around. When Laurene said the word, with her clear diction, I knew there was nothing I'd rather not be than a loser. Laurene was from New Jersey, and I got the idea that people were more normal in New Jersey. They didn't have Birkenstocks and gurus and talk of reincarnation. Around this time, she said a man had followed her around the Palo Alto Whole Foods, saying he was reincarnated from a bumblebee.

Now, upstairs in the house in the muffled silence, I wanted to find out her secret.

I walked into her closet, which had a full-length mirror, a chest of drawers, a rod for hanging clothing. A carpenter had come to build these closets with light-colored wood. On the chest of drawers were two tubes of lipstick: one mauve, the other a light, shimmering pink, both carved by repeated application into pointed crescents so high and thin the top might break off. I tried the mauve. It felt wet and smelled of wax and perfume.

I opened her underwear drawer. Different cottons—white, nude, black—lumped together the way mine were lumped at home. In the depths of the far-right corner was a loop of ivory. I pulled the loop—a web of elastic and lace unfurled in front of me. A garter belt. I knew what it was, maybe because I'd seen one in *Playboy*, but I'd never seen a real one before.

In the drawer below was a pair of charcoal wool shorts I recognized from a photograph in which she stood in the Stanford Quad, her hair bright blonde and cascading around her face, her feet turned out at ten and two from the heels, one in front of the other, confident. My father kept the picture on his desk. My mother liked candid photographs; I liked them head-on, as in a magazine. I wanted to be Laurene, and if I couldn't be her now, I wanted to be her later.

I slipped off my trousers and pulled on the shorts. They bagged around my legs; I had to hold them up with one hand so they didn't slide off. I put on one of her shirts, a sleeveless cream with black stitches around the neck and arms. I tucked the shirt into the baggy shorts, then looked at myself in her mirror from the side and back, hoping that changing the light and the angle would improve the form. I turned my feet out like hers, ten and two, heels in a line, one in front of the other, hid my nail-bitten hands behind my back.

I pursed my lips. I looked nothing like the person in the photograph.

I took everything off, rearranged the lipsticks. I slipped the garter belt into my pocket, walked down the stairs, down the hallway of windows, past the pantry, through the kitchen, and out the door.

◆

That spring, my father invited me on a trip to New York with him and Laurene.

"She's a great dancer," he said on the flight. Laurene and I flanked him in the leather seats at the front of business class. He looked at her and ran his hand over her hair the way you might with a sleeping child.

"I'm an *all right* dancer," she said, but I knew she must be better than I was, as he'd seen me perform once in a concert and didn't mention that I danced too.

Laurene had taken me to lunch once before this in her white VW Rabbit convertible, taking time out from Stanford's business school, where she was in her final semester. She seemed rushed, didn't talk to me or look at me as she drove, but looked straight ahead, as if she wasn't sure how to relate to a child. She held the gearshift differently from my mother, with less grip, pushing it forward with the heel of her hand. She was pretty, but a different pretty from Tina, who didn't wear makeup and who didn't seem interested in the way she looked.

We walked through the Stanford Shopping Center. She walked fast, with her feet pointed out to the sides; she wore black suede shoes with metal clocks on the tops. "Let's go to the Opera Cafe," she said. "They make a great chicken Caesar salad without much fat." This talk of fat was new and enticing—another, more sophisticated world I wanted to be part of in which women watched the amount of fat they ate. I didn't think of myself as thin or fat. I didn't go out to eat very often, and looked forward to sampling one of the outlandishly tall cakes so large they looked unreal, like sculptures by Claes Oldenburg. I hoped we'd get more than salads.

But we had to eat quickly; we didn't have time for dessert. Laurene's blonde bangs fell over her forehead, curling out from a cowlick at the hairline. When she touched objects, she did it firmly, with precision, as if she knew what she wanted to take before she touched it. I liked the way she held the menu, the steering wheel, the tube of lipstick.

At first, New York City smelled of yeast. Warm pretzels, exhaust, steam.

Laurene took us to Wall Street and showed us around the trading floor, where she'd worked just out of college.

"They used to switch the phones," she said, of a circular bank of white telephones, each one with a white twisting cord hanging down, "as a joke. They'd hang the earpiece of one phone on the base of another, crossing the cords. So when someone needed to do a trade, and they were in a rush, they'd pick up a phone, dial the number, and then realize they were using an earpiece that didn't match the keypad."

Laurene's friend Shell, a large brunette woman who wore red lipstick and spoke loudly, with a New York accent, came to visit us at the suite at the Carlyle Hotel. She stood beside the piano, playing a few notes. They talked about people I didn't know, calling them "total losers."

That afternoon, my father said, "There's something I want to show you two." We took a taxi to a tall building and then a freight elevator with blankets for walls up to the very top. My ears popped. The elevator opened onto a dusty, windy space, full of watery light.

It was an apartment at the top of a building called the San Remo. It was still under renovation, and it took me a few minutes to grasp that it was *his* apartment. The ceilings were at least twice the height of ordinary ceilings. Pieces of cardboard covered the floor; he lifted one up to show us the marble below, a glossy deep black that also lined the walls. He told us that I. M. Pei designed the apartment in 1982, and when one of the quarries ran out, they'd had to find another one and replace the old marble with the new marble. Otherwise the blacks wouldn't match. Construction had lasted six years and it was still unfinished.

"It's incredible," Laurene said, looking around.

Other than a bank of windows along two sides, all the surfaces in the apartment were black marble. I swept up a line of dust with my finger; the marble gleamed beneath. We stood in the main room, with its triple-height ceilings and windows, gaping fireplace, black walls and floor. The staircase looked wet, dripping down from the second floor, each level of stair opening wider than the last, like molasses poured from a jar. He said it was based on the design of a staircase by Michelangelo.

It was hard to tell how a person could possibly be comfortable in such a place. It was hard-edged like rich people's apartments in movies. It was opulent, the opposite of the counterculture ideals he talked about, a showcase made to impress. Yes, he had the Porsche and the nice suits, but I'd believed he thought the best things were simple things, so that looking at this apartment felt like a shock. Maybe his ideals were only for me, an excuse not to be generous with me. Maybe he was bifurcated, and couldn't help trying to impress other people in the obvious ways rich people do, even as I'd thought, with his holey jeans, his strange diet, his emphasis on simplicity, his crumbling house, he didn't care.

"It was supposed to be the ultimate bachelor pad," he said sadly. "Oh well."

We went out onto the balcony, a line of stone balustrades like candlesticks wrapped around the corner. From up this high, New York smelled like nothing. The wind made a sound like a sheet flapping. Below us, Central Park looked like it was cut out of the concrete.

"It's a great view, isn't it?" he asked.

"It is," I said.

"This is amazing, Steve," Laurene said, with a lightness to her voice I wished I felt too. He grabbed her and I looked away. I felt stuck, unable to talk, my feet heavy on the ground.

◆

Soon after I returned, my mother and I bought a couch, a chair, and an ottoman at the mall.

Wings made of white feathers hung in a children's store window display. "When I was a kid, my mother told me all children are born with wings, but the doctors cut them off at birth. The scapulae are what remain. Isn't that strange?"

We walked past Woolworth's, with its tubes of watermelon-flavored lip gloss and packets of press-on nails, past the restaurant Bravo Fono, where we still went sometimes with my father, and into Ralph Lauren. The store was half outside. Cement planters came up to my waist and held impatiens with swollen green seed pods that popped open when I squeezed them, spraying tiny yellow seeds and springing back to a horizontal curl.

"Hey, what do you think of this couch? Do you like it?" she asked. It was two cushions wide. I sat; the cushions did not spring back, but sank slowly under my weight.

"I like it," I said. "Is it expensive?"

She looked at a price tag pinned to the side and took a sharp breath.

I knew she hated the couch we had, the one we'd taken from Steve's house years before; it was nothing she would have chosen for herself. It made her feel, I think, like her life was composed of the castoffs of other lives.

She bought the couch, along with its matching chair and otto-man, on her new credit card. It was, by far, the largest purchase we'd ever made. To reduce the cost, she took it in the natural cotton linen it came in—the color of sand—instead of having it re-covered. We were both giddy afterward, as if the mall was a different place to us now, opened up.

We must have more money, I guessed. Why else was she buying big things? She'd wanted a new couch for a long time. Where was she getting the money? I didn't know. She said no, always. This time, yes. If I asked why, it might pop. She seemed happy and confident, and I thought this is how we should have been at the mall all along, and maybe this is what the future would be like.

At Banana Republic we tried on the same jean jacket in different sizes. It was nicely boxy, with a collar made of stone-colored corduroy. I tried not to act excited; I knew not to push. But she bought them both. Both! Compared with a couch, two jackets were nothing. We walked out of the store with the weighted paper bags.

"That," I said, pointing to a sweater and skirt in a shop window. The small, minimalist shop sold expensive clothing from Switzerland. The long skirt was dark gray cashmere, the sweater was made of maroon angora with fabric teddy bears appliquéd. "*That's* the kind of thing you should wear." It maybe could have done without the bears, I thought.

"Where would I wear it?" she asked.

"Anywhere," I said. "To parent-teacher conferences. Out to dinner or lunch." I imagined another life for her.

"I don't really like it," she said.

"Just try it on. You can't tell on the hanger." I'd heard someone say that in another shop. When she came out of the changing room, still ambivalent, she looked exactly right. I insisted, the saleswoman insisted, and she bought the set.

When we were almost home, we stopped at the stop sign of the four-way intersection before the turn to our block. My mother began to make the turn, but continued to spin the car past ninety-degrees, missing our street as if by accident. "Oops," she said, the steering wheel kinked as far as it would go.

She made a full circle, and we came back to our starting position. But again, when the time came to turn, she missed it.

"Oops again!" she said, laughing.

She spun us round and round, as if we were caught in a vortex: sidewalk, lawn, tree, house; sidewalk, lawn, tree, house.

"Turn now!" I yelled each time we approached our street.

"I just . . . can't seem . . . to turn!" she said. Bushes grew halfway up the houses, so they looked like faces with beards, watching us as we spun. She went round and round until we were both dizzy, and then—finally—she made the turn and took us home.

At home that night we heated up chicken potpies in the microwave and watched *Masterpiece Theatre* sitting on the floor in front of the television. She wanted to read Andy Warhol's diaries out loud to me in bed before sleep, even though I was too old to be read to, and I let her.

"You're a Simpleton," I said, as a joke, a few days later when we were stopped at a gas station filling up and she said she liked the smell of gasoline. I'd never called her that before. I might have gotten the word from the Mock Turtle's Story in *Alice in Wonderland*, parts of which she also liked to read aloud to me. When I said the word, I wanted her to deny it. I wanted her to get mad at me: how dare I call her Simpleton—it wasn't true. But she only laughed.

A couple months later, the new couch, chair, and ottoman arrived upholstered in the dun-colored linen with down-filled cushions and pillows. She gave the old ones away. She wore the skirt and sweater together a few times, for me, and then she must have given those away too. I called her Simpleton when she made mistakes—forgetting directions, insisting that Italian ice cream wasn't different from or better than the American variety. It made her laugh. I'd been spending more time with my father and Laurene, absorbing their ideas, their sophistication. I'd been to New York, I understood the importance of low-fat, watched Laurene add oil carefully and sparingly to salad dressings. I'd learned that gelato was different from, and better than, ice cream.

One day, driving somewhere, I noticed a speck of paint on her jeans she hadn't noticed to wash off and said it again: "You're a Simpleton." This time she burst into tears, pulled over, and leaned on the steering wheel, surprising us both, and I never said it again.

My father's wedding took place in Yosemite, at the Ahwahnee Hotel.

Kobun, a Buddhist monk my parents knew, officiated. During the ceremony, Steve and Laurene stood before three large plate-glass windows through which you could see the mountains, the forest, and the falling snow.

Laurene's dress was ivory silk; my father wore a jacket and bow tie with jeans, as if he were one of those puzzles where each part of the body is clad in a different outfit.

That morning Laurene had been downstairs in the hotel lobby wearing black leggings with a flower pattern and black-rimmed glasses. In my idea of weddings, brides hid before the ceremony, worried about their beauty, and I liked the way she was playful and among us.

Kobun had asked several people to give short speeches, and I was to be one of them.

There were only forty people invited to the wedding, and afterward we would go for a hike in the snowy forest, wearing fleece jackets they'd given out as gifts. The dinner would be in a room with rectangular tables arranged in a U-shape, a classical guitar performance, and bouquets of wheat.

My mother wasn't invited, but my father called her the day after the ceremony, something she didn't tell me until years later. When she did tell me, the fact of the call surprised me because I didn't realize they were in touch; they could be distant and then close in a pattern I didn't understand.

My father gave a speech in which he said that it wasn't love that brought people together and kept them together, but values—shared values. It was delivered to the crowd and to Laurene in a tense way, like a lecture, or an admonition. A few more speeches and then Kobun called my name, and I walked forward toward my father and Laurene, who stood in front of the windows, a thick snow falling slowly behind them that gave the scene the look of being a snow globe. I was holding the paper on which I had written something about how it was rare to get to see your parent get married (a friend suggested this idea), and as I walked toward them, reading the speech at the same time, I started to cry. My father gestured me closer, and I hugged the two of them until Laurene whispered, "Okay, Lis. C'mon."

I'd been looking forward to the wedding: I would get to eat the food and cake (it was shaped like Half Dome, and tasted of banana), and there might be dancing (there wasn't). I was prepared for these details, the surfaces of the ceremony. I was unprepared for how it would feel to be this close to the buzzing wire of what I wanted. I hoped to be the very center of it, the matchstick girl who had imagined a scene into being. This wedding was *for* me. I would be the daughter of married people, even if Laurene wasn't actually my mother.

When the ceremony was over, however, I felt empty. I was *not* the center of the affair. I wasn't invited into most of the wedding photos. My father seemed absorbed with Laurene and everyone else. During the dinner after the ceremony, I braided Laurene's hair, standing behind her at the table.

Later I wandered down to the lobby and looked around the gift shop. I found a small photo album, the cover made of a piece of cloth that looked like a tapestry of pixelated trees.

"Would you like to pay with cash or charge it to your room?" I'd learned at some point that hotels let you charge to rooms. The woman seemed earnest, not aware of my scheme.

"The room," I said. I zinged with excitement, my palms got clammy, at the prospect of having a photo album. But my father might see it on the bill. I hoped he would be too busy to notice, or that he had too much money to notice money.

I was sharing a hotel room with my father's sister, Patty, the sister he grew up with who was also adopted. My father wasn't very close with Patty—he'd become closer to Mona in the years since they'd found each other in adulthood. I felt upset to be rooming with her, as if it meant she and I were in the same category.

Most of the guests left on the Sunday after the wedding, except for Mona and her boyfriend, Richie, who would stay for a week with my father and Laurene, sharing a honeymoon. Richie and Mona would marry the next year at a ceremony at Bard College, and also share a honeymoon with Steve and Laurene, but then it seemed to me that there was no reason, if Mona stayed, that I could not stay too. Kobun and his girlfriend, Stephanie, were also still around, but would be leaving that afternoon.

"If you're staying, I want to stay," I told my father.

"Maybe," he said. "Let me think about it." He seemed conflicted, the way he rarely seemed when he said no to me.

But a couple of hours later he said I had to ride home that afternoon with Kobun and Stephanie.

Before I left, he requested the bill for the room I'd shared with Patty at the main desk in the lobby. I stood near him. I didn't want to be anywhere but at his side.

He looked through the bill and frowned.

"Is this yours?" he asked, pointing at the charge.

"It was Patty," I lied. I was afraid of him, deeply sad to leave, and terrified of what he would say to me if he found out it was me. "I told her not to get it, but she did."

Shortly after the wedding, a fight that had been simmering between my parents on and off for more than a year exploded. Before this I had hardly been aware they were fighting, only that the rapport had cooled between our house and theirs. I attributed this to the fact that my mother was having a hard time with her own life. A few

years before, my father had hired a man to do gardening at the
Woodside house. The same man had recently started to do some
work as an assistant gardener at the Waverley house too, and my
mother had found out. My mother heard through acquaintances
that this man had been accused by his children of sexually molesting
them, and the issue of my proximity to him became a catalyst for a
larger disagreement between my parents. They had become friendly
again over several years without resolving or discussing how my
father had neglected us years before, how he had not protected me
when I was little. And now he was not protecting me again, and it
must have reminded her of his other abandonments and neglect and
made her enraged. When they discussed it, she lost her temper and
she could hardly speak. She had asked him several times already to
fire the man, but he refused.

The final argument happened one evening when I went over
to the Waverley house for dinner on my own. My mother knocked
on the door, white with rage. It seemed to me completely out of the
blue. I watched as the two of them argued, both standing outside
the gate on the sidewalk on Santa Rita near her car. I understood
the fight was about the man, but it didn't make sense to me why
she should be so upset, why she should be almost incapacitated with
anger over what seemed to me to be such a small issue. I remember
wishing she would go away, stop humiliating herself.

"How dare you. How dare you," she repeated, crying. "Promise
me you'll fire him."

"Nope," he said. He stood tall, impassive. He looked good, a
new black T-shirt, jeans that had not yet sprouted holes. She was
wearing shorts and tennis shoes.

Next to him she looked ragged and disheveled. When she spoke,
sobbing, she was hardly intelligible. Looking back, I'm ashamed to
see that I just wanted her to act neat and quiet—to preserve the
semblance of friendship and normalcy that had been established
between them. I didn't want my father to think I was anything like

her. If he did, he might not want me. She seemed too dramatic. Crazy, even. I wanted her to feel less, express less. I was embarrassed by the ways her feet kicked and her face contorted.

At some point she got into her car, slammed the door, and drove off. He shrugged, walked back into the house. I followed, pretending along with them, for the rest of dinner, that nothing had happened.

After that night, my father no longer stopped by our house on Rinconada, and my mother wasn't invited for dinner at Waverley again. The gardener continued to work for my father, and my parents stopped interacting.

◆

The news that Laurene was pregnant hit me like a slap. I thought they'd wait to conceive—for several years, at least. Although I could not have articulated it, I thought *I* was what they wanted. A house, a woman, a man, and a daughter: now, finally, with the wedding ceremony over, we might enjoy it.

They invited me for dinner. We ate the same food as on other days: vegan food. On this night, vegetable sushi with brown rice. He'd kissed her on the lips like he was Mr. Passion when he came in the door; she had to bend back awkwardly and steady herself on the island. It looked painful for her neck. I said so afterward, and he laughed.

He said that he was a good kisser, and lots of women told him so.

"It looked more like suction than a kiss," I said.

Laurene raised her eyebrows and nodded at me, in agreement, behind his back.

Now we were in the den, and they had become serious. I wondered if I was in trouble.

I sat on a chair. Laurene sat on an ottoman, my father on the floor.

"We're having a baby," he said. I looked at Laurene to see if it was true. She nodded.

The light was dim in that room at dusk—only the lamp on his desk and a weak one overhead and royal blue in the windows.

"That's great," I said. I felt the muscles in my face melt and twitch so that I wasn't sure anymore what the resting position of a face was supposed to be and how to get back to it.

"We're very excited," he said, and put his arm around her.

I walked home. The lights were on, two yellow eyes. The house was small now, and far away. It was nothing, my mother was nothing. She was not part of the family and new baby and she couldn't stop it.

"They're having a baby," I told her the next day in the car, both of us looking forward so she couldn't see my face. I'd kept it to myself, the night before, crying in bed after she said goodnight. When I was with her now, I felt as if I was too much like her, the part of the family that was set aside.

"Good for them," she said.

"But I didn't think they'd want—they never mentioned having a baby," I said.

"That's why people get married," she said. "To have babies."

This baby would have my father from the start, and the right mother. It was born into luck. The baby was not to blame; this made it worse, somehow. I wished that I were that baby instead, and that Laurene was my mother. Soon Laurene's stomach became round and tight as a drum. Her belly button poked out like a doll's ear.

I went over to the house, into my father's study, and saw my father had typed out the name—Reed Paul Jobs, three names, three syllables—in many typefaces, fonts, sizes, filling his computer screen. Garamond, Caslon, Bauer Bodoni. He wanted to make sure the name would be good enough for a whole life of use.

My brother was born with long fingers and curling fern hands that grasped my finger, miniature fingernails with white tips. How I loved him! It was involuntary; I couldn't help it. The way he smelled, his proportions—his perfect heels and loose-skin knees. I went over to visit him after school and on weekends. I changed his diapers. I wondered who he would become. Curled on his stomach, I noticed the downy hairs on his back, his abdomen flaring out under his ribs like a roasting chicken. Dark straight hair grew around a soupy area on his skull that pressed in like the center of a pie. His lips were pink and made of a different kind of skin, like a clean pink worm that contracted. His tiny diapers made him seem even smaller, spindly thighs and tiny feet shooting out of a big white casing. He had an old, dreamy look in his gray eyes, like he came from a wiser place.

Sometimes, in the evenings, creditors called. "What's your name," my mother said, when she picked up the phone, frowning into it. "I want to get *your* name. You're not allowed to call at this hour. I'll report you."

"Who was it?" I asked when she'd hung up. At the time I believed they were people calling to sell us things. Later I learned it had been the purchase of the couch, chair, and ottoman at Ralph Lauren that day that led to the debt she could not pay, then to the stress of creditors calling; and later, when I was in high school, unable to pay off the cards, she went through bankruptcy.

I heard her complain about the carnations Ilan sometimes brought—he might have sprung for better flowers. Later she told me that one night when he said he had to work late, she bought a ticket to an opera at Stanford, went alone, and saw him there with another woman. Over the course of the next couple of years they were off and on, sometimes fighting, sometimes separated or back together, broken up for the last time before I started high school. When they weren't getting along, she and I fought more too.

"You know Ilan's pinkies? How they twist inward?" she asked me one day in the car. The second joint of both his pinkie fingers bent in at a thirty-degree angle. "It's a sign that someone isn't faithful."

I felt myself above the menial tasks she wanted me to do. I felt humiliated and bored taking out the trash or doing the dishes, and so I would perform these tasks with lethargy and carelessness, doing a sloppy job and then rushing back to my room to work at the earliest opportunity, lazy about anything that didn't result in academic praise. One night she was still in the kitchen when I came back from dragging the trash to the canister at the side of the house, waiting for me with an air of expectancy.

"Look at the counter," she said.

I looked for the sponge, but she'd already grabbed it and wrung it out, and was furiously wiping crumbs on the countertop into her cupped hand.

"All I'm asking," she said, "is that you do the dishes and wipe the counter. Dishes, counter. Get it?"

"I'm sorry," I said. "I'll do it next time."

"No, you'll do it *this* time," she said.

"But it's already done," I said.

"You need to change the behavior."

"I will," I said. "I promise. I'm sorry."

"*I'm sorry*," she said, mimicking me in a high baby voice. "Little Miss Princess," she spat.

At the beginning of these mounting arguments, I would try to reason with her, in case I could calm her down. Later, when it was clear she wouldn't stop, when it was clear that the fight would go on and on, I stood very still and stopped speaking.

A few times before, the phone had rung at the beginning of a fight, interrupting it; she took the call in her room, where I could hear muffled noises. Her friend Michael or Terry had called. Later, when she came to say goodnight, she was no longer upset. I was innocent, I thought, her unhappiness nothing to do with me—she was lonely. This is what I believed and told myself when she started screaming, and it was one of my excuses for being lazy with the dishes, and unhelpful around the house, and contemptuous of her.

"Do you think I'm your *maid*?" She said it through her teeth, snarling.

"Mom, call a friend," I said. "Please."

Besides me, the people my mother yelled about during our fights were Jeff Howson, my father's accountant, who sent the monthly child-support checks that I was acutely aware were lifelines and, increasingly those days, Kobun. (Compared with how much she mentioned these two men, she rarely brought up my father.)

"Kobun said he'd take care of us, then left me to *rot*." Her voice was almost gone. "That crook," she said, wrinkling up her face.

I didn't know what she meant. As far as I knew, Kobun didn't have much to do with us. He was just a Zen Buddhist monk my parents had once known, who'd officiated at the wedding, and who hardly spoke.

Only later would I learn that because her own mother was mentally ill and my father was unresponsive, it had been Kobun my mother had turned to when she got pregnant, asking him what he thought she should do.

"Have the child," Kobun had advised. "If you need help, *I'll* help you." But in the intervening years he had not offered any help. No one had promised as much as Kobun or had seemed, to my mother at the time, as trustworthy. At the time, my young father had also trusted Kobun, who told him that if I turned out to be a boy, I would be part of a spiritual patrimony, and in that case my father should claim me and support me. When it turned out I was a girl, my mother later found out from others in the community, Kobun had told my father he had no obligation to care for my mother and me.

The next evening, we had the same fight.

"Oh, poor me, poor me," she said in the mimicking baby voice. And then, yelling, "You have no idea what I've done for you."

"I promise I'll do a better job," I said. "I'll do the dishes and I won't complain at all. And I'll do the counters right." She wanted me to wipe hard, and hold my hand underneath the spot the sponge swiped to catch the crumbs.

"It's not the counters, you ignorant little *shit*. It's this fucking life." She began to sob, taking in big breaths like gusts of wind.

I stood very still and tall and kept my face the same. I couldn't feel anything below my head. I was standing like a house I saw in Barron Park, knocked down with the exception of the facade: viewed from any angle other than straight-on, there was nothing to it. No rooms, walls, substance.

"I'm very sorry," I said again. "I mean it."

"Sorry means nothing!" she screamed. "You have to prove it. You have to change the behavior *now*."

She hit her flat palm against the kitchen cupboards, against the counter—slap, slap. She took another long, deep breath through a closed throat as if she had asthma, as if she could hardly breathe.

"You know what I am?" she screamed. "I'm the black sheep. I'm the one who has done everything for you. But nobody gives a *shit*." She extended the "*shit*," at full volume, for a long time, gravelly, so I was sure the neighbors, the whole quiet street, would hear.

"I'm the *Nothing*," she yelled, starting to cry. "First with my family, now with you and Steve. That's what I am. The Nothing."

She turned on a lamp in the kitchen, a gesture remarkable for how ordinary it was in the midst of this. On nights we weren't fighting we turned on lights in other rooms, and the house glowed on the dark street beside other glowing houses.

"No you aren't," I said, deadpan. My feet hurt.

"Fuck you, universe. Fuck you, world." She stuck out her middle fingers on both hands, pointed at the ceiling.

She went and stood by the screen door, her back up against it, sliding down it so that she was squatting with her head in her arms, the way she did when the fight was nearing an end.

"I don't want to go on," she said, crying softly.

She made it sound like it could just happen, not going on, the way my ankle sometimes gave out and curled under when I was walking and I fell.

Without her I would cease to exist; there would be only emptiness.

I crouched down beside her and put my hand on her arm. "What do you mean, you don't want to go on?" I asked.

"This life," she sobbed. "I can't do it any longer. You have no idea what I've been through. You have no idea how it's been, raising you, with no help from anybody. I'm trying so much, but I don't have enough support. It's too hard."

Every denouement felt like the end of a long, tiring journey, disorienting, gravityless. Sounds around us returned. Smells. By that time I could no longer feel the outline of my body.

She stayed on the floor in front of the screen. The fight was over. She wasn't angry anymore, only sad, and I couldn't imagine, now that the storm had raged through and left her weak and defeated, how I had ever wanted anything but good for her.

As my mother foundered, I fantasized about living at my father's house. To traipse around the clean white rooms—still with hardly any furniture—and to sample from the bowls of unlimited fruit. Laurene was starting a business called TerraVera with a petite man from business school, making vegan wrap sandwiches on whole wheat lavash bread. She was chipper when I asked how her day was when she walked in before dinner, with the mane of blonde hair, a leather satchel she carried with papers. Her jeans were cut unevenly on each side, a frayed line at different heights above her ankles, which stuck out below, like the tongues of bells.

Around that time I also began to walk with my toes facing out. My feet, on their own, pointed straight. I was different when I walked this way, more in charge, more promising, more deliberate.

The fights continued for months, becoming more frequent, so that soon they happened almost every night for several hours. When we were together but not fighting, I watched her face for when her mood might turn.

I would tell my teachers, Lee and Steve, of particularly bad fights. This worried my mother, who was mortified if others were talking poorly about her, and who then started bringing Lee up in our fights, mocking me for running, always, to complain to Lee.

She hit the wall, hurt her hand, yelled so that blood vessels rose around her face, her neck turned into sinews. Doors slamming, charcoal half-moons below her eyes. A couple of times she grabbed the top of my arm and shook it hard.

"I shouldn't have had you," she said one Saturday afternoon, toward the end of a fight. "It was a mistake to have a child." She wept, not looking at me, then got up, went to her room, and shut the door.

I knew other parents didn't say such things to their children. If I'm ruining her life, I thought, why does she often follow me around from room to room, as if we're chained together?

I tiptoed quickly to the front of the house, went out the front door, down the steps, across the lawn, onto Rinconada toward Emerson.

Nobody was out in the quiet afternoon, the houses like blank faces, cars gone or in driveways. I walked quickly to the corner, self-conscious of how I was walking, wearing a skirt and flat shoes, looking back in case my mother was coming. She probably hadn't left her room or even noticed I was gone.

I turned east, south, east, toward Embarcadero, toward Highway 101. Once past the corner, where I might have gone straight, or turned, where she would not have been able to find me easily, I began to breathe. I felt elation and freedom I hadn't expected, an exciting shiver in my knees. More than escape: relief.

I was light, becoming myself again, feeling the lines around my body where it met the still air.

I looked at my palms. It was true: my left palm was like a thicket of sticks with no clear path. The lines on my right palm were not clearly defined either, but the lifeline was better. I knew the bubbles weren't good, but how was it possible to tell when one would happen, how far along I was on the line? I kept her vision of my future, even as I cast her off.

At some point, I had to pee. There was a round front window as tall as a person, with rosebushes planted close together on the front lawn of a putty-colored Spanish-style house. I looked both ways—no one around—and peed quickly on the dirt underneath the rosebushes.

I walked around until dusk. I'd been gone for hours, it seemed; there was nothing to do now but go home.

A block away, I saw people on our lawn and heard a sound like insects: walkie-talkies, chattering and static. Lights in our front windows, the porch light, a police car.

A woman in uniform saw me half a block away and started walking toward me. My mother stood with her legs apart on the lawn, her arms crossed.

"You're back," she said.

"Yes," I said.

She approached me cautiously.

The female officer spoke to my mother. A male officer, also buzzing with a walkie-talkie, stood farther off, talking into the handset, looking away.

"Thank you," my mother said, nodding to the policewoman, who nodded back and walked toward the car.

"You shouldn't have done that," she said, after the cops were gone. "You can't just run away."

"You shouldn't have yelled at me." I stood strong, with my legs apart, like her. Some new power I wouldn't have guessed I had.

"I'm sorry I yelled," she said.

◆ ◆ ◆

That night, before I went to sleep, she came into my room. She'd washed her face, and when she leaned over me and said, "I'm sorry," she smelled like soap. "Are you hungry?"

"A little," I said.

She cut apples and cheese in the kitchen and brought them back to my bed on a plate and we ate them together propped up against pillows with our legs under the covers. "You'll tell everyone," she said. "You'll make me out to be an ogre. You'll tell Lee."

"No I won't," I said emphatically.

The next morning, I found Lee. She was behind a partition in the big classroom.

"Look," I said, pointing to a bruise on my upper arm like a smudge of dirt. "And she told me I shouldn't have been born."

"She shouldn't have said that," Lee said. "She doesn't mean it."

"The fights take hours," I said. "By the time they're finished it's late and I can't focus on homework. I ran away. But then I went back."

Recently, my mother had started to have some wine with dinner.

"And she's been *drinking*," I said.

"Really? How much?"

"A glass of wine, some nights," I said darkly.

Lee's face changed; I understood this detail was not as compelling as the rest.

"That's not a lot," Lee said. "But we do want you to consider where you might stay during finals—the trip to Japan is right around the corner." The next week, I stayed at Kate's house in Burlingame. My mother drove me to school on Monday with an overnight bag, saying she also needed a break. Kate's mother picked us up after school. She was large and tall; her glasses hung from a long beaded necklace that rustled pleasingly when she walked.

"Good things come in small packages," she said when we reached the house and she examined me, looking down at me in the white tiled kitchen.

"Thank you," I said, all at once aware of how small I was compared with them.

◆

We flew into Kyoto and stayed in rooms in a gated temple, the girls in one room, the boys in another, the teachers in a third. We slept on futons on tatami mats, folding the futons and storing them behind shoji-screen closets in the morning, and pulling them out again at night.

In the mornings we ate breakfast on our knees at a low table in the courtyard surrounded by trees. On the third day, we discovered microscopic silver fishes mixed in with the morning rice.

We were supposed to keep track of our spending in the same journals in which we wrote about our experiences. I wrote expenses scattered around the pages as they arose, in a disorganized way, including, on the first day, three hundred yen to make a wish at a temple at the top of Mount Hiei, so that toward the end of the trip, when it would have been useful to count up what I'd spent, it was difficult to find the numbers hidden around the pages.

At the temples, Japanese girls came up to us, giggled, asked to take photos with us. When they laughed, they covered their mouths. They held out bunny ears behind one another's backs before the click. I paid to write wishes on slips of paper, pushed them through an opening in a granite stone to be burned later by praying monks.

We traveled to Ikeda, where we stayed for a week, and one evening we went to a bathhouse. We brought towels into the baths for modesty, but I found I wasn't uncomfortable. It seemed like nothing to be naked here.

The room was large, with three different baths, a sauna in the back, a warm, hot smell of sandalwood and steam. There was a hot pool, a cold pool, a dark sauna that made a ringing sound from an electric grate. There were young women and thin old women, with skin dripping down, bones showing through. Women with towels around their chests leaned back in the hot pool with closed eyes.

A few hours later, when we left through the metal turnstile into the night, the heat of the pools clung to me, insulating me against the night air. We all gave off steam.

Toward the end of the trip, we arrived in Hiroshima.

Inside the dark hallway of the museum were lit cases containing fingernails, hair in boxes, burned pieces of kimonos, black-and-white photographs of children abandoned and crying. Some children had been vaporized immediately; others survived but then lost their hair in large tufts, lost their fingernails, even their fingers, in the following weeks. The bomb created tornado-like effects. Radiation was carried by the wind in irregular patterns.

For school, I'd read a book about a mother and daughter on a bridge. When the bomb hit, the daughter had become a soot smear on the ground, while the mother was left naked, her skin charred with the shapes of the dark flowers on her kimono. The image haunted me.

That afternoon a few of us went to look at the epicenter of the bomb, a fenced-off area with an old building that remained standing. There were cement benches surrounded by planters looking into this fenced-off area, and sycamore trees with mottled trunks dropping leaves that curled like hands on the asphalt around the benches.

I bought a tray of unagi on rice from a mini-mart nearby and sat on one of the benches. Inside was a plot of land covered in scrub grasses. The land around the building was more expansive than other plots of land I'd seen in Japan, except at the temples. It reminded me of the empty lots between buildings around Palo Alto off El Camino Real, weeds sticking up in the dirt.

In the middle was an old see-through structure, a curved dome made of only panels of steel, like scaffolding, or a dressmaker's form. This was a building standing on the morning the bomb was dropped that had been reduced to its skeletal structure below paint and plaster,

like a dry leaf worn away to a system of brown veins. It remained
because, given the physics of the bomb, the place at the epicenter
of where the nuclear bomb was dropped was not destroyed.

We left Hiroshima and went to a town in the countryside where we
stayed in a low, flat building with a meeting room in the middle.
We'd already been to many temples in the mountains, green and
smelling of peat and rain. We'd been on the bullet train, so smooth
it hardly felt like we were moving.

I'd been thinking about my mother and our fights. It was a
relief to be away from her. I knew that when I returned the fights
would continue.

On the second day in the countryside, near the end of our trip,
a man walked through the door and into the meeting room. It took
me a moment to realize who it was: my father, barefoot, flipping the
hair out of his face.

"*Steve?*" I said.

"Hey, Lis," he said, smiling. The whole class looked. "I was
nearby on a business trip. I thought I'd come find you."

"But how did you know I was here?" We were far from Tokyo
and Kyoto, where he went on business trips.

"I have my ways," he said.

I looked at Lee, who winked.

How young and handsome he was. I felt the same zing I would
feel when I saw his face on the cover of magazines.

That afternoon, I was not required to participate in regular
activities. We were left alone in a room with a rice paper screen, a
window, and pillows on the tatami floor. I drew my hands across the
shiny reeds woven in a herringbone pattern with cloth seams. Being
with him was awkward at first, the way it was with boys, when it
was clear we liked each other and yet there was nothing to say.

"I'm so glad you came," I said.

"Me, too, Lis. I wanted to spend some time with you."

At some point I was sitting on his lap. I was too old to sit on laps—I'd just turned fourteen—but I was small for my age and sometimes sat on my mother's lap too. When I sat on my mother's lap, I accidentally dug my ischial bones into her thigh, but I didn't want to do that to him, I didn't know him well enough, so I sat as carefully as possible, curving my spine.

I was shaking a little. Was it fear? Excitement? I couldn't tell. I was afraid of him and, at the same time, I felt a quaking, electric love. I hoped he didn't notice how red and hot my cheeks were: to have a father now, the way I'd hoped for so long. Having a father, as far as I understood, felt not like being ordinary but like being singled out. Our time together was not fluid but stuttered forward like a flip book.

How close are you supposed to be with your father? I wanted to collapse into him, to be inseparable. In his presence I wasn't sure how to hold my hands, how to arrange my limbs. Other daughters would have known this by now.

In the cool, quiet enclosures of the temples, I'd felt as if I were more than just myself, part of some larger and benevolent system or plan. I wondered what I would do when the trip was over and life resumed with my mother. Would my father say I could live with him?

"Do you believe in God?" I asked now, to find out if he'd had the same feeling I'd had at the temples. I was too scared to ask about living with him, in case he said no. I would impress and distract him with grand curiosity unlikely to come from a young girl.

"Yes, but not in the ordinary sense," he said. "I believe there's something. Some presence. Consciousness. It's like a wheel." He moved to stand, and I got off his lap. He crouched on the ground and drew a circle on the tatami with his finger, and then a smaller wheel within that. I crouched down too, my heart beating fast. This was closeness! I wanted more of this! For him to talk to me as if he was interested, to say what he thought, knowing I could understand because I was his daughter. "The wheel has nodes at different points, something greater on the outside, the outside and the inside connected." He drew two spokes between the smaller circle and the larger one. "I don't know if that makes any sense."

It seemed he had also become confused. "Anyway, it's simple," he said.

That night, I wrote in my journal: "When I tell him events, they come alive. When I don't tell him, they don't exist."

"My insides are jumping," I wrote.

Later he rode along with a group of us on bikes into the sleepy town, the houses and shops made out of dark wood, rice paddies all around, the hills carved into shelves. We went to a soba shop and sat at a booth. I ordered kitsune udon, broth with a few globules of fat floating on the surface beside a strip of fried tofu, thick noodles almost visible beneath, like white stones at the bottom of a murky pond. He ordered cold soba with dipping sauce.

"Can I borrow some yen, Lis?" he asked. He'd brought only dollars.

"Okay," I said. I gave him some of mine from the amount my mother had given me, the amount our parents were instructed to give, calculated by the teachers to cover the days we were free to buy our own lunches and snacks, temple wishes, and transportation.

"I'll pay you back before I go," he said.

After lunch we went to a bank; from here, he would catch a train back to Tokyo. Japanese rooms were small but smelled of open spaces, food glistened in separate lacquered compartments, pachinko parlors clinked, the doors open to the street—all of it different, strikingly foreign. But this bank looked like any big bank in California, with carpeted floors, red-rope divisions in scalloped shapes with brass attachments, a line of people waiting for a teller. "Here," he said, after he talked with someone behind glass who counted out a stack of bills. He handed over a bill of a denomination I'd never seen before—10,000 yen—an amount almost half as much as I'd brought for the whole trip. Other bills were rumpled; his were crisp. "I don't have a smaller bill, kid. Sorry."

"Wow. Thanks." We said goodbye, the bill in my pocket making the day spark.

With the new cash, I bought gifts for my father and Laurene, including four porcelain bowls of different pastel colors, thin-lipped and small, fitted in a wooden box with four compartments. Incense in an oblong paper box that smelled of the forest and resin. "Cedar," the woman at the counter said. She took the bills I had left over, bowed, returned many fewer bills. For my mother I bought a cotton *yukata*, size small, in indigo blue with a pattern of opening white fans and a cloth belt of the same fabric. The robe came in a plastic cellophane envelope and cost less than the gifts I'd found for my father and Laurene.

"Did you get them better gifts than you got for me?" my mother asked. We were in her bedroom. I'd brought her gift out of my luggage, still in its plastic sheath.

"No, I got you different gifts—nothing better or worse."

"But you spent more on them," she said. How did she know? I should have bought her the best gifts because she had less money and couldn't buy them for herself.

"I like the *yukata*. It looks good on you," I said. She'd put it on over her clothes in the bedroom while I sat on her bed and watched.

"I don't like things that tie like this," she said. "It's too big. Anyway, I'm your mother and you should be more honoring toward me."

"It's a size small," I said. "And I am honoring—"

"But what did you buy *them*?" she asked, interrupting.

How to explain to her that I'd bought them the more expensive gifts because I worried they didn't care for me and I wanted them to like me, to love me, even? With them together, the feeling I was loved and belonged was tenuous, superficial, my place in their family not essential or fixed. They did not ask me questions about myself, or seem interested in me the way my mother was, and this made me hunger to impress them.

My mother already loved me. Even when she screamed at me, I knew it. I wasn't so sure about them.

◆

Reed was six months old by now. I went over to see them the week I returned from Japan, and my father asked me to change his diaper. "It's part of being in this family, Lis," he said. "You haven't done it for a while."

I took my brother on my hip, walked past the bank of French doors in the hallway and up the curve in the stone stairway, careful to hold the railing. In the rooms upstairs, my father had replaced the floors with foot-wide boards of Douglas fir, a silky, soft texture to the wood. In my brother's room, a carpenter had built a set of wooden shelves in the same wood that connected to a high changing table.

I set my brother down on the table, opened the straps on the sides of the diaper, cleaned him, then turned to grab a diaper, as I'd done before.

In the three weeks I'd been in Japan, he'd learned to roll. No one had told me. I heard the *thunk* of his skull hitting the wooden floor. I looked down at him, face up on the floor. There was a pause, and I thought that maybe he wouldn't cry, and they would not notice, and everything would somehow return to normal. One second later, he began to wail. I scooped him into my arms and heard the sound of their bare feet running from the kitchen.

On the way to the hospital, Laurene nursed him. I sat beside her in the back seat, hoping there would be a chance to be helpful. I wanted to go back to the moment just before it happened.

My father drove. He was silent. Finally he said, venom quiet: "Lis, you should learn to understand the impact of your actions on other people." It couldn't be undone. I'd meant to protect Reed; now this mistake would become part of the lore, as if I had done nothing good before or after.

But the changing table did not have a lip or fence. The cushion was flat—the curved foam pads that dip in the center had not been invented yet. And the diapers were stacked out of reach.

"I'm sorry," I said. "I'm so sorry."

◆

"I want you to consider moving in with our family," my father said a couple of months later. We were in his Mercedes, driving back to his house from Country Sun, where we'd bought some Odwalla apple juice. My mother and I had already talked about our need for space from each other, in calmer moments realizing we couldn't keep fighting like this. She needed a break, she said.

He said it sharply, as if I'd done something wrong. I had worried they wouldn't want me to live with them after my brother fell, but since then they'd had me change his diaper many times, and even asked me to babysit several nights as middle school drew to a close and summer began.

This was what I'd been hoping for. It had happened. He'd asked me to come live with him. But his tone didn't have excitement or joy in it.

"Yes," I said. "I'd like to live with you, for now. If you want me to." I had the idea that if I moved in with him, we'd look at old photographs together to understand what we missed, urgently, like we were cramming for an exam. Also, it would be a novelty, the big house, a family that looked right. I was his daughter, lost to him for a time like Perdita in *The Winter's Tale*, now returned; I had noble qualities (I imagined) and was perhaps beautiful, from some angles, and worthy. All this he would see and recognize. It would be glorious. There would be dresses and bowls of fruit.

Later, I heard that when I was in the last year of middle school, when the fights with my mother got bad, the school had called to tell him that if he did not take me in to live with him, they'd call social services. I'm not sure whether this story was true or exaggerated, but in any case, the story repositioned him—after all this time—as my savior.

"It's not *for now*," he said. "If you're going to live with us, you've got to choose. Her or us. I need you to really give this family a chance. If you choose to live with us, I'd like you to promise you won't see your mother for six months. You need to give it a real shot," he said. It wouldn't work if I was going back and forth, it wouldn't *take*. He'd decided that a clean break would be the right way; my mother didn't agree with him, but those were his terms. It was almost summer now, which meant I wouldn't be able to see her until December. "Otherwise," he said, "the deal's off."

"I do want to live with you," I said, with a surety I didn't feel.

"You've made a very important decision," he said, with solemnity. "This is one of those life moments, one of those *adult* moments."

I would leave my mother—I'd said the words out loud. I felt giddy and guilty and numb. Maybe this was the origin of the guilt that seized me later and left me hardly able to walk sometimes, after I had moved in with them: having stolen her youth and energy, having driven her to a state of perpetual anxiety, without support or resources, now that I was flourishing in school and beloved by my teachers, I cast her out and picked him, the one who'd left. I chose the pretty place when she was the one who'd read me books of old stories with admonishments not to believe in the trick of facades.

We turned from Waverley onto Santa Rita into the driveway of the house. The fancy car, the young, handsome father, the prettiest house in Palo Alto. I was aware of being part of this picture when I was in it, as if I was also watching it from outside. None of their surfaces spoke of shame or imperfection, and that itself would be a great relief, to relax inside the appearance of the good. When the picture looked pretty, you didn't have to brace against what others might think, you didn't have to charm or compensate. He took the apple juice by its hollow handle and walked through the gate toward the house.

"I'm proud of you," he said.

Small Nation

A few weeks later, on a weekday morning in June, my mother and I packed my things and drove to my father's house. A four-block journey with a single kink in the path.

She parked on Santa Rita in the shade. We walked through the metal gate with the metal ring on top that clanked and echoed through the yard. I knew we didn't belong here together, although no one had said so. The side door was unlocked. "Hello?" I called. No one. My father was at NeXT, Laurene at TerraVera. My brother must have been out with Carmen, his babysitter, who came from nine to five on weekdays.

We stepped inside. The house was moist and cool, like the shadow beneath big trees.

"Follow me," I said. Left at the low hallway under an arch, then left again at the first door into my new bedroom.

The room was square, with brick walls painted white and a window looking out onto the rose garden and driveway. I could reach up and touch the box-shaped rice paper lantern hanging from one of the fat wooden beams. There was a futon on a frame, a desk, a chest of drawers; an adjoining bathroom in green tile. It didn't feel like my room. I didn't want to touch any of the surfaces, or sleep in the bed, or use the shower. I'd chosen the room for its proximity to the kitchen. The kitchen was where they spent time together, feeding my brother. I wanted to be as near to my father and Laurene and my brother as possible.

When I first saw the house, before they were married, I'd told my father I wanted the bedroom near theirs, lying down on the floor and imagining it was mine, with its windows on both sides, a fireplace with a curved hood made of painted brick. I liked the way the light shone into the room, and the idea that I'd be close to them. "You can't have that one," my father said, and then, "We might expand." It did not occur to me that Laurene was pregnant, or what he might mean by "expand." When I asked him about it, he said, "Sorry, kiddo." Only later, soon before I moved in, after my brother was born and slept in the bedroom I'd originally picked, he said I could have a bedroom too, and told me to choose between the two that were left. Both were far from their room. One was over the garage at the end of a long, dark, musty corridor. The other was downstairs, near the kitchen.

"It's small," my mother said, "but I like the view. And you know I love these tiles." For years she'd been talking about wanting terra-cotta tiles.

She walked to another small room at the end of the hallway. I was starting to worry that we'd be caught—that the front door would jangle open and my father or Laurene would find us here together. I wished she would hurry. At the same time I didn't want her to leave. I needed her to stay close and protect me.

"There still isn't any furniture," my mother called out, her voice echoing in the hallway.

"I know," I said. "I wish they'd get a couch or something." Most of the rooms were empty. Sound traveled unobstructed and bounced off glass and clay and brick, did not catch or absorb or muffle. For the years I lived there, I longed for more furniture; the longing would grow into a feverish craving for the furnished rooms I'd seen in other houses.

"All right," she said. She was standing in the doorway of my room, her eyes watery. "I'm going to miss you. I hope this is for the best." We hugged. "Don't worry about me, I'm going to be fine."

"You'll go to Greece," I said.

"Yeah. I'm not looking forward to it right now," she said. Her skin became luminous when she was sad, like it was backlit.

"It'll be great," I said.

In October, she left for three weeks to travel in Europe, in Italy and Greece, a trip my father had promised her as a kind of restitution when I moved out. He'd given her ten thousand dollars.

She would be traveling alone, going to Venice and to a yoga retreat in Greece. My mother had taken up yoga for the first time since I'd moved out.

Later she would tell me how lonely she'd been, how she cried the night she'd arrived in Venice—absurd, foolish, all that water instead of streets!—but how the next morning she'd flung open the layers of curtains, then the shutters, then the windows, and there it was before her, shimmering in the morning light, the coruscating Grand Canal.

But over the next months when we weren't talking for the first time in my life and I didn't know how she was doing, guilt would be heavy on my chest, like a large animal hunched down. Some crime I'd committed but couldn't quite remember. Leaving my mother? Dropping Reed? Sometimes I would be unable to speak, terrified to say the wrong thing and wound others with the slightest mistake.

I followed her out of the house and stood near the door. At the gate she turned and waved: the flap of a bird's wing in the sharp white light.

My mother and I had agreed to his conditions. I sensed it was a drastic rule for two people who'd hardly missed a few days together for thirteen years—and that the formation of a new family needn't hinge on the eradication of the existing one. Secretly, I also felt relief. It gave me the perfect excuse: I would not have to see my mother for six months, my mother who was angry at me, and yet it wouldn't be my fault, because he had required it, even if later I would feel guilty and complicit.

Also, I figured that if I demonstrated such loyalty to my father, it would impress him, and make him love me more. In fact, I was so convinced that he would understand the extent of the sacrifice he'd required, that when, later, he did not seem to understand but said I did not give *enough* to be part of the family, I was confused. I'd thought it was clear: I'd given him everything.

That first summer away from my mother, I continued to go to Lytton Gardens, an assisted-living facility, a couple of days a week for a volunteer job I'd started the year before. I took the old women for walks, pushing their wheelchairs through the leafy streets near University Avenue. Mostly, I took one of two women, Lucille or a woman who called herself Zsa Zsa, who often sang "Tiny Bubbles" as we walked. The women seemed to enjoy our time, but they didn't remember me between visits.

I ran into my mother a few times near that part of Palo Alto, once on Hamilton on my walk back from volunteering, when she was getting into her car after a yoga class. She called out to me, and we talked for a few minutes, small talk. I was careful to leave quickly. When I saw her, I was filled with simultaneous feelings of longing and dread. I tried to get away as fast as possible, so I wouldn't be caught. I was afraid of someone seeing us together and reporting it to my father, afraid of going against the rules, and also afraid of her anger.

I did not want to admit how much it had been a mistake, how horribly lonely I was already, how I needed her again. And I didn't see a way to get out of it.

My father hadn't forbidden calls, and some evenings in the fall, after the rest of the family was asleep, after school had started, my mother and I began to talk on the phone.

I pulled the box of the landline phone as far as it would go on the wire, and then pulled the looped cord behind the dish rack and wedged the headset between my head and shoulder. We talked as I washed the plates. I worried she would say I had betrayed her, but she didn't. These nights on the phone, her curiosity and warmth lifted me up. We did not talk about the fact that we weren't supposed to see each other. We didn't argue. She didn't let on, but later she told me that she was worried about me, and that she began to stay at home in the evenings so she'd be there to pick up the phone in case I called.

My father commissioned a low split-rail fence to run like a brace around the cornered front yard of the house. The grass was torn out and only dirt remained. A tree would be planted there on the Waverley side.

"I like East Coast oak trees," Laurene said in the car, when they were talking about what to plant.

"Do you know about the East Coast kind, Lis?" my father said, glancing at me in the back seat. He usually used the words "East Coast" as a synonym for "inferior."

"What do they look like?"

"There," he said, pointing to one growing between the sidewalk and the road. It looked nothing like a California oak. Its leaves were larger and shaped like they'd been perforated around the edge by a large hole puncher.

In the end, they chose to transplant a mature copper beech. The tree was inserted with a crane into a deep hole. A huge trunk, a wiry ball of roots. The beech stood as tall as a two-story building, taller than the top of the house, the limbs reaching up and sideways like a broom, dead leaves dangling on otherwise bare branches.

When I left the house in the mornings, and in the evenings when I returned from school, I looked for evidence of life—leaves, buds—something to indicate the tree would grow and flourish. After about a month, the tree still hadn't changed. It didn't leaf out or unkink to become symmetrical like other trees, but still listed, bare. One day, a crew of men arrived, sawed the trunk and branches into sections, and took it away.

A friend of my father's, Joanna, came over for lunch—she'd been part of the original Apple team and had a son who was about nine months old, like Reed. Steve gave her a tour of the house. "These,"

he said, pointing to the silvered wooden beams on the ceiling of a
small alcove, "were used to build the Golden Gate Bridge." I thought
he meant they were part of the structure itself, but later I understood
they'd been part of the scaffolding.

"Don't you worry about protein, Steve?" she asked while we ate.
She spoke with a pleasing accent. She talked about children's developing brains, how a vegan diet might not contain enough protein
or fat. You could tell she was a worrier.

"Nope," my father said, with a calm authority. "You know breast
milk—what a baby drinks during the time they're developing most?"

He began this line of reasoning with anyone who asked about
our vegan diet.

"Yes?" Joanna said.

"Well, guess what? Breast milk is only six percent protein," he
said. "So, getting a lot of protein can't be that important."

He delivered his conclusions so convincingly that I didn't question them for years. He believed dairy products were mucus forming;
mucus blocked spiritual clarity the way it blocked a nose. It was diet,
most of all, that he used to differentiate himself from other people.
He'd been a little more relaxed about his diet when I was younger,
occasionally even having a scoop of ice cream at the Häagen-Dazs
shop at the Stanford Barn. Now he'd become even more rigid than
he was before, not wanting a single animal product to pass the lips
of anyone in the family, especially Reed's.

I noticed the way Laurene seemed confident; her face was symmetrical and serene, whereas my face was composed of uneven halves,
the eyebrow, ear, and eye of one side higher than those on the other.
Without my permission or knowledge, my face would fall into expres-
sions that revealed thoughts and feelings like weather patterns. I
began to imitate the way Laurene tossed her long hair. She wasn't
a hippie or bohemian. She had fended off two marriage proposals
and then captured my father. Because of this I supposed she could
do other great feats. My father talked about her to me in the third

person when he grabbed her to kiss her, "She was a cheerleader, you know?"

For lunch my father made pasta, and on a serving plate I arranged a TerraVera burrito—black beans, salsa, and avocado wrapped in lavash bread—sliced into sections like sushi rolls. At that moment, I liked the purity and abstemiousness of our diet, the sparse furnishings of the house exposing the beauty of its bones, beams like ribs, the entrance left unlocked, so that anyone could wander in. The gardener had planted chamomile in between the paving stones, and when you walked across, the scent drifted up. We ate our wholesome food at the round wooden table in the kitchen, my brother's high chair pressed up against the edge, and at moments like this—with a guest over, my brother slapping his plastic tray, my father humming, serving his pasta topped with avocado cubes and drizzled with his fancy olive oil—I felt like I was part of the family.

The only problem was my hands. Since moving here they'd become detached-feeling, conspicuous. They fluttered and lifted in an embarrassing way, as if they too, separately, wanted attention; otherwise they hung dead at the ends of my wrists in an obvious, strange way I was sure everyone noticed. I was severely conscious of them. When we sat down to meals I begged them, silently, not to betray me. Yet almost every evening at dinner I broke a glass.

I was terrified my father and Laurene might tell me at some point how insignificant I was, what a disappointment I was, sloppy and repulsive, breaking things like a baby. They already had a baby. How little I fit into the picture of family. I could see it and feel it. They'd made a mistake in allowing me to live here; I was unsure of my position in the house, and this anxiety—combined with a feeling of immense gratitude so overwhelming I thought I might burst—caused me to talk too much, to compliment too much, to say yes to whatever they asked, hoping my servile quality would ignite compassion, pity, or love. They had taken me from a drab life and brought me into this perfect house: she was strong and intelligent, he was glinting with genius and aesthetic mastery.

I fawned over Laurene, pulling lantana blossoms off stems in the garden and throwing them at her, making a shower of blossoms around her when she came home from work. I was trying, and failing, to express gratitude and worthiness by becoming the long-lost daughter they might want. Yet my hands continued to feel as if they might float up and disappear, and I kept breaking glasses.

One day, after school, I rushed over to where my father and Laurene were standing beneath the Juliet balcony in the courtyard, the green-leafed wisteria vines winding up fat wooden beams. They were discussing the landscaping.

"How many Californians does it take to screw in a light bulb?" I asked. I didn't usually tell jokes, but I'd heard this one at school and thought it might impress them. The joke hadn't seemed particularly funny, but the other students had laughed.

They looked at me, expectantly.

"How many?" my father asked.

"They don't screw in light bulbs," I said. "They screw in hot tubs." The moment I said it, I understood for the first time the double meaning of *screw*, and something in my face changed even though I willed it not to.

Neither of them laughed.

"I don't think she gets it," my father said.

"Oh, I think she does," Laurene said, studying me. "I think she definitely does."

That evening I broke another glass at dinner and ran to my room.

I hid in the closet with the light out, crouched on the floor. My father followed me and found me there, like I hoped he would.

"Hey, Lis," he said. He'd crouched down beside me for a while, and then pulled me up. "I'm sorry I wasn't there for you, you know. When you were younger."

"It's okay," I said, too fast.

"I'll love you until the cows come home," he said.

"Hey, Lis," he said one day as we passed in the hallway. "Do you want to change your name?"

He was barefoot, wearing only a black shirt and white cotton underwear—his uniform around the house. He was vain about his slim legs and wore this uniform even when people came over so that it became something I teased him about.

"Change it to what?" I asked. Sunlight streamed through the bank of leaded-glass windows that made up one wall of the hallway, falling in bright rectangles on the floor, warming the tiles.

"*My* name," he said.

For a moment I thought he meant Steve.

"You mean . . . Jobs?" I asked.

"Yeah."

I paused. I didn't want to offend him. When offended, he became distant and wouldn't acknowledge me, sometimes for days. I'd been Lisa Brennan my whole life. The thought of not only deserting my mother but also replacing her name was too much—as if he'd suggested that we perform a kind of theft.

"Maybe," I said. "I mean, my mom . . . let me think."

"Let me know," he said, and walked off.

I thought about it that night, and went to find him in his study the next evening and told him I'd like to take his name but keep hers too, and connect them with a hyphen.

A few weeks later, a lawyer arrived. All of us, including my brother, gathered in the living room around the coffee table. My brother stood and smacked his hands against the glass. There were two Eames lounge chairs, a Tiffany lamp with dragonfly wings, a large patterned rug, but no couch. We sat on the floor.

We signed the certificate, first him, then me, making official my new, joined surname. The lawyer put the papers in a briefcase.

He would later replace my original birth certificate—on which my mother had drawn stars—with a more official-looking version, watermarked, yellow and blue, starless. It was the same lawyer who had argued in the California court against my father's paternity years before, though I didn't know it at the time.

I'd already started high school under my old name, but I began to write the new name at the top of my papers.

"Should we frame it?" my father said, getting up. "We could put it here." He pointed to a space on the wall where the hallway met the living room. He was ebullient; I felt important, and giddy too; all this fuss over adding a line and four letters. A lawyer had even been summoned!

"What do you think, hon?" he asked Laurene.

"It might be a little strange," she said tactfully. "To hang up a birth certificate."

Laurene seemed to understand the division between strange and normal in a way we did not. Near her, he and I were at a disadvantage. We were ragtag. He was adopted and had dropped out of college. He didn't seem to know what people did or didn't do, nor did I. Unlike me, he said he didn't care. About rules of civilization and decorum, he was usually dismissive, or even contemptuous. (But he was unpredictable. I'd worn a cardigan one day and he said, sternly, "You're supposed to unbutton the bottom button," and it surprised me that this once he not only knew but cared.) My mother was also apathetic about many conventions, and that's why when I was little she'd let me dress myself. As for my bad spelling, she preferred to enjoy it rather than correct it. She didn't try to steady and null the confusions of the world but navigated inside them, and for this I hated her now, wishing to know its precise codes.

What a relief it was to have Laurene, with her knowledge of etiquette and protocol. Who knew people did not frame birth certificates and put them up on walls.

◆ ◆ ◆

That night, I set the table for dinner while Laurene fed my brother. They had blue-and-green-striped cloth napkins and thick French glass cups (the ones I broke) with petal-shaped indentations around the lip that caught the light.

"Where do the knives and forks go?" I asked, a bouquet of cutlery in one hand. I was determined to learn, from her, what went where. Her mother had been an English teacher; surely she knew what was done and not done, would find it easy to say, "Do it like this, not like that."

"The fork on the left," Laurene said, "knife and spoon on the right."

"Which outside, which in?" I wanted to know unequivocally.

"Spoon on the outside," she said.

My brother sat up to the table in his high chair, gumming his food, splattering it around with his open hands. Feeding my brother meant spooning mush into an O-shaped mouth, swiping what did not make it from the sides of his lips and cheeks, and spooning it in again, like spackling a hole—until he was finished and without warning released the remains in a great whirring noise from his lips.

"What about the napkin?"

"Napkin under the fork."

Years later, I would live in Italy, where every finer point was known, and learn as much as I could—only to discover that these rules weren't very important to me after all. Which was what my father might have been saying, and hoping for me, when he taunted me with the phrase I hated: "Lis, you're gonna be a hippie someday."

The next day my father and I went to Country Sun to get avocados. "I'm really good at picking them out," he said, cradling each in the palm of his hand for a few seconds, closing his eyes.

At the register a man with long brown hair in a ponytail looked at him. "Does anyone ever tell you that you look like Steve Jobs?" he asked. I kept a straight face.

My father was looking down, getting change out of his wallet. "Yep, sometimes," he said, handing over the change. And then we left, me following him out to the car. How cool it was that he hadn't claimed it. Even a regular errand with my father was edged with glamour.

In the car on the way home I finally built up the courage to ask him if the Lisa computer was named after me. I'd been waiting for a moment alone with him to ask—if he said no, I wouldn't be humiliated in front of others, who might have assumed.

"Hey, you know that computer, the Lisa?"

"Yeah?" he said.

"Was it named after me?" I asked. We were both facing forward. I didn't look at him; I tried to sound curious, nothing more.

If he would just give me this one thing.

"Nope." His voice was clipped, dismissive. Like I was fishing for a compliment. "Sorry, kid."

"I thought it was," I said. I was glad he couldn't see my face.

◆

I'd become fixated on the idea of going to college, and I was sure that one secret to getting in was a profusion of after-school activities. I was going to a private high school called Lick-Wilmerding in San Francisco, about an hour away, which I attended with four friends I'd known from Nueva. The school building was modern, cement and glass. In the mornings it would be encased in white fog; in the afternoons, when the fog burned off, sunlight streamed through the glass and onto the whiteboards and industrial rugs. Together with the other Nueva kids' parents, my father arranged for a car that picked us up, one by one, at various stops along the Peninsula. The car made the return journey in the afternoons—but it wasn't possible to do an after-school activity and still catch this ride home.

The next weekend, Laurene took me clothes shopping.

"We'll have to go quick," she said. "Just one store." We had an hour. With my mother there was time but no money; with Laurene it was the opposite, and I figured I could keep as much as we found, like a game show my mother told me about, frantic contestants grabbing from shelves and throwing as much as they could into a shopping cart before a buzzer went off.

As we backed out of the driveway in the white BMW convertible my father had bought for her, Laurene slid on sunglasses that were small and rectangular, made of a brushed brown resin with greenish lenses.

"I like those," I said.

"Oh, they're silly," she said, which seemed incredible, to dismiss the glamorous while inhabiting it.

When we got to the mall, a car backed out of a space directly in front of Gap Kids. "Providence!" she said. We went inside and I selected clothes from the circular racks and hung them on the pegs in a dressing room. I modeled a ridged yellow shirt that hugged my chest and black cotton slacks.

"Those are great on you," she said. "Let's get them."

I found yellow socks to match the yellow shirt, a gray shirt, a blue T-shirt, a pair of jeans. She liked everything I liked. I was shy at first, but she didn't seem to mind when clothes were tight or possibly sexy.

By the time I finished, the changing room was a shambles: shirts draped on hooks, pants on the floor. I'd leave it—assert my entitlement along with her. She and I were queens of this realm; other people would pick up the clothes and hang them. Anyway, we were in a rush.

When I pulled open the curtain, she frowned.

"What a mess," she said. "You can't leave it like that."

She came in and started pulling shirts over hangers and squeezing pants into metal clips. Her movements were forceful and quick. I hurried to join her.

I'd failed to get a part in the fall production of *Guys and Dolls* and had been assigned the role of assistant stage manager instead. My friend Tess was stage manager. We carried black binders, each scene annotated with props, stage directions, and lighting cues.

"Can you give me a ride home?" I asked my father, assuming he could pick me up on his way home from work at Pixar, where he went on Fridays instead of NeXT. I'd hardly noticed, living with my mother, how easy it was to get from here to there; I just arrived at place to place as if by magic. Despite our fights, there was never any question that she would drive me to and from friends' houses, doctor appointments, dance classes, and school.

"Nope," he said. "You're going to have to figure it out."

A couple weeks later, it was opening night. In the lead-up to the play, I was probably gone for a night a week, and would have loved to stay late at school more often but did not because if I missed the car, I couldn't get a ride. On rehearsal nights, I stayed overnight with a friend. Sometimes, when I was at home, my father didn't talk with me or look at me during dinner, and even Laurene seemed distant and displeased. They did not explain themselves, so I thought they might have just been upset for other reasons. But then my father began to complain that I wasn't around enough.

For the opening night of the play, I planned to spend the night at Tess's house. Laurene let me borrow her black leather shoes: Joan & David oxfords with a buckled-over strap. We both wore size six and a half.

The girl playing Miss Adelaide had a long neck, a nasal voice, and black hair cut like Louise Brooks's that glistened under the lights. I'd developed a burning crush on the star, David, who had an English accent and played Sky Masterson, and who did not seem to notice me as I rushed around with props and papers.

After the play, a group of stagehands and actors and I ran outside. The lawn was dark, damp from sprinklers or dew or fog. We played capture the flag with two sweaters for flags. It was the first time, at the new school, that I was happy and unguarded. I didn't think about the shoes on the wet grass. In the morning, I noticed they were scraped in the heel with vertical grooves, as if a blade had cut stripes into the leather, and the leather had swelled, soaked in water. How could blades of grass be strong enough to cut leather? I put the shoes back into Laurene's closet when I got home, hoping she wouldn't notice. If she did notice, I figured she could certainly afford to buy another pair. She noticed the scratches a few days later, asked what had happened, upset, but then didn't mention them again.

I left my things in piles around the house, the way I had when I lived with my mother: shoes, sweatshirts, mango skins on cutting boards, papers, crumpled socks like droppings. Maybe I thought they'd find it endearing, or that I'd claim some of the attention allocated to my brother. When Laurene came into the living room one evening shortly after I'd ruined her shoes, and saw the socks and sweatshirt I'd left on the rug, she said, "Lis, I'm going to need you to pick up all your things from now on." She said it coolly.

"Okay," I said. It was a reasonable thing to ask.

"I have enough on my plate now with a new baby and starting a company," she said. "I can't be picking up after you."

Her words felt like stabs. Perhaps I'd left those piles unwittingly as a kind of call-and-response, as if I'd asked her to claim me as her child, and she'd replied that she would not. I was humiliated and exposed. I was sloppy; she was not.

My father called the school Lick-My-Wilmerding. I laughed and rolled my eyes.

"You know I wrote you a pretty great recommendation letter to Lick-My-Wilmerding," he said one morning.

"Really? Can I see it?"

"I thought you were going to save it and give it to her when she's older?" Laurene said. I could tell she didn't want me to be arrogant or claim the center of attention. The problem with saving things for later, though, without experiencing them, is that they get lost, or are forgotten.

"Nope. I want to do it now," he said, went to his study, returned with a sheet of paper, and—standing in the kitchen, barefoot—he read the letter aloud.

I don't remember the bulk of it, only the last line: "If I were you, I'd snatch her up in a second."

I decided to run for freshman-class president and began stapling flyers to notice boards around the school. I'd made some new friends and I started an Opera Club, organizing group trips to the San Francisco Opera at group student rates. It was a lark. I didn't know anything about opera. Before this, I'd never been to one.

On the night of the first performance, my father asked me to save him a ticket, then picked me up at school and drove us to the show. "I'm so proud of you for doing this," he whispered as the curtain went up. I hoped winning president would please him too.

The election was held a few weeks later, the four contenders giving short speeches. My voice was almost gone from laryngitis. I wore corduroy pants for good luck, and a thick cable-knit sweater. My classmates huddled close, and I felt the surge of goodwill that sometimes happened when I was sick and no longer had the energy to be formal, instead letting others lean in to support me.

That night I missed the car ride home and stayed at a friend's house in Potrero Hill. I called my father to let him know. I dreaded these calls. Recently, when I'd stayed overnight at a friend's house in San Francisco, he'd been short and distant on the phone, sighing heavily. Laurene was working hard to start a company, and he worked a lot too. They had Carmen until 5 p.m., but my father didn't allow employees in the house after he was home from work, and my brother wasn't sleeping through the night. I wonder if my absences stirred up conflict between them.

"I missed the ride home," I said when he answered. "Because of the election."

"You're not putting in the time, Lis," he said, his voice grim. "You're not acting like you're part of this family."

"I'll be back tomorrow," I said. "The elections were held—"

"I don't care. I gotta go." He hung up.

Later that night, I got another call.

"Guess what?" It was Tess.

"What?" After the call with my father, I'd forgotten everything else.

"C'mon, guess."

"I don't know."

"You won, silly," she said. "You're class president."

This meant I'd have to attend after-school meetings for student government about once a week, spending the night at a friend's house or trying to cadge a ride from the parents of my friends.

"This isn't working out, Lis," my father said the next day, when I told him I'd won. "You're not succeeding as a member of this family. You're not pulling your weight. You're never around. If you want to be part of this family, you need to put in the time."

It seemed strange that he could insist on my continuous presence, having been absent for so long himself. At dinners on the nights I was home now, he and Laurene were aloof. I assumed this had to do with me, but of course it might have had just as much to do with the difficulties of a new marriage, a toddler, and sleep deprivation. My father would make pasta, plain or with avocados, and eat carrot salad. I would slice a black bean burrito and help steam broccoli as Laurene fed my brother. As soon as dinner was over, they went upstairs to try to put him to sleep. I felt their disappointment in me like an augmentation of gravity in the room, and if I made any mistakes, it was a tick on the wrong side of a ledger, creating the sense that I would be forever outside of this thing I wanted: family.

What was the inside like? It would have an adhesive and ordinary quality; once inside it, I could not be dislodged. I'd become indispensable, if only I could get in.

He wanted me to be around, but in another room, in his orbit, not too close. I was supposed to occupy the path drawn by a compass circling around the point that was him.

During this period when I was increasingly away and he was increasingly angry with me, I mentioned to my father that the schoolwork was not rigorous compared with Nueva's. Sometimes I got bored and doodled in class.

"Doodling?" he said. "That's not good. That's not good at all."

"In history, we're learning about the Renaissance. But I already learned about it."

What followed was a strange flurry: he and I driving up to the school to meet with the head of the school, the admissions director, and several teachers, and him telling me to repeat the story about doodling, about how I was bored sometimes in class. In my imagination I became the kind of extraordinary student for whom certain private schools are woefully inadequate. My father indulged the lie, becoming indignant on my behalf, perhaps believing me, perhaps seeing in my vanity a way out of the after-school-ride conundrum. Emboldened by my father beside me, I believed my own stories: the top-rated school wasn't academically rigorous enough for me.

I was too afraid to admit, even to myself, that the problem wasn't the school but the fact that I couldn't participate in it, or see friends, or leave the house without feeling that I had betrayed some essential agreement.

On the way home from another visit to the school, he suggested that we stop at Palo Alto High School—"Paly" for short—just to see what it was like. It was late in the afternoon and school was out. For a few minutes we walked around the empty quad. Many of the buildings looked like bunkers. I felt uncomfortable, as if we were trespassing. But then we heard music coming from somewhere, and we followed it over to where a tall boy was standing beside the door where the music was coming from. I was too shy to speak, but my father asked, "What's going on in here?" and the boy said, "It's the paper," and we peered into the room. There were lots of people inside, working on computers and lounging on beanbags, and I thought, if I did decide to go here, I'd work on the paper too. "You know what's great about going to a school nearby your house?" my father asked as we left. "You can walk to it, like I did. And if you walk a lot, over the course of time, you get to see the seasons change." He said it in the same slow way he spoke of beautiful women. Walking to school didn't sound very romantic to me. I decided to transfer anyway—it seemed like the only way to make it work at home.

It was midyear when I decided to transfer to Paly, and my father drove me over to sign up for classes. The administrative offices were off a long, glossy corridor that smelled of the same cleaning fluid as the public library, and had the same combination of muffled sounds and sharp echoes. I felt the glow of nearness to my father, his attention on me. Walking beside him down the corridor I felt protected; he was confident in this school.

We sat down in the office of a registrar who helped to fill out my schedule, sometimes placing me in classes I needed that were already full.

"Is there a student government?" I asked her.

"Yes," she said. "Maybe you could run for representative. There are two per class—the elections are soon." A demotion, I thought. I'd run for president instead.

Several Christmas wreaths arrived from Smith & Hawken. Three were the size of small bird's nests. My father carried one through the kitchen, to hang on the wooden beam between the banks of French doors in the hallway. He didn't want me or anyone else to touch the wreaths, or any of the Christmas decorations he'd ordered. Even the tree lights— which he insisted on hanging by himself, looping the twisted cords around the branches of a Douglas fir in a process that took him the whole day—were off-limits. He fussed about the small round wreath, adjusting it on the nail, stepping back; adjusting it, stepping back again.

I laughed, watching him. "I guess you have to get it *just right*," I said.

"If it's not just right," he said, in a high falsetto, rolling the *r*, "I will *perish*." When he was happy, he became goofy, able to laugh at himself and his fastidiousness.

Sometimes my father sang extemporaneous rhyming songs about me to me—the way Bob Dylan did in the recording studio, he said. My bike and hike I liked to school, my books, my looks, my life as a wife of a fife.

He adjusted the wreath one last time and lunged for me, wiggling his index finger under my rib cage. I reached for him too, trying to dig my hand into his armpit to tickle him first. He got me, I laughed—a shrill laugh that did not sound like part of me. He jumped away so that I couldn't reach him, sashaying, his bare legs tapered, silly-looking, like a frog's.

He'd recently bought a CD he played for me, a recording of the last castrato, who didn't sound like a woman or man, but had a haunting high kind of voice in between, like someone singing after sucking on a balloon. "Perish, simply perish," he sang again in that high voice, on the way back to his office to make a series of work calls under the spotlight of a desk lamp that looked, bent and hovering, like a praying mantis.

For Christmas he gave Laurene a ball gown from Giorgio Armani and a pair of shoes, too narrow for her feet. He gave me only the pair of shoes, the same ones he'd bought for her—slim black loafers, also from Armani. They fit me perfectly. He was cold toward Laurene after noticing the shoes didn't fit, as if her wider feet were an indication of some deeper offense. I was jealous of the ball gown, which was diaphanous, long, and unfolded out of the box. I felt superior about my feet, though, for a little while, as if their slim shape was an indication of something noble and pure.

It had been more than five months since I'd seen my mother. I was angry with her; I missed her. I hated her, I pitied her, I wanted to eradicate all the signs of her in myself, I missed being touched by her. She didn't know what I did every day now, how I babysat my brother and sometimes he cried and I didn't know what to do or how to soothe him.

During the months we didn't see each other, my mother had a recurring dream of a nuclear attack in which she would throw a sheet over her head and run over to get me.

Finally, for Christmas, my father agreed we could see each other again.

As soon as I felt I could leave, I walked to the Rinconada house and opened the front door. It had a smell, warm wood and soil and paint, that I hadn't noticed when I lived there. I hopped into her lap—I was still small enough for that—and she grabbed me, felt my shoulders and my head, my arms and legs, my fingers, and smelled my hair. Later she described that moment for her, a shock, a relief, to hold me—that some part of her, after not seeing me for so long, had felt as if I were dead. I remember that she wouldn't let me go.

I started school at Paly after the holidays, using my new name.

The Paly quad was grass worn away in places to stubble or bald dirt. I went to the classes in the sequence the registrar had arranged for me, using the textbooks with holes in the cover where brown cardboard showed through, notes from previous students written in the margins.

I'd never had trouble making friends before; now I was cripplingly shy, doubting myself before raising my hand in class. I didn't have a single friend.

The algebra lessons at the new school were different from the ones at Lick-Wilmerding, based on formulas I didn't know, more difficult. Most evenings for a couple of months I asked Laurene to help, and she would get up with a sigh, we'd go downstairs, she'd work out the problem in a businesslike way, and then tell me the procedure to follow to get the answer.

At night, after they went upstairs, I was incredibly lonely and cried myself to sleep. I was also cold. I discovered the heating didn't work in my part of the house.

I might have asked to move into the bedroom upstairs, the one located over the garage, with slanted windows along the roof. It was the room my father had first offered to me, thinking I would like it the most because it was large, with a fireplace, and its own Juliet balcony with stairs leading down to the courtyard. When he offered it, he said I might sneak out at night, and winked. But that room had since been turned into a guest room, and when I finally asked to move, he said no.

"I'm cold," I said to my father in the kitchen in the morning. "Would you get the heater fixed?"

He pulled an apple juice from the fridge. "Nope. Not until we renovate the kitchen," he said, "and we're not going to do that any-time soon."

◆

The next weekend, I parked my bike outside a clothing shop called Roxy, a white cube with English punk music blasting at noon, racks of clothing hanging so high the clothing brushed against my cheeks: short, loose jackets with shoulder pads, pleated pants, T-shirts in bright pastels. I'd been there with my mother, among the pleated, silky pants and patterned shirts and music, and I'd come back to feel the familiar surroundings. When I walked out of the shop, the bike was gone.

I figured my father would get me another one, now that he didn't have to pay for the car service or the private school. Also—although I couldn't articulate this—I had a feeling he owed me. I thought he and Laurene would come to understand that, and try to make it up to me; that he would pity me, eventually, and it would hit him.

The feeling of being owed was like a cloud darkening the air around me that would lift and disperse when my father was kind to me, but then settle again, thickly. I couldn't get it to go away for good.

Anyway, I needed a bike now that I was supposed to get myself around.

"Lis," he said, when I told him about the bike, "you're not doing a great job keeping track of stuff." It was morning at the table with my father, Laurene, Reed, and me.

"I'm trying." I hoped Laurene would come to my rescue.

"You're letting things slide," he said.

"It was a mistake."

"Well, I have an idea. I'll get you a new bike if you do the dishes. Every night. And babysit whenever we need you."

"Okay," I said quickly. It was a bad deal and I knew it. I should have negotiated. I was certain he knew it was a bad deal too, but I thought that if they observed me take it anyway, they'd be more generous with me. It would compensate for the way I was absent before. It would give me a chance to prove my dedication.

The dishwasher that came with the house was built into the kitchen island and didn't work, and my father said he wouldn't replace it, so I did the dishes by hand with a sherbet-colored sponge. I stood on the cold terracotta tiles, seeing my reflection in the window turned into a mirror at night, and lined up the plates to dry in the slats of a wooden rack. The requests that had seemed oppressive and Sisyphean at my mother's house—to make the bed, set the table, clean the counters, write thank-you notes—I did now, mostly, without anyone bugging me.

When I finished the dishes, I looked through the family photographs in a shoebox kept in a kitchen drawer, noticing how many pictures there were of my brother, how few of me. I flipped through the stack, removing the pictures of myself I didn't like. Maybe they'd notice there were too few and realize their mistake in not taking more.

After they put my brother to sleep, my father would come down to his office to work for a few hours. Sitting at my desk, I could hear when he left his office again to go up to bed. I listened to his feet on the tile as he turned left at the staircase and went upstairs. It would have been easy for him to walk a few more steps, duck his head into my room, and say goodnight. But I was fourteen, too old to need a goodnight. My mother had always done so, a part of our pattern that was, I thought, infantilizing, and that I could have done without. Here I burned for it.

What did I want? What did I expect? He didn't need me the way I needed him. A dark and frightening loneliness came over me, a sharp pain beneath my ribs. I cried myself to sleep, the tears turning cold and pooling in my ears.

♦ ♦ ♦

Yet even in the middle of my most profound, heavy-legged self-pity, I was aware of the fact that my bedroom wasn't *that* cold—it was California—and if the house cleaner didn't wash my dirty laundry, she did wash my sheets every couple of weeks, and some pictures *did* contain me.

After school, Carmen sometimes braided my hair in the kitchen while my brother napped. She was loving toward me. She knew how to make a variety of braids, including a braid in a circle around my head like a crown. Her braids didn't fray or slip but remained for a couple of days, despite the fact that my hair was fine and slick. I wore them until they became loose, muzzy with escaped hairs that formed a halo in the light. I sat in the kitchen chair as she shivered my scalp with her fingernails pulling strands. I closed my eyes. I liked being touched. In those moments I thought she and I were lucky to be in this house, with its brick and sparkling windows, the jasmine vine that bloomed around the front door and gave off a quenching smell like you could drink it.

As my brother slept one weekend afternoon, my father, Laurene, and I went to sit outside at the table in the courtyard. Laurene cut watermelon and brought it out on a plate. Before she ate each piece, she rubbed it around her lips like a gloss, wetting them with the juice.

My father was sitting beside her, watched her wet her lips, then grabbed her shoulder and pulled her toward him, leaning across the chair. I wanted to leave, but my feet were heavy on the brick, as if some invisible external pressure compelled me to stay. The two of them formed a tableau; him pulling her in to kiss, moving his hand closer to her breasts and the part of her leg where her skirt ended, moaning theatrically, as if for an audience. He'd done the same with Tina. Why didn't these women push him away, I wondered. I felt my aloneness in the courtyard acutely, how there was no one else there to say, Stop.

The emotions didn't feel real, but like a performance. Like Cary Grant in *North by Northwest*, kissing Eva Marie Saint on the train.

I could see a scythe of her white cotton underwear between her legs under the hem of her jean skirt. My mother had taught me to close my knees when I wore a skirt; I wondered, did her mother not teach her that? I was angry that she was doing something like a child and an adult at the same time, letting him kiss her like this in front of me, and that she didn't know, or care, to close her knees.

I started to rise, finally, and moved toward the door of the house. They detached. "Hey, Lis," he said. "Stay here. We're having a family moment. It's important that you try to be part of this family."

I sat still, looking away as he moaned and undulated in the side of my vision. It was not clear how long it would go on. I looked into the grass of the courtyard, at the blooming crab apple tree that grew beside the curving brick path, a profusion of tiny white and pink blossoms hovering above the trunk.

Although I couldn't have known it clearly then, I hoped Laurene would fix our family, pry my father open, demand his full heart and attention, and get him to acknowledge what he'd missed.

If I was angry, now, that she was also human and flawed—she didn't close her knees, didn't push him away in front of me—it was because of the immensity of the job I had in mind for her. She was the last resort, after everyone else had failed. But in this girlish lapse, I saw hints that she might not choose or even be able to inhabit the role I'd assigned her, that she was not here to fix my father for me.

◆

My mother and I planned to meet for brunch on a Saturday. Since our reunion at Christmas, we'd seen each other twice, but these visits had devolved into fights. I picked Il Fornaio because it was close enough that I could get there and back on my own—a twenty-minute walk to my father's house. I didn't have a new bike yet. If she lost her temper, I could leave. When I arrived, she was already waiting. We hugged. She was wearing a new dress. The maître d' with the gray mustache said, "Follow me," and walked us into the courtyard, past the fountain, to a round metal table near a potted tree covered in purple flowers. He didn't seem to recognize me, even though I'd come here many times with my father to pick up marinara pizzas with onions, olives, and oregano.

My mother faced out and I faced the back of the courtyard, where there were no more tables. We put our napkins in our laps. We weren't connected anymore but separate. I wasn't sure how to let her know that I was still her daughter. If she yelled, I would get up and leave; just imagining it, the boldness of it, made me feel giddy and guilty both.

"How are you doing?" she asked.

"I'm okay," I said. "How are you?"

"I'm fine. I miss you. How do you like Paly?"

"It's all right." It was terrible. "I mean, I think it will get better," I said in a cheery voice.

The formality could not continue. I knew she would break it.

"So it sounds like everything's just great," she said—a hint of sarcasm.

The waiter came and asked if we were ready to order, jolly, as if he was interacting with any mother and daughter on any morning. I ordered the pancakes with stewed peaches and whipped cream.

"You just seem like this strange, distant person," she said, when the waiter left. "Completely different. It's like you're not even my daughter anymore since you moved out." She sounded curious about it, and the curiosity hurt me—as if she noticed but didn't care. I wondered if it was true; I might be worse than I thought, irreparably changed. Near her I was a perfect shell that even I could not break.

"I moved out because we were fighting," I said. "I didn't want to."

"Oh, come on," she said. "You just worry about yourself. Your perfect life. Things get tough and Lisa goes with the rich people. Poof."

My life didn't feel rich; maybe it looked rich, or richer, from the outside. It was true I had nicer clothes now. Not a lot of clothes, but better ones, and newer. When we went for Indian food at the mall, my father would sometimes guide us into Armani Exchange, where he would buy me a T-shirt or a pair of trousers. Before this, when I got something new, I'd wear it a lot and wear it out until it looked like the other things in my closet, but shopping with them worked differently: small and more frequent renewals, nicer fabrics, and because most of the clothes came from the same shop at around the same time, they went together. Blue, white, charcoal. For the first time, when I looked into my closet, I could find something newish that fit and could be worn with something else newish that fit. I knew my mother would have loved to have this same feeling, and I felt guilty to have it first. "You have a real problem, Lisa," she continued, growling through her clenched teeth. "You know what's wrong with you? You want to be like them so much that you have no idea what's important in life."

In fact, I wanted to be just like them, but it wasn't possible, hard as I tried. I stuck out. I did not blend, needing more than I was given and hoping to hide it.

My mother began to speak in a high, piercing voice meant to mock mine.

"I'm just so delicate, such a princess," she said.

"You're like them," she said. She began to raise her voice and speak angrily. "Cold, and heartless, and phony. I guess you might as well *be* with them."

I looked around at the other tables—no one was sitting too close, but a few people looked. "This isn't okay," I said, standing. "You can't yell at me anymore. I'm leaving."

She looked at me, stunned. I walked through the courtyard, through the belly of the restaurant past the row of chefs, the bustle, the warmth, and din. I was self-conscious about my back and my legs. Everything she could see as she watched me go—the way I moved, my clothes, the way I walked—might confirm what she'd said about me. I tried to walk as I'd always walked, the way I'd walked when I was with her, so that she would see this walk and understand that I was still who I was before. I quickened my step as soon as I was out the door, in case she was following me to yell more. I wanted her to follow me; I was terrified she would.

I walked home. My hands were shaking. I'd abandoned my mother. I'd left her all alone. The street was empty and peaceful. I felt a strange sort of calm, too calm; I was a girl walking and a girl who watched a girl walking. I was what she said I was, the kind of person who left the people they loved.

I kept looking back. In between looks I stepped carefully to avoid the hard fruits from the sweet gums. The trees were fiery orange and red, with star-shaped leaves, and because it had rained the day before, there were leaves on the ground, unnaturally bright on the gray sidewalk. The fruits were the size of cherries, brown with brown spines. They left rust-colored marks on the sidewalk. These same fruits had fallen from the tree in the backyard at the Rinconada house, *thonking* on the deck—so many that it had been impossible to walk without losing my balance until my mother came outside and swept them away.

When election season arrived a month or two into the semester, I handed out flyers announcing my candidacy for class president. Passing them around, I realized the problem was that I didn't know the other students, who all knew one another, and they didn't know me. I wore a black skirt that fell to my mid-calf; they walked by in jeans, in groups of two or three, and gave half-smiles. Some took my flyers. Some smirked and said, "No, thanks."

"Sorry, who are you?" a girl said.

"A new freshman," I said. "I just transferred in."

"And you're running for president?"

"Yeah," I said, realizing at that moment how absurd it must have looked.

She took a flyer and walked away.

At Lick-Wilmerding, students had come from a variety of schools; here most had known each other since kindergarten. The gossip circulated that I was Steve Jobs's kid, which likely made my run for president even less attractive, but at the time, I wasn't aware of it. I was only embarrassed, and a little ashamed, driving for the position of president with stubbornness—as if, with enough willpower, I could re-create the triumph from my old school.

When the votes were counted, a boy named Kyle had won. He wore plaid shirts and khakis and had a strong, definitive voice, a large Adam's apple, a long neck.

That night my father and Laurene went to a dinner party, and I looked after my brother. They had me babysit a lot, telling me at the last minute as their plans resolved. I loved my brother and didn't mind watching him, but I felt unseen as they put him into my arms without asking and left. My father had already left me when I was little; now he made me care for the next one as he walked out the door.

I fed my brother as he squirmed, delightfully, read him books he tried to rip, and tried to sing him to sleep. He would not sleep. He cried, unconsoled by the milk I'd heated and tested on the inside of my wrist. He wailed for what seemed like hours, his face crimson, his cheeks wet, his mouth wide open.

I called the number they'd left. No one picked up. I paced back and forth with him in my arms, in front of the windows that became mirrors at night, wondering if this is what it had been like for my mother, alone with me.

A week or so after our brunch at Il Fornaio, my mother and I talked on the phone. She said she was sorry, that she shouldn't have yelled, that she wasn't mad at me and understood why I'd moved out. She'd been offered a lucrative job painting stenciled images and signage for a large women's and children's hospital in Los Angeles, which meant she'd be gone most of the time for a month or so and we wouldn't see each other, but we'd continue to talk at night.

When she returned, she would start making canvas stick-on animals for the walls of children's rooms. A hospital nearby hired her to do stenciled murals covering the walls of several rooms, and for another hospital she was hired to paint trees with stenciled donor names on the fruit. She hired an assistant to help with the larger projects, and they worked together in her converted garage, playing the Cranberries, Talking Heads, Paul Simon, Ladysmith Black Mambazo.

My parents would see each other around town occasionally, at Country Sun or Whole Foods. I heard about these encounters from my mother, who didn't relish running into him, but reported that they'd been kind to each other, saying hello or mentioning something about me, or him asking her to say hello to Tina.

Tina and my mother were still friends, and they sometimes had breakfast at Joanie's Cafe on California Avenue. When I asked how Tina was doing, my mother said that my father had been calling her ten or twenty times a day, leaving messages on her answering machine about wanting to get back together.

One morning my father read the newspaper and then sang "This Old Man" to my brother, identifying the paddy-whacked part and rolling my brother's hands for the dog and the bone, my brother squirming to get free.

Laurene left the kitchen to change clothes for an aerobics class; my father stopped playing with Reed for a moment and looked at me.

"Hey," he said, "how do you think Tina's doing?" He had begun to ask about Tina when the two of us were alone, or alone with Reed, asking each time like it was the first time, as if the question had just occurred to him. It soon became the only topic, then, that he spoke with me about directly, making me feel important, so that even though it made me feel furtive, I also liked it.

"I think she's doing okay," I said. I didn't let on that I knew about the phone calls, or that I understood that his question was less about Tina and more about himself. I knew too much. I didn't want to give him so much information that he stopped asking. I felt a strange and wonderful power; knowing about Tina I was useful to him, even if I was disloyal, and sneaky.

"I really miss her," he said.

When Laurene returned, we played with Reed in the kitchen and made lunch. My father left the room and returned with his camera, the big-lensed, expensive camera no one else was allowed to touch. I wanted to be in the pictures he took. I wanted it with an unseemly desperation.

I also wished to be my brother instead of myself. It didn't matter if I had to give up my life until now because that was nothing. The way I imagined it, this would not be death but just, lucky me, I get to *be* him, this time born right. I could imagine the exhilaration. The wish was more powerful than any wish I'd felt before, and had an unfamiliar, urgent force, and because of this difference from ordinary life, I believed in some small way that it *could* happen. I searched my palms for a hint of when or how.

"Lisa, step aside," he said, in a business voice, holding his camera in front of his eye, the lens like a marble or a deep, still pool.

I jumped toward the sink, out of the frame. From behind him, I continued to coax my brother to smile, so my father wouldn't know it hurt.

"Lis can come in, Steve," Laurene said. She held her hand out to me. "C'mon, Lis." I went to stand beside her. I was so grateful to her it made me shake.

Early one morning Laurene took me with her on a trip with the Audubon Society. We rode in a van full of people to a nature preserve, with thin, tall trees on either side of a sand path, birds moving the branches.

A few days later, my father came into my room. He was distraught, pacing.

"What is it?" I asked. "What's wrong?"

"What matters in life," he said, "is only what you do with your own hands."

"I don't understand," I said.

"That bird trip," he said. "That sort of—*thing*." What did he mean? The trip had seemed innocent, the quiet footsteps, heads up, carrying binoculars, looking for the origins of the trills.

"These sorts of things don't mean anything. They aren't real."

"I know," I said, emphatically, though I didn't. Later, I understood the trip had been given to us with the hope that he or Laurene would contribute money to the Audubon Society, and this bothered him profoundly.

I didn't want to be his conscience—the one he confided in when something went wrong, the one with whom he shared a stricter value system. I was some grainy old photograph from before he'd "lost himself," as my mother had said. The photograph got dusty, and he'd return sometimes to look at it, to wipe away the dust and look, but then he'd leave again and forget.

"People who aren't born here"—he meant California—"they just don't *get* it."

Sometimes, when I left the house, Laurene would slip me a twenty-dollar bill where he couldn't see it. She told me I looked pretty.

I asked once if he gave to charity, and he snapped at me, saying it was "none of my business." Laurene had bought a velvet dress for her niece on his credit card, and he gave her a hard time, reading the bill aloud in the kitchen. I assumed his frugality was part of the reason we didn't have much furniture, and that the reason he wouldn't hire more help to take care of my brother or clean the house was that he was tight, although this may not have been true. He made calculations out loud about what things cost, at the grocery store, and at restaurants and the Gap, and what a normal family could afford, and was indignant when things were too expensive and refused to buy them, when I wished he'd just accept that he wasn't normal and splurge. I'd also heard of his generosity, how he'd bought an Alfa Romeo for Tina, and a BMW for Laurene, and paid off her school loans. I thought he was mostly frugal with me, refusing to get me more jeans, or furniture, or heat, and generous with everyone else. It was hard to understand why someone who had enough money would create a sense of scarcity, why he wouldn't lavish us with it.

Besides the Porsche, my father kept a large silver Mercedes. I called it "Small Nation," a nickname I made up.

"Why 'Small Nation'?" he asked.

"Because it's big enough to cover a small nation, heavy enough to crush it, and expensive enough to feed the population for a year," I said. It was a joke, but I also wanted to hurt him for what I thought was his extravagant spending on himself, throw him into self-reflection, bring about some revelation.

"Small Nation," he said, chuckling. "That's really funny, Lis."

One day at home, passing me in the hallway, my father said to me, "You know, each of my girlfriends has had a more difficult relationship with her father than the last." I didn't know what to make of the statement, or why he'd said it.

Like me, most of the women I knew did not have fathers when they were growing up: fathers died, divorced, or left. Not having a father wasn't unique, or even significant. My father's significance was elsewhere. Instead of raising me, he was inventing world-changing machines; he was famous, mingling, accruing, driving stoned in the South of France with a billionaire named Pigozzi, dating Joan Baez. I figured no one would think, *Hey, that guy should have been raising his daughter instead.* What presumption. To whatever degree I felt grieved by having lost him for so long, and to whatever extent this grief arose powerfully in me, I suppressed it, or was not fully aware of it: it was wrong, selfish; I was nothing. I dismissed the fact of my own importance to him, his importance to me, or even the importance of fathers and children more generally—a dismissal so familiar to me then that I didn't even notice it: it was part of the air.

It was only recently, when an older friend, a father himself, called to tell me about his daughter's engagement, that I understood something new. His daughter and her fiancé came to tell him the news and he'd cried, surprising himself.

"What was it that made you cry?" I asked.

"It was this: since the day she was born, it had been my job, our job, to protect her and care for her," he said. "I realized that from now on it would be someone else's job. I was no longer on the front line, no longer the main person."

When we got off the phone, I started to suspect I'd underestimated what I'd missed, what my father had missed. When I lived with him, I'd tried to put it into the language of dishwashers and couches and bikes, as if to reduce his absence to things. I felt owed trifles, so resolutely, so achingly. In fact it was something bigger—something I'd felt for a gut-visceral moment on the phone as a whole intricate universe: the kind of care and love we'd missed that can occur between a father and child.

When I was reading, I was not lonely or self-aware. I felt upheld by the stories. I read a whole stack of fiction at one time, alternating between books so I could finish all of them together, the multiple endings crashing around me like the cymbals in a musical finale. When I stopped reading, I felt lonely again, like a window had been thrown open.

The same carpenter who built my brother's changing table also built the bookshelves on one wall of my father's office, carefully matching the back side of each shelf to the dimpled indentations of the white-painted brick. Some nights, after he'd gone to sleep, I went into his office and perused the books, including one about Noguchi, and *The Rise and Fall of the Third Reich* and *Autobiography of a Yogi*. On his desk beside the NeXT computer was a box that contained twelve new black uni-ball pens. He used these pens, always, and usually had one in his pocket. I took three. In his office, with everyone else in the house asleep, I sat on his rug and read with a pen in my hand. Here was a feeling of abundance and freedom, any book I wanted, pens, no one bothering me or following me around.

Around that time I read a copy of Salinger's *Franny and Zooey*. It was a matte white paperback with black text and two stripes of color across the front. I read it repeatedly until my copy frayed, the cover collecting dirt from my hands and my backpack. Trains, frigid train stations, coats, dorms, diners, drinks—here was the East Coast, the Ivy League, Harvard—a different planet, a different class. Did it exist like this, really? I doubted it. The characters used words foreign to me, clipped and slick. Nonetheless, I wanted to be Franny. She was real enough. She gushed with "absolutely" and "lovely" and "love." Trains were numbers: the ten-fifty-two. They arrived on cold platforms where you could see your breath. Against the cold, people wore overcoats, topcoats, raccoon fur coats, buttoned wool linings.

I decided I would go to Harvard, because that was the college they talked about in the book. I would leave, get away from this town, the world of my parents. I wouldn't let them know how fixed my plan was, because they might try to stop me.

It was different from anything my parents had done, but might impress them nonetheless. This seemed like the answer: a plan to get out that was above reproach. I didn't know what I wanted to study or how I wanted college to be, really, but figured if I went to Harvard, those things would become clear.

I started collecting coats, not realizing why, asking for coats as gifts for birthdays and Christmas, even though it was often too warm in Northern California for the kind of coats I received. As the school years progressed, I understood I was collecting for college, and I collected with decisive fervor (even if it would turn out that these coats, although too warm for California, wouldn't be warm enough for the East Coast).

I didn't tell my father about how determined I was because it was too delicate a plan to withstand him, too unfinished. I sensed he wouldn't like it when I left and didn't understand how soon it would happen—even as he joked about my future marriage to Biff and Tad and the rest. I'd have to get out by stealth. That even if he did not believe in raising the kind of child who would hang around and never leave, feeding off his charisma, he might try to create that kind of child anyway, despite himself.

For a joke, my father would turn his back, moan, and move his hands up and down until they seemed disembodied, like someone else's hands.

When he spoke to me directly about love and sex, he was curious and interested, the two of us equals, a team.

I did not feel the same revulsion I did when talking about sex with my mother. Maybe it was because I hadn't grown up with him.

"Let's go over the bases again," he said, in a kind but officious tone. We used the language of baseball, a game neither of us knew or cared about.

"You mean—for making out?" I asked.

"Yeah. So first base is kissing . . ." he prompted.

I knew it was ridiculous, but I liked it. He asked me about once a week, as if he'd forgotten in between. This was a repetitive exercise. I didn't have a boyfriend and wasn't making any progress but I went through what I knew. He continued to prompt. The only confusion I had was third base, called "feeling down," which may or may not have included oral sex, so I didn't mention that part and hoped he wouldn't want more details.

"And which base are you at?" he asked.

"Second," I said, "from Nueva."

"Ah," he said. "Great."

One evening when Laurene got home I went outside to meet her, near the roses beside the gate.

"You know that computer, the Lisa?" she said, closing the gate, the ring clanking, her hair flashing in the sunlight, a large leather satchel on her shoulder. "It was named after you, right?" We'd never talked about it before and I wasn't sure why she was asking now. Maybe someone had asked her.

"I don't know. I think so," I lied. I hoped she'd drop it.

"It must have been," she said. "Let's ask him when he gets back."

"It doesn't really matter," I said. I didn't want him to say no again. Though maybe if she asked him, he would say yes?

A few minutes later, he came in the gate and Laurene walked up to him. I followed.

"Hon," she said, "that computer was named after Lisa, right?"

"Nope," he said.

"Seriously?"

"Yup. Seriously," he said.

"Come on." She looked him in the eye. I was impressed and grateful she kept pushing when I would have given up. They faced each other, stopped on the path on the way to the door.

"It wasn't," he said.

Then I wished she hadn't asked. I was embarrassed for her to discover that I wasn't as important to him as she might have thought.

"Well then, who was it named after?"

"An old girlfriend," he said, looking off into the distance, as if remembering. Wistful. It was this dreamy quality that made me believe he was telling the truth, because otherwise it was quite an act. I had a strange feeling in my stomach, the same one I got when something was fake or phony, but I was getting that feeling a lot lately. And why would he lie, anyway? His true well of feeling was clearly reserved for the other Lisa. I'd never heard of a girlfriend named Lisa from when he was young, and when I mentioned it to my mother later she said, "Hogwash." But maybe she didn't know, maybe he'd kept the first Lisa from us both.

"Sorry, kid," he said, patting me on the back, then walking into the house.

My father opened a large, thick-paper envelope—an invitation to a wedding in Napa.

"Hey, Lis, you wanna come?"

Often when my father and Laurene went to parties, I babysat for my brother. This time I would be included, in public, part of the family! The daughter, the sister. I thought of what dress to bring, and how I'd have to buy nylons, an ecstasy of decision-making. A few weeks later, the date of the wedding arrived.

On the way we stopped for sandwiches at a fancy grocery store, and later, on the road, my father shook a water bottle when I said I had to pee. My brother sat beside me in his elevated seat.

Shortly before we arrived, my father delivered a lecture about Risk and Consequence that seemed like a performance. "Lis, do you know about Risk and Consequence?" he asked. "It's a way of evaluating whether to do something, a sliding scale. For example, if the risk is low, but the consequence is high, you might decide not to do something."

"Right," I said.

"Even laws," he said. "They aren't about what you can and can't do. They're based on whether or not you get caught. For example, cars can do one hundred twenty miles an hour, way faster than any speed limit in this country. You can drive as fast as you want—as long as you don't get caught."

I remembered a story my mother told me about how, before I knew him, he'd drive home so fast down the roads in Woodside, and without license plates, that for almost a year the cops couldn't catch him. He was the cool one, the fast one, telling me how to break rules. I could see the freedom of his intelligence, how it made you lighter on your feet.

The ceremony would be held at the Meadowood Napa Valley, with its grand curving entrance, somewhere near the golf course, past pools and suites that looked like wood cabins.

When we arrived at the hotel and got into the room, we all got ready. Laurene put my brother in a light blue cotton confection, pantaloons with straps over the shoulders. She wore a dress made of vintage Japanese kimonos stitched together; my father wore a black formal jacket, a white shirt, and jeans.

"Okay, we're off," he said, almost to the door.

The idea that I was invited to the ceremony had been implied but never explicitly stated.

"Hold on. I'm not ready yet," I said. I'd just hitched up my stockings; damp skin made them stick midway.

"That's all right," Laurene said. "Take your time. Here he is." She handed Reed to me in a way that suggested she was in motion and I would be still.

By her tone and movement, I understood. They were moving quickly, as if to flee. No time to mention what we should eat for dinner. When I realized my mistake, I felt ashamed most of all to have presumed. But in the car when I'd hung the dress, they might have told me I wouldn't need any dresses.

"Why don't you two head out, maybe to the pool?" Laurene said, as they walked through the door.

I changed into jeans. Outside the door of each room was parked a red wagon. I put Reed inside, leaving his fancy outfit on. He wanted to be pulled, and then carried, and then pulled again. The weather was damp and cool, too cool for swimming. "Ky," Reed said, pointing up. Bug, tree, pool. The light was muted under a thin layer of clouds like tissue paper that made it diffuse, everywhere and nowhere.

When we reached the place where the pavement ended and the field began, I lifted him out of the wagon and he ran forward, toward the edge of the pool, almost tripping on clods of dirt in the grass but managing to stay upright, always on the cusp of falling, like a marionette held under the armpits by strings. I ran after him and caught him, helped him lie belly-down on the concrete lip so he could touch the water. I crouched beside him, grabbed a leg. He smacked his hands against the surface of the water.

"Slap, slap, slap," I said.

"Lap lap lap," he repeated.

Behind us I heard a motor and laughter. I looked up to see a convertible drive past, an old sports car, chrome and cream, limbs hanging out the windows, teenagers. The car crackled its way up the long drive that curved from the hotel to the road under a double row of trees with high, arching branches that created a different sense of scale—a huge enclosed room, light shining through the bright green foliage.

I don't want to be here, babysitting, I thought. That is where I want to be instead. In that car, with them.

♦

One night, after putting my brother to bed when Steve and Laurene were out, I rooted around upstairs. I searched Laurene's dressing room, where I hoped to find some trinket or item of clothing or old photograph. Some secret she had that I didn't. I found a pot of white skin cream, dimpled on the surface where she'd touched it, a tall, thin triangle of perfume with a glass marble stopper, a few photographs of my brother. The full-length mirror warped to make me big-hipped. Her closet was disappointing in its refusal to reveal more about her.

I walked through the bathroom to my father's closet. His shelves contained socks, ties, sweaters that crinkled with inner tissue paper. In his drawer on the left side I noticed the glossy lip of a small manila envelope.

I looked inside: a stack of one-hundred-dollar bills, two inches thick! More cash than I'd ever seen. It gave me a shock, like when I'd come upon an infestation of ladybugs, a hundred or a thousand crawling around a branch, having seen them only in ones or twos.

I flipped through the stack, my heart pounding. Each bill was new and crisp and gave off a whiff of alcohol and burlap. When I furred the edges, they fell in clumps.

I took one bill, folded it, and put it in my pocket. Then I closed the drawer and went downstairs. My palms were sweating; I wiped them on my jeans.

Had there been a camera? Had I left fingerprints? I was jumpy, as if someone might leap out from behind a door; there was a strange, rubbery quality in my legs, pleasurable electricity racing through my arms.

I was a thief. But I wouldn't take any more, ever. I wouldn't push my luck. That was it. If my father found out, he would have proof I was unworthy to the core and deserved any distance he put between us. The knowledge that I had committed a crime made me more eager to please them than ever. I went out and cut flowers in the yard, arranged them in vases around the house.

From that night on, whenever my father said, "Lis, we have to talk," or even just "Lis," I braced myself, ready for the accusation.

At the mall, on a mannequin in a window, I'd seen a pewter-colored Benetton trench coat the silvery color of the underside of a leaf. It was seventy-nine dollars. It was unlined, made of the kind of fabric that might be used on a windbreaker, but instead had been made to tie at the waist, appealingly, and with its adult silhouette it reminded me of something Candice Bergen might wear in the rain on the way to an important meeting.

The next time they went out, I crept back up to my father's closet, shaking with fear and excitement. I couldn't tell whether the quantity of bills had changed since the last time.

This time, in case I never returned, I took two.

The trouble came with cashing the hundreds. They weren't accepted everywhere—the first bill I'd stolen had been refused at a café across from my high school. I worried shop owners might become curious about why I had such a large bill, and word would get back to my father. As a result, I was furtive when trying to cash them, never going to the same shop twice, attempting to look nonchalant and confident at the same time.

At Benetton, I braced for the woman to refuse the bill. Instead, she took it without looking up, folded the jacket around itself, dropped it into a paper bag without any tissue paper, and handed me the change. I walked out, the jacket almost as light as the paper that held it. A sensation of floating—the thrill of money transformed into possession.

When I got back, I hid the jacket deep in a drawer. I couldn't wear it; they might notice. It was one more in my collection for college.

I didn't save the money because I didn't understand what savings were for. Instead, I looked for things to buy and spent it all right away. Other than a few things for myself, I bought gifts, mostly, for my parents, Laurene, and my brother, for birthdays and Christmas. I listened to people talk about saving money in order to buy something they wanted in the future—but it didn't make sense to me because I might find an object I burned with desire to own right away, and what was the point of savings if they accomplished the exact same purpose, only later? I also heard people talking about saving money for emergencies, or saving just to have savings. In the case of an emergency I figured I'd find a way to wiggle out of it, to hustle and charm. I'd outsmart the savers.

At dinner that night, my father said a photographer would come to the house soon to take pictures of the family. My hands began to flutter. I broke another glass.

When the photographer arrived one morning, he and his assistant fastened a roll of white paper to a rafter in the living room, pulling it down to the floor to create a backdrop. First he took pictures of my brother alone, sitting up on the white paper, wearing a jean jumpsuit. Then he took pictures of all of us together, me standing behind them; then of Laurene holding my brother, both facing forward. She wore a long, patterned vest with a fringe, and platform shoes.

"Hey, Lis, we're going to need you to step out of this next photograph," my father said.

I stepped out and watched, pretending I didn't care. At some point during a few shots of my father holding my brother, Reed started to wail, and Laurene took him upstairs to change his diaper.

My father slipped away to his study to work, vanishing as he often did in between moments.

It was one of those days when the light was diffuse and watery, the sun a yellow smudge behind clouds. The photographer looked at me, standing beside him. "Can I take some pictures of you?" he asked.

"I'd love it," I said, even though I sensed it was not allowed.

I was wearing the jeans my father told me to wear. "Wait," I said, and ran down the hallway to my bedroom and pulled on a dress of my mother's from the seventies that hung in my closet. It fit like a muumuu: long sleeves that buttoned at the wrists, a pattern of small gold and cream flowers on a black background, and thin gold piping around the neck and the sleeves. From a high flat placket in front it hung down to my ankles.

I'd wanted a professional photograph for years—I saw them framed on walls at friends' houses; now it was happening, but without my mother. Wearing her dress was a way to have her there too. Who cared if the dress was old and unfashionable.

I ran back down the hall, barefoot and, breathless, stood where he told me to, beside an Eames chair and ottoman. I knew I was getting away with something, stealing the spotlight like this; he might have sensed it. A flurry of clicks; the faster we went, the more photographs we'd get. I smiled big, showed my teeth, made my eyes bright.

My father emerged from his study. "What are you doing?" he asked, looking at me up and down, in the dress.

"He said he would take—"

"Stop it," he said to the photographer. "Stop it right now."

One night, doing dishes and talking on the phone with my mother, I mentioned that I had a dentist appointment, and she offered to pick me up and take me. I accepted her help, guiltily, sensing that my father and Laurene would not approve of her ferrying me places. I would be under her influence when I was supposed to be under theirs. I might have biked to my appointments, as they said I should, but I was too lazy for the forty-five minutes across town to the dentist, the doctor, the therapist, especially if my mother would give me a ride. Was it these sorts of tasks that had made my mother unable to care for me? Now, burdening her, I might push her past a limit.

She insisted it wasn't a problem.

"I want to help," she said. "But don't be late. I don't like waiting in front of that house for you to come out."

On Saturday, all of us were in the kitchen, the windows looking out to Santa Rita, where she would park and expect me to run out. I hadn't told my father or Laurene she was coming.

This morning, in the kitchen, we coalesced into a family.

"This old man, he plays one, he plays knick-knack on my thumb," my father sang to Reed, who was sitting on his lap, slapping at his knees. My father took Reed's hands in his and twirled them around each other. Reed had recently grown another tooth. Why, Reed asked over and over, in response to whatever one of us said. Whywhywhy? He was elbows and knees, bright blond hair, red lips, a dimpled chin, and miniature biceps. I loved his laugh with his head thrown back, his spaghetti arms twisting out of grasp. He was three, but he still did not sleep through the night. He woke me up in the early morning, running into my room and tickling me awake under the armpits.

Laurene and I made bruschetta according to her recipe. "Good job, Lis," she said, as I added the garlic and dripped the garlic and oil on the bread. I was filled, at that moment, with a sense of real family, the joy in the kitchen. We had reached an eminence.

My mother was probably already parked out front, waiting for me; I knew I was supposed to be outside ready to go. I wished I'd never made the plan with her, wished I could somehow get her to go away. I hoped she would wait patiently; maybe she would understand that nothing could be more important than this.

She leaned on the horn, a long honk like a foghorn. Wasn't she worried about the neighbors? Wasn't she ashamed? When she honked like this, I had to rush out of the house as fast as I could. Why did it seem these minutes of what felt like family closeness always came at the moments my mother was there to take me to an appointment?

By the time I got out to the car, she was fuming and spoke between her teeth.

"You promised," she said.

"I know, but—"

"I don't like waiting in front of that house like I'm your maid."

Not only did she drive me places, but also I'd started to stay at her house, for one week every two weeks. It was the space in between that was perilous, the walk to her car, the four blocks, the few days of adjustment—as if my parents (who had similar values, diets, and mystical beliefs) were not only separate people but operated on contrasting principles. The houses were close but their atmospheres so starkly different it reminded me of something I'd read about the surface of the moon, how if you put your hand on the line where the light meets the shadow, one side will freeze and the other will burn.

Soon I reduced the transfers between houses, extending my stays from one week to two weeks, to a month, to two months.

◆ ◆ ◆

"I'd like to stay at Mom's house more," I said to my father at the end of the summer before my sophomore year. "Maybe half the time." Because my parents had never been married or divorced, there was no official custody arrangement. And now that we'd fulfilled his requirement of not seeing each other for six months, I figured I was allowed to decide where I went. He didn't seem happy about it, but he didn't say I couldn't. He wouldn't give me rides between the houses, though, and when I stayed with my mother, he'd give me the cold shoulder for several days around the transfer.

The first two days at my mother's felt excessively warm, almost cloying, as she followed me around, tending to me, cooking with what I'd recently understood to be an excess of oil, and profligate butter. I felt superior. I knew things she didn't know. I had aesthetic refinement she didn't have, I thought. She touched my hair and came in to say goodnight to me, when I had already learned to do without her. I hated how needy she was, how vulnerable, wanting to be with me even when I said I was fine alone; I hated the fact I was related to her, that because of her I was unable to belong in the other house. It was messy, I noticed, her kind of love. With her affection, I felt how she wanted to please me, and I thought less of her for it.

I wanted to be someone else, to be prettier, blonde, tall, worthy—but she seemed to love me, to like me, as I was. I doubted her taste.

I hoped she would not notice how I judged her. I bit my tongue and spoke in a brittle, condescending voice, pitied her strangeness and her adoration of me.

Then we would get into a fight, and she would sob, saying that she was hurt and I treated her badly, and I would see her as human again, some defense would fall, my perspective would shift, and I'd feel close with her again. We couldn't help repeating this pattern every time, even after we became aware of it.

"Steve doesn't love me," I told her. "I was born too early." We were sitting outside on the side steps, under the wisteria vine, eating half a watermelon with spoons.

"He does love you," she said. "He just doesn't know it. You, you are what is important to him."

Her words produced a great bloom inside me.

"He knows it," she said, "he's always known it, but he's disconnected from himself. He doesn't know his own heart, because he lost it."

I wasn't nothing; I was something. I thought of how he asked me about Tina: he doesn't know what he has until it's too late, and the pattern is overlapping. He uses me to find out about her, and later he will use someone else to find out about me, and on and on—the tragedy, for him, of no two points connecting.

"It's better to do your own job poorly than to do someone else's job well," she said. It was from Hinduism. She also said, "Mama may have, papa may have, but God bless the child who's got his own." That wasn't Hinduism; it was part of an old song.

There was a stack of papers on her desk, bankruptcy paperwork. I was hardly aware it was going on. I saw a man's sweatshirt in the back of her car. "Just a friend's," she said, her dating life not part of our visits. I found out later she'd dated and broken up with a mathematician and was attracted to someone in her yoga class, a software engineer from the Bronx with a black belt in karate, but she wasn't sure if he'd noticed her. On Thursday nights, the yoga students would go out for salad and pizza at Vicolo on University Avenue.

By the end of each visit with my mother, I felt some other part of me rise out of a shell—maybe my soul—the texture of it all around me again, some calm, warm authority. When she had errands to do that didn't concern me—going to the art store, grocery shopping—I rode along in the car with her, just to be close.

♦

When I was staying with my father, I babysat for the neighbors' son, age three. They lived on Waverley, a block down. The family had a two-story wood-shingled house painted light blue, with a white picket fence and a backyard littered with trucks and robots. The parents, Kevin and Dorothy, were both lawyers. I looked forward to eating crackers, soy cheese, and cookies—foods we didn't have at my father's house—and reading in a chair under a lamp.

We'd met in the neighborhood one weekend on a walk with my father and my sleeping brother. From the sidewalk my father called out to Kevin, who worked on his car in the open garage, visible from the street. This reminded my father of his father, Paul. Kevin looked and seemed like someone from a lineage of more upstanding, straightforward men. My father and Kevin became friends, going on walks around the neighborhood. Sometimes on weekends we'd drop by their house and sit in the backyard. The car was a Morgan, with a long, vented muzzle, black lacquer paint, glistening chrome exhaust pipes, and a fine red stripe.

Kevin and Dorothy seemed to like me, and overpaid me for babysitting. They invited me to join them one Saturday afternoon on a drive to the ocean, and we wound up the curving road through flecks of light to the clearing at Skyline, passing a restaurant called Alice's, where swarms of motorcyclists also stopped to eat. Then farther, toward the beach, the landscape changed to hills.

Dorothy lent me a scarf to wear over my hair, Kevin lent me a windbreaker.

"How's it going over there?" he shouted over the roar of the wind and the engine. He meant my dad's house.

"It's all right," I said. "Maybe a little cold."

"Cold?" he shouted.

"There's no heat downstairs," I yelled over the wind.

"What?"

"He won't fix it." We'd reached a stop sign at the crest of a hill. "I have to do the dishes every night and they don't have heat down there. Or a dishwasher. I mean, it's broken."

"Why don't they get a new one?"

"I don't know."

This would change during my last year of high school, when, tired of doing the dishes by hand, I thought to call a dishwasher repairman. He fixed the machine in ten minutes for forty dollars—it was only a rubber gasket, decayed into lace. When I told my father that the old brown machine was working again, he frowned, and the next week, after years without a working dishwasher, a new Miele dishwasher was installed.

"Like Cinderella," Kevin said. This was the kind of sympathy I was going for, and what I believed about myself sometimes, looking through the photos late at night.

"And they make me babysit a lot," I said.

"Oh," Kevin said. He seemed to sympathize, but it was clear this was a lesser offense, and diluted the rest.

"And they won't get a couch," I said. Later, I would learn which complaints worked, and which ones, however strongly I felt aggrieved, didn't trigger much sympathy in others.

He won't even get a *couch*, I said, to anyone who would listen.

The fact was, there were other places to sit—the Eames chairs with ottomans, a grand oriental rug, the kitchen table, my desk—so that my insistence on getting a couch, and my strong feelings about the lack of one, confused even me. But I didn't stop insisting. Whatever we'd lost before would be regained, we could catch up—if only he'd get a couch.

"The worst thing is," I said, "I get really lonely at night. I just wish my father would say goodnight sometimes. Like, even once a week."

Kevin shook his head and smiled. He smiled like this, not saying anything and shaking his head, when something made him angry, I would learn later. He had long eyelashes, sparkling eyes, a cleft in his chin, and seemed like a real adult to me then, another species of person from my father, who was more boyish—even though they were around the same age.

Much later, after I'd spent a lot more time with them and even lived at their house, Kevin and Dorothy would go against my father's wishes and pay for me to finish college. I think they did it for their own reasons—connected to their own history and sense of justice. It made them furious that my father might get away with cutting my college tuition payments, just because he had more power.

"I wish there was someone in that house who was thinking of you," Dorothy said. "Someone thinking, What does Lisa need?"

Complaining to them, about the heat, the goodnight, the couch, was a relief, and gave me a dual role: I was not only in this pitiable situation, but watching it; I was both the one hurt and the narrator of the hurt. I was meek, wishing someone would make my father do the two or three things I could not get him to do myself; telling others about it—and receiving their sympathy—gave me a power I didn't have inside it.

We got back after the drive, windswept, and they made tea.

◆

"I'm so lonely," I told Mona on the phone. "He doesn't come to say goodnight."

I relied on Mona to be an intermediary, a role that continued past high school into my adult life, when she would carry bits of information between us. Her place in the middle seemed like a mercy; he might listen to his sister.

"Really?" Mona said. "Have you asked him to?"

"No."

"Why don't you ask?" I hadn't asked because I knew there was something wrong with needing it. I needed too much. There was a difference between the way I knew I should be feeling and the way I actually felt.

"The thing is," I said, looking out into the emerald garden through the small window—at the cup-shaped roses, their centers densely stuffed with petals like pages in a waterlogged book—"the thing I don't understand is . . ."

"What?"

"It *looks* so good here," I said.

"It's a nice house," she said. When you looked into the windows of other houses, beautiful ones, the people inside the light, you imagined happiness for them. Now I was inside it.

"How can it look so good but feel bad?" I asked. It must be me that was wrong, I thought. Not it.

"What else is money for," Mona answered, "if not to make it *look* good?"

"Hey, would you guys come say goodnight to me sometimes?" I asked my father, standing in the kitchen. I'd built up the courage, after talking with Mona.

"What?" he asked.

"Just a couple nights a week," I said. "Because I'm lonely."

"Nope, sorry," he said, without pausing to think. He was bouncing my brother in his lap, sitting in the rocking chair in the kitchen.

A few days later, I asked Laurene, separately.

"Sure," she said.

I was flooded with gratitude and relief, the same feeling as when she pulled me into photographs, the same feeling that made me shower her with rose petals and lantana blossoms when she walked through the gate after work, so grateful it made me shiver as if from cold.

That night she came down first, sat on my bed, and stretched out her legs. When she stretched her legs, her almost pointed feet looked like a mannequin's feet, shaped to fit into a high heel. I put my own feet out, imitated the shape. "He'll be coming down in a minute," she said.

"So how was your day?" I asked. I'd turned the overhead lamp on, although I usually kept it off at this time of night. I wanted to make things pleasant, so they wouldn't think of it as a burden to come down, more like a treat. I wouldn't have minded if they simply tucked their head around the door—I only cared about the fact of the goodnight, not its duration.

"Great, Lis. Tell me about what you're reading." She eyed the stack of books beside my bed, all of them partially finished. She was a reader too. I was reading *Franny and Zooey* again, and the last book in the Cairo Trilogy. Also a book called *When Nietzsche Wept*, with fictionalized accounts of psychological revelation, including one about an overweight girl who seeks therapy during the process of weight loss and who, with each successive pound lost, relives the difficulties she faced at that exact weight. It left an impression on me for the idea of cell memory—that whatever we undergo is stored within the physical body, even when conscious memory of the event has disappeared.

My father came down and sat beside Laurene on my bed. The joy and relief of this event made it hard to relax, like trying to breathe in a high wind.

"All right, well—goodnight, Lis," my father said grandly as he got up, as if to underscore it. We hugged.

After that, they didn't come down again. I asked one more time, my father said no, and I stopped mentioning it.

Marketable Skills

I joined the debate team. It was one more thing I might do to get into college, and like the other activities I did for that purpose, it consumed me until I'd forgotten why I started to do it in the first place. The type of debate I chose was called Lincoln-Douglas, named for the famous debates between Abraham Lincoln and Stephen Douglas. The debate topic was printed on a long, thin sheet of paper: "Majority rule versus minority rights." What did it mean, exactly? And how would we make questions about a statement? I didn't know.

After we had prepared our arguments for both sides, done many practice rounds, and gone to one small competition at Stanford, which I'd lost, a small group of us left for another debate competition at a school called Lincoln, an hour away. Debates were held in empty classrooms, moderated by volunteers, parents, and teachers. After each round, paper assignments were posted on the wall with the next classroom assignment. In between we found each other, the four people from our school; we bought snacks, sat on the lips of concrete planters, this school much larger than ours, with charts on classroom walls that seemed more sophisticated and difficult than our charts. We whispered stories about the inanity of our opponents' arguments.

When I argued, my cheeks got red. When that happened, I felt as if I were floating and sparking. Ideas seemed to be delivered to me, the right series of words in the right time allotments. While my opponents spoke, I had ideas for how to crush them rhetorically. The issue of minority rights or majority rule felt personally important to me. The only debate I was pretty sure I'd lost was against a boy in the first round.

That night, we returned home. The following day, Sunday, was the second and last day of the tournament. We left early, in the same van.

"We'll return home as soon as we've all lost or, otherwise, we'll wait as long as someone is still being placed in tournaments," the coach said. I'd told my father I'd be gone for another day; he seemed wary, as if I'd made up the debate team. "I should be back by dinnertime," I said.

But I kept winning. My cheeks continued to burn, so hot that as I formulated my counterarguments, I put a hand on my cheek, alternating between left and right, to cool them down.

I called home in between rounds, letting Laurene know that I would be later than I thought. I could tell from her flat voice that my father wasn't pleased.

"You can talk to the debate coach, if you'd like," I said. "To verify."

"No, thanks," she said. "We'll just see you when you get back. We might be asleep."

If I won, I could show him the trophy. I'd never won a trophy before, and it began to seem necessary to get it.

Day turned to night, the number of competitors who remained on the white sheet of paper pinned onto the wall after each round dwindled to very few, and when I walked into a room for what I heard were the semifinals (it wasn't clear), there were three judges instead of one.

I don't remember the look of any of the contestants I debated except the first, but I do remember the feeling in the room, during the final round, when I knew I was winning. It didn't take long. By that time I didn't care which side I got, my opinion papers were wrinkled from use. Any arguments could be overcome; I knew them all. We shook hands at the end. I felt a great magnanimous love for my opponent as well as for all the competitors who had come before.

Twenty minutes later, we gathered for the awards ceremony. "We have two winners in the Lincoln-Douglas category," the man said. He was holding only one trophy in his hand. I started up from my seat. "Unfortunately, we only seem to have one trophy, so I'm afraid it'll go to whoever gets up here first."

I was already scrambling up the steps to the stage, trying to look graceful and nonchalant. The other winner, I saw now, was the boy I'd debated first, who had probably won the first round, meaning that his opponents had been more difficult after that. But he had not been quick, and as I neared the podium, the man reached out with the trophy. I grabbed it, transferring it to my left hand as the boy arrived behind me. We shook hands, and smiled.

The next day, in the car with my father, I mentioned the tournament.

"I won the whole thing!" I lied. I'd pulled out the trophy that morning, but he hadn't seemed sufficiently impressed, so I'd brought it up again.

"I know, Lis. Maybe that's all you need," he said.

"What?"

"You're done. You proved it," he said.

"But that was just one. There are others. It might help me get into college."

"Better to debate in real life," he said. "Better to save it for when you need it. The club's kind of lame."

Off Highway 101 was a squat building set at an angle to the road. The marquee said Ruby's, with an image of tipping martini glasses.

"That's where Lis is going to work," my father said, pointing to it as we sped past, all of us in the car, me and my brother in the back. He'd made the joke before. Now I understood the place was a strip club. I pictured women in scenes from movies, women writhing naked on countertops inside. There were hardly any cars in the parking lot.

"Ha," I said, trying to play along.

When we got home, he played a CD in the living room. He'd been saying he wanted to play something for me for a while. "Listen," he said, chuckling, "This one's for you, Lis."

The song was "Short People," by the composer Randy Newman, who was writing the music for Pixar's *Toy Story*.

Toy Story would be the first fully computer-animated feature film, he said, bringing home tapes every week as work on the movie progressed. The tapes included drawn sketches interspersed with computer-animated segments and blank spots. There were various voices for the characters, some rough, some polished, some movie stars and some people filling in for movie stars—a patchwork movie in progress.

The lyrics to "Short People" made me laugh in spite of myself: I was five-two and wouldn't get any taller. As it played, he bobbed on his heels and looked at me and tried to sing along with the lyrics. He knew some of them. He tried to grab me to dance to it. My father was six feet, Laurene was five-seven. They'd measured my brother's height and doubled it, a trick Laurene knew, and it seemed he'd be tall as well. Height seemed to matter so much to them, as a sign of worldly promise.

◆ ◆ ◆

One day, when I got home from school, a computer was set up on my desk. It was matte black, with a pleated side vent and huge screen.

"I thought you might want one," he said, coming into my room. I'd been asking for a NeXT computer since I'd moved into his house; he and Laurene each had one. But he'd said no. It was too expensive, too nice, for a kid.

"Wow," I said. "Thanks." Why had he decided to give it to me now, without an occasion? I flipped the switch in the back; the computer didn't respond. "How do I turn it on?" I asked.

"Like this," he said, reaching around and ruffling the same switch. Still no response. I clicked a letter on the keyboard, clicked the mouse. Nothing. He took the screen by the corner and tipped it a few inches on the desk, toggled the on-off switch again. I crouched down under the desk, pulled the plug out, and pushed it back. He checked my desk light to make sure the outlet was working. It was.

"Well, Lis," he said. "I don't know."

When I returned from school the following day, the computer was gone, and it was never replaced.

For the entire year after my sixteenth birthday, whenever we were together, my father sang me the song about being sixteen and turning seventeen from *The Sound of Music*. He sang as he ascended the stairs, in his usual black shirt, white underwear, bare feet uniform, flinging his hand out over the banister like he was performing in a Broadway revue: "Innocent as a *ro-o-o-se*." I rolled my eyes, standing at the bottom of the stairs in the middle of the afternoon. But I loved it.

One Saturday my father, my brother, and I went for a walk, my father pushing my brother in his stroller. The air smelled of the overgrown rosemary in yards, and the asphalt, hot and cracked. "Wouldn't it be terrible to be impaled on that steeple?" he said when

we passed the church with its high cement point. He made a farting
sound with his cheeks: a steeple piercing the intestines.

The light and air seemed to have a golden presence, alive with
many lit particles. Pollen, maybe. We passed a park with pine trees
and suede-leaved magnolias. "You know, Lis," he said, "people from
the East Coast don't really understand the West Coast. They try, but
they just can't. It's not inside them." On the East Coast, he said,
people wore khakis to be casual. People there were nothing like us,
he said; they were phony and too formal, without the quality of holy
surrender we had because of these fragrant hills that smelled of
pepper and eucalyptus, all this watery sunlight. We wore jeans with
holes, he and I, and Birkenstocks.

I bobbed between different ideas of myself: on a weekend morning I was my father's confidante, the one like him, true like jeans,
the Stanford hills, Bob Dylan.

His cheek sometimes pulled up into a dimple at the top; I could
make the same dimple appear in my cheek. I avoided meat, butter,
cream, the foods he avoided. I'd started to walk like him, in admiration, falling forward at each step, and saying "sort of" this or that,
like him, because I thought it sounded sophisticated. My impression
of ways in which we were Californian and the ways in which we
were similar blended together.

We ended up at the corner of Cowper Street and North California Avenue, in front of a house with a split-rail fence. A rosebush
filled in the fence so it wasn't possible to see the house from the
sidewalk. The bright green stems with bright green thorns grew
straight out like spokes. The roses, not large, were every color of
sherbet and sunset: white, orange, baby pink, hot pink, magenta, red.
Each rose contained a variety of these colors different from those
of the rose beside it, and because of some trick of light or hue, they
seemed lit from within.

"These are so beautiful," my father said.

"I know," I said.

Neither one of us moved. We gazed at them, my brother asleep in the stroller. He and I see these the same way, I thought. We have the same vision. A great relief, to have someone besides my mother—and different from my mother—who saw things the way I did.

A few minutes later, a man walked out the front door of the house.

"What are these roses called?" my father asked.

"Joseph's coat," he said. "I guess because they're all different colors."

When we were back at the house, sitting at the table, I suggested that we switch eyeglasses. I was wearing the ones he'd bought for me—dark rimmed, by Oliver Peoples. They were large and bold on my face, with oxidized metal flourishes. His were rimless, two thin metal lines to the ears.

He removed his glasses slowly, using both hands.

"Careful," he said. "If you torque them, it ruins the lens." In my hands his glasses were thin-boned and alive, like an insect. Still warm from his face.

We put them on, looked at each other, and, at the same moment, we both chuckled. Our prescriptions were almost identical—nearsighted with an equivalent astigmatism in the left eye.

"Never pluck your eyebrows, especially not the middle part," he said. My brows grew in an uneven wave, one side rising up to the crest, the other crashing down. The edge of one reached toward the other. "If you pluck them, the hairs stop growing back, and then at some point you have to draw them in with a pencil." He contorted his face in disapproval or contempt. "You'll see," he said, reaching out to touch the middle where they met. "Those eyebrows are your best feature."

"Hey, I drew you a bath," he said, a few days later, in the evening.

I went into the bathroom and saw he'd lit candles and placed them on the shelf above the sink and along the rim of the tub. Rose petals floated on the surface of the water, which glowed yellow-gold from the candles. He must have torn petals off the roses outside.

One morning around then I walked into the kitchen. He was reading the paper; Laurene was looking through the mail. When I stepped into the room, he lowered the paper and looked at me.

"Lis?"

"Yes?"

"Do you masturbate?" The question hung in the air. The answer was that I didn't. I'd never tried it. I knew what the word meant, but wasn't sure how to do it myself. Once in dance class years before in the middle of a series of moves, a gust or wind of pleasure had overtaken me, unbidden, and I ran out of the dance studio into the changing room, flushed and confused.

I didn't say anything and stood very still.

"Well, you should," he said, and lifted the paper back up again.

♦

In the fall of junior year, when the pressure to get the grades to get into college was at its peak, my father asked me to go to Hawaii with the family. Mona would be coming too.

"I don't think I can get out of class," I said.

We were sitting together in the hallway, on a dark wooden bench with wide planks, one of the only pieces of furniture in that part of the house.

"If you can't manage to go on this trip," he said, "you shouldn't consider yourself part of this family. Lis . . ." He paused, as if about to say more, then pinched his lips and shook his head.

"Okay, I'll go," I said, quickly, to stop him from elaborating.

The following day I lied to my teachers, who were required to sign a form for my absence, saying I was going on an extended trip to visit colleges. The chemistry teacher, Ms. Lawrence, shook her head, but signed. The history teacher, Mrs. Warren, looked at me with surprise, but signed nonetheless. How would I be able to visit colleges, I wondered, now they thought I'd already been? How would I report on towns I had never seen, when they asked? How would I hide freckles and suntan?

I'd have to figure out how to spin it once I got back. Maybe I'd stay inside.

The day we arrived in Hawaii, I followed my father down to the beach, the sand flecked with lava crumbs and hot under my bare feet. Beneath a few palms was an open structure with a thatched roof called the Beach Shack, where you could borrow equipment and sign up on a clipboard for activities: snorkeling, catamaran rides, scuba lessons.

Here the sand was cool. In the shade beside the shack, standing on a pole between two beams, was a bright green macaw with a black tongue. My father had saved a piece of a roll from lunch, and now he held it out to the parrot. The bird leaned forward, jutting out its neck and chest, black-skinned talons gripping the pole. It arced forward as if on a hinge, stepping and clutching the pole and opening its black beak to reveal a stub of tongue shaped like the topmost joint of a pinkie. The tongue lifted in anticipation, and then—my father pulled the bread away. The parrot swung back and stood straight on the pole, closed its beak.

"Hey," I said. "Let him have it."

"Wait a sec," he said.

Again, my father presented the bread, just out of reach; the parrot leaned forward, slowly opening its hinged beak, the black space inside large as a pillbox. Again, my father pulled the bread away before the parrot could reach it.

"This is boring," I said.

He kept going, developing a rhythm. The parrot leaned, he withdrew, the parrot straightened again, ruffling his green feathers. Each time, I worried the bird would tip and spin down around the pole—its wings were clipped.

"It's not nice. You're torturing him."

"It's an experiment," he said. "To see if he'll learn."

I waited to see if my father would listen and stop or get tired of the game, or if the parrot would wise up. Neither thing happened so I left.

I saw him later, smiling and looking refreshed. "Isn't it wonderful here?" he said. All around us the birdsong was continuous and varied, the trill patterns overlapping.

Dinner took place in the same hall where breakfast was served. We were seated at one of the round tables at the front of the hall near the door and the big windows that were mirrors in the dark. Hawaiian music was piped in from a small band of three outside, sad-happy harmonies. Our waiter, a petite woman with long, dark hair flecked with gray, came to take our order. I'd seen her earlier, walking with a little boy I thought must be her son.

My father ordered a carrot salad. "I'd like it shredded into pieces this size"—he held his fingers an inch apart—"with half a lemon on the side. Can I also have a large glass of orange juice, fresh squeezed? Not those little glasses. The big one." He gestured the shape of the glass, the top and bottom. He lisped when he enunciated carefully.

"We'll do the best we can with that, sir." She'd said it kindly, dismissively, looking down and writing on her notepad. My father leaned his chair so far back that his chin was almost level with his knees. I sensed danger.

She looked up at Mona, ready for the next order.

"I'd like a white fish," Mona said. "What would you suggest?" Mona was polite, her voice small and sweet.

"There's the ono, a white fish like snapper," the waitress said. "Or the ahi, also fresh today, although that's a denser fish."

"I'd like the ono please. Could I have it poached, with no butter and just a tiny bit of olive oil? And a few steamed vegetables on the side?"

Fish and vegetables, no butter? It was as if she'd peeled off from my contingent to become one of the adults; as if she would be less my friend on this trip, more theirs. Laurene ordered simply too, a salad. I ordered the fettuccini Alfredo.

"I did a little experiment on the parrot," my father said. "The one on the beach. It turns out they are just so dumb."

"He tortured it," I said.

"They can't really learn," he said. "They just have this set pattern. It's fascinating."

The waitress returned with the food, his salad a pile of matchstick carrots cut by machine and set on a side-salad plate like a sloppy garnish. The carrots were oxidized, raspy white at the edges. The surface of the lemon—a wedge, not a half—pulled in at the rind

and would crack when squeezed. The waitress handed out the rest
of the dishes. I showed my contentment more than I might have at
another time, as compensation for whatever had changed in the air.

My father was looking at the carrots. He touched one of them,
then pulled his hand away as if repelled. "Wait," he said, as the
waitress walked off. "This isn't what I want."

"But you said—"

This woman with her kind face and her tired eyes—she should
not have argued back. She wouldn't see the difference between what
he wanted and what she'd brought; you could tell she found his request
tiresome and extravagant. I knew she'd have to appear interested in
what might please him. Walk away, woman, I thought at her.

"I can try to change it, sir," she said, too formally.

She pulled the plate away, and while she was still within earshot,
my father said, "It's too bad the dinner is crap here. Everything else
is so great. And then this shit."

"Steve, try the fish," Mona said. "There's no butter." She pushed
her plate toward him. He looked but didn't taste. I could tell, by his
tight half smile, that he was preparing for an attack.

Near him was the safest place to be when he attacked someone
else.

I wanted to move permanently across the invisible line between
being in danger and being safe, from the outer to the inner circle—
and the price of the possibility of safety was having to watch him
attack this woman. Suffering did not diminish or grow but was
allocated, redistributed from person to person. If I leapt out to defend
her, he might turn on me. An attack on one person had the effect
of lifting the others up; for me, the relief of being safe in the midst
of danger created a floating sensation.

On the first trip to Hawaii with Laurene, he'd pointed to my
bathing suit and said, "Why don't you get one like hers?" comparing
us, and I'd felt, despite myself, like the best person for having the
right thing.

Later I thought of how each of us at the table had, at some point when we were young, lost our father. He was the patriarch, and he'd paid for all of us to be here. The mood was tense.

The waitress returned with a bowl, more carrots—fresh and old, combined. She brought a new lemon wedge and the orange juice.

"Is this what you were looking for?" she asked, as if she thought it might be right.

"Actually, no," he said. "This isn't at all what I was looking for. Does anyone know how to do their job here?" he said. "Seriously. You don't. I asked for fresh carrots."

"Sir, I've asked the kitchen to do the carr—"

"No. No. You obviously *haven't* asked. This is the same shit you brought me last time."

"I'm sorry," she said, a tremor in her voice. "I'll take it back."

"I think that would be a good idea," he said. "You should think about why you're here and whether you are actually doing your job. Because so far what you're doing is crap. Everything you've done is crap. You just bring this shit again and again. I would like shaved carrots and lemon in a bowl." He made a gesture to show the size of the bowl.

"Yes, I understand, but—"

"All I'm asking for is the *simplest* thing. Do you have carrots."

"Yes, but—"

"Do you have a lemon."

"Yes." She stood very still.

"Do you have a grater back there in the kitchen." He leaned his chair back and looked toward the kitchen opening across the carpeted floor.

"Yes."

"Okay. I'd like you to tell them to take three carrots and grate them like this," he motioned pressing a carrot down a metal grater. The ends of his words were sharp as whips. "And then bring it out with a lemon."

"The kitchen grates the carrots in advance." She was crying but trying not to show it. "I'll ask them what they can do." She started to walk away. He moved in slow motion, looking down at the disappointment on his plate as if he'd suffered a tragedy.

"You know what," he called out to her across the carpet. "Don't bother about the carrots. Can I see the menu again?"

She brought it and waited near him.

"I'll just have this." He pointed to a pan-seared fish. "Except I'd like it to be steamed, not fried. I don't want any butter or any cream. I don't want anything with it. Just the plain fish."

She wrote it down. She didn't say anything. This fish would not please him, either, without the ingredients that gave it taste. I knew this. He liked butter, he just didn't like the idea of it. He should have ordered what Mona had. This resort kitchen would not get it right when he invented the dishes and had so many rules.

The rest of us had almost finished when she returned with his fish: white on a white plate with a cloudy drip of cooking water leaking from the side. This time the manager came out and stood beside her, a squat man with a mustache.

With the edge of one tine of his fork, my father pulled up a piece of white flesh the size of a matchstick and put it into his mouth. He winced.

"It's not any good, but thanks anyway." He dropped the fork. He looked wounded.

"We're sorry it's not what you wanted, Steve," the manager said. "What can we do so you'll be happy with your dinner?"

"Nothing. You can't do anything. Too bad your dinners are so bad," He leaned the chair back, smiling the tight smile. "But, you know, the rest of this place is great. So I guess that's just the way it is."

"We'll do everything we can so this doesn't happen again," the manager said.

As we walked back from dinner, the geckos chirped, their bodies twirling around the poles of the low lights beside the white sand paths. Laurene wore a white dress that glowed in the near-dark. Walking along the paths, I felt we were all inside the movie *Citizen Kane*. My father had come over a few afternoons when I was younger and whispered, "Rosebud" to me, like a growl, before we went to see the movie at the newly reopened Stanford Theatre. I hadn't thought much of the story, but the sets, the palm fronds and long shadows, the glowing white clothing, the torches, reminded me of this place, so that I felt swept up in a fantastical world.

The next day we discovered that a friend of my father's, Larry Ellison, was at the resort too. He wore a straw hat. After lunch I sat with Larry and my dad at a table on the lava rocks that jutted out near the ocean. Larry said he'd been reading about how evolution didn't happen in gradual stages but bounded and stuttered—that, if you looked at the fossil record, there wasn't a linear progression. It was impossible for animals to have adapted at the rate they did through gradual random mutation.

They made business jokes I didn't understand. Larry had a low voice but he laughed high and fast as if he'd sucked on a balloon, as if the man who spoke was a different man from the one who laughed. He'd arrived with one woman who flew home on a United flight that day. Another woman was flying in to visit him tomorrow, he said. The second woman also wore high heels, and was unaware of the first.

My father grabbed me and squeezed. His affection surprised me, seemed complete, and then vanished, and then reappeared, like the two different landscapes on the island.

"What do you think, hon," I overheard my father say to Laurene the next day. "If you gave a kid a trip to this resort in Hawaii every year or sent them to college, which one would be better?"

"I don't know," she said. "This place is pretty great."

"I think it might be best to just bring them here every year. That might be better than college, if you weigh the two."

Were they joking? He didn't mind being strange compared with other parents. At restaurants, he blew his nose right into cloth napkins. I should have asked about college before coming on this trip; I hadn't considered the possibility that in agreeing to one, I might be forfeiting the other. I am a girl who goes on vacations, I'd thought, *and* I am a girl who will go to college. It was an entitled way of thinking, I knew, and I liked thinking it. Both. Now, so many virgin piña coladas in, the trip was spent. How much did it cost to come here? It must have been less than college. I didn't know. I regretted everything about it. The smells and the trees and the birds made me sick.

"Yes, I think that would be worth it," Laurene said, "in the balance." She said it in her joke voice. Maybe she thought he would never do it, not really. How ridiculous, I wanted her to say.

"What did you tell your teachers?" my mother asked when I called her on the white resort phone, one of two phones stationed in a room near the reception office.

"I told them I was going on a college trip," I said. "If I'd told them the truth, they wouldn't have let me go."

"I'll tell them," she said. I hadn't imagined there was a way out of it, other than continuing to lie. I'd been staying inside, to avoid tanning.

I gave her the names of my teachers, the classrooms, and the following morning she went to the school and spoke to them, telling them I could not find a way out of it and had lied because I was ashamed. When I returned to school, I got a few quizzical looks from teachers, and Ms. Lawrence teased me, but soon the matter was forgotten.

On one of our last nights in Hawaii, I stood on the place where the lava overhung the ocean, near the restaurant. Below me I watched a series of tiny waves lapping, illuminated by a dim lamp attached to the bottom of the overhang. The warm wind swirled, and I saw a fish lit up and swimming out toward darker water, a bright star hanging far above it. In that moment I saw—sensed, really—a cord strung between the fish and the star, connecting them. It was silvery and strong, like a rope, distinct, obvious, as if it were really there.

There was no unimportant, no negligible, being, I felt, just then; something as small and seemingly insignificant as one fish in the slapping ocean was connected to the galactic immensity.

I told Laurene and my father about the fish and the star soon after we returned to Palo Alto. We were sitting in the car, in the parking lot of the Tower Records in Redwood City, where we'd come to buy CDs. My father turned off the engine. My brother was asleep in the car seat beside me. To my surprise, they remained in the front seat and let me finish the story, speaking from the back seat. Usually they were in a rush. They sat very still, facing the windshield, listening.

♦

If I hoped Laurene would save me, I also wanted to save her, and imagined myself as her savior, powerful and generous. One day she had turned to me in the kitchen and said, "I was too young."

"For what?"

"Marriage," she'd said dryly.

She'd harvested cauliflower from the garden and put it to steam in the new Alessi pot my father had recently brought home, about which he'd been excited, showing us that it rounded out at the sides instead of being straight, a cauldron-shaped pot that was made of the same materials, at the same price point, as an ordinary pot. But you could see the impact of a better design. "It's so simple, and so beautiful," he said, turning it under the kitchen lights.

Laurene had gone upstairs and forgotten about the cauliflower, and the water at the bottom had boiled dry and ruined the pan. The idea of getting another one didn't occur to me, and I had no idea where he'd bought it or even how much pans cost, and anyway we didn't have time to buy another before he got home. The kitchen was filled with smoke. "Oh shoot. *Shoot*," she said, opening all the windows and the door and fanning furiously with a newspaper. I'd never seen her panic before; she was usually calm. I helped her fan. The house smelled like sugar and carbon and burnt metal. We both fanned furiously.

He sometimes pointed out how she came from New Jersey and had wide feet, and how she liked the wrong kind of trees. The cauldron pot might symbolize a whole realm of aesthetics he felt she didn't have. ("She doesn't have taste," he'd said to dinner guests, after she left the room.) When he saw the burnt pot, he might be unkind to her for it, as if here was further evidence that she would lay ruin to his refinement.

She could do better than him, I thought. I would rescue her; we could rescue each other, drive off in her white BMW, like in *Thelma & Louise*. I was overcome with affection for her, how in spite of it all she kept being positive, kept working hard to make her company succeed. She understood that life took a certain relentlessness, she continued despite his disapproval, and this forward motion was a model for me. If she was hesitant to leave because she thought no one else noticed, or she doubted her own perceptions, *I* noticed, *I* saw. I wanted her to have fulfillment and joy, I believed in her capacities, and I thought that my confidence and my encouragement might be just what she needed to escape.

Afterward, the close feeling between us did not remain. It surprised me, each time we were close, that it did not stay, but snapped back and became more formal. My father, displeased about the burnt pot, was taciturn for days.

I was still seeing the same therapist, Dr. Lake. I'd been seeing him once a week since I was nine, my father paying for the weekly sessions. His office was a room on Welch Road near the Stanford Hospital. He was tall, with dark hair and a kindly face. When I'd first started coming to him, he'd let me paint a doll with nail polish and ruin it, not complaining when I gave her a short skirt, scissored her hair into a frizzy zag. Now I sat on a daybed against a wall, and he sat in an Eames chair facing me. Sometimes we played checkers or chess. He had a jar of Oreo cookies; part of the reason I'd agreed to keep seeing him years before was the accessibility of these cookies, which I was allowed to eat at will. Before he worked on Welch Road, when he worked at a different office, we would sometimes walk to the Fosters Freeze down the road, talking as we walked. Now we sometimes walked to the Häagen-Dazs in the Stanford Barn where he bought us ice cream. "Freud would roll in his grave," he joked.

After asking for several months, I finally persuaded my father and Laurene to come along with me for a session. I had a crazy idea that Dr. Lake would say something to them, or he would be silent when they said something, and they would just *get* it. Then they'd agree to all my (reasonable, I thought) ideas, like getting a couch, saying goodnight, and heat. His presence would make them unable to deny how *reasonable* I was.

My father and Laurene had dressed for the occasion—how coupled and taut they looked, walking in—she smelling of soap and pressed linen, wearing a crisp white shirt and the small, gold-rimmed glasses my father had bought for her. My father had put on a new black shirt, and jeans without holes. It looked as if he'd just gotten a haircut.

Dr. Lake had arranged four wooden chairs with black foam-covered arms around a wooden desk. They sat down, backs straight. I had long since abandoned formality around Dr. Lake, and I hoped they would find him comforting too, with his teddy-bear nature, his corduroy trousers, his messy but thoughtfully designed office.

"We're here to talk about Lisa," Dr. Lake said.

Silence. I knew Dr. Lake was good at allowing long silences, and sometimes, in order to get him to speak, I would have to let time pass, an uncomfortable pause beyond what seemed reasonable.

I cleared my throat. "I've been feeling so lonely," I said. "I was hoping that you could . . . that we could figure something out." I paused and looked at Laurene, who held her face very still, as if it was a representation of her face and not her real face.

"I'm feeling terribly alone," I tried again. Still they didn't speak.

I looked at Dr. Lake; he didn't speak either.

We waited. I wished that I wanted less, needed less, was one of those succulents that have a tangle of wiry, dry roots and a minty congregation of leaves and can survive on only the smallest bit of moisture and air.

After what seemed an interminable silence, I burst into tears. I hoped it would soften them, that my messiness would give them permission to be messy. I wasn't perfect or straight-backed or smooth; I didn't require them to be so either.

Laurene finally spoke. "We're just cold people," she said. She said it dryly, like a clarification.

You're allowed to say that? I thought. How incredible; that's what struck me later: that she had dared to say it. How good it would be to know one's limitations and say them with unapologetic conviction. Her tone was deadpan. I had thought I could shame them for being cold and absent. Now I was the one who was ashamed, for ignoring the simple truth.

How obvious it was—they were just cold people! The clarity of the pronouncement stopped my tears. I looked to my father, who did not speak. He isn't cold, I thought; he just withholds his affection in a pattern I can't predict or control. In the end, maybe it added up to the same thing.

Our time was up. We filed out of the office together, Dr. Lake surprising himself, he told me later, by what he said to them in the hallway between the office and the waiting room as they walked out: "You were just as I expected you to be."

"You've got to trust in your life," my father said, coming into my room that night as I sat at my desk copying notes in small handwriting on small note cards for memorization. "If you trust your intuition, and listen to it, it will speak louder. Ever heard of the concept Be Here Now?"

What did it mean? Something about existing in the moment. But I had homework to do. I found most of the work boring, motivating myself with the idea of Harvard. To be here now was to be miserable.

"Lis," he said.

"What?"

"You should smoke some pot," he said.

I was too serious, was the implication. But I didn't trust him. I was a junior. Grades mattered.

"I'll do it with you," he said. "If you want."

"No, thanks," I said. He'd make me lose my motivation in a stupor of weed (or so I imagined). Then he could say, See, she wasn't worth it.

"You'll be a hippie someday," he said. "Trust me."

"No, I won't," I said. I knew he meant the word as some kind of shorthand for peace and relaxation. But I'd known hippies before I'd known him—men who wore brown and let their hair grow. The memory left a dusty taste in my mouth.

"Suit yourself," he said, and walked out of my room, springing on the heels of his Birkenstocks, whistling, as if to parade his own peace and happiness before me.

Later that night I dreamt that a classmate I hardly knew named Josh and I hovered, side by side, above the hills that wrinkled up west of the town. Josh and I were in the same English class and also on the staff of the school newspaper, but we'd hardly ever talked. In the dream we were wearing special backpacks that allowed us to float. We bobbed in the air, lazily, looking toward San Francisco in the distance: the spikes and glints of high buildings and Victorian houses in slanting pastel arcs and, beyond them, the bright, friendly Pacific Ocean lapping against the shore. The city was more vivid than in life, both far away and near, the perspective foreshortened, the way certain atmospheric conditions will make distant things appear alternately far away and very close.

In the dream I looked at Josh, joy welling up like a balloon rising from my chest into my throat. I was so excited I had to be careful to say the words slowly, to not let them rip out: "Let's go," I said. We bobbed slowly forward toward the great metropolis—the most thrilling city I knew.

The next morning in class, I leaned over my desk and tapped him on the shoulder before Mrs. Paugh arrived.

"Hey, I had a dream about you last night."

He turned around to face me. "Uh-oh," he said, smiling. "What was it about?"

"We flew to San Francisco. Floated, actually. I mean we had these flotational backpacks."

"Well, we should do it then," he said. "We should—" but then Mrs. Paugh arrived, and Josh turned to face the front, and class began.

At my mother's house I was vaguely aware that at some point, maybe when I left for college, the child-support checks from Jeff Howson would stop arriving. My mother had no other reliable source of income. She must have been aware of this too, and also wanted to be independent of my father.

She approached each new moneymaking idea with fervor and optimism. She admired Mrs. Fields, who made the chocolate chip cookies, and Nancy of Nancy's Quiche, women who'd made a fortune in business. But what she failed to account for is that it wasn't just the quality of the product that turned ideas into money, but business savvy—marketing and strategy know-how.

Once my mother planned to have a garage sale, but until the day before, she didn't put up any signs. We had nice things to sell, nicer things than in most garage sales, but few people knew about it; almost no one came. She was likewise not methodical about selling her art. When her stencils didn't sell at Neiman Marcus or Smith & Hawken, or get snapped up via word of mouth, she was discouraged, and put her hope in a new project, floor cloths—paintings that went on the floor. They were colorful acrylic squares and rectangles of unmounted canvas—deep plum and rich orange and all different shades of green. Ripe fruits, blossoms, and leaves in patterns, some stenciled, some painted, lacquered with expensive Jolly Glaze she poured over the paint to protect it that cracked pleasingly like the surface of old porcelain. She and her friend were both working on them, but her friend had no artistic training; hers were far better.

Canvases were strung up along the walls of her studio in various states of completion, along with used stencil patterns hanging up to dry. I liked sitting in the garage with her as she painted. She seemed to forget about me and dissolved into a deeper part of herself.

When she tapped the stencil brush up and down, it sounded like a faraway woodpecker.

I picked at the splotches on the board she used as a palette—indigo, carmine, white, gamboge, which seemed to be a dull, pasty brown but when mixed with water became electric yellow, the color of a mosquito whine. The top layer of the glob of paint was hard, but if I pressed, wet paint inside came oozing out. To clean the paintbrushes, she knocked them against the inside walls of the metal jar of turpentine.

When we heard my father call out, we left the garage and went to find him in the house. He hadn't come over for years; I wasn't sure why he'd come this day. He stood in the middle of the kitchen, too straight, wearing a gray sweatshirt with a hood threaded with a red cord that hung on either side of the neck. He looked around as if mildly disappointed.

"Steve," she said. "How are you doing?"

"Great," he said. "What are you working on?" He moved his shoulder and scapula like he was carving a semicircle in the air.

"Floor cloths," she said.

"What's that?" he asked.

"They're paintings, but underfoot," she said, toeing a pomegranate painted on a piece of canvas under the sink. "They're mats, really, for in the kitchen, or wherever, but they've got a protective coating. Anyway, I'm doing them with a friend, and we think there's definitely a market. We might sell them at Macy's or Neiman Marcus."

I knew she wanted his approval and recognition; we both wanted it. He knew about business; he knew about money and the world; he was a success. She became voluble but also unsure, especially when he was about to be unkind—as if she knew he was going to be cruel and knew how to smoke out the meanness first.

I watched them take their places as if in a familiar choreography: she had said she wanted to be free of him, and he had said he wanted to be free of her, but yet, after all these years, they were still entangled; they would thrash around in a single net, becoming more stuck.

"I'm also doing stencils," she said.

"Show me," he said. She took him through the screen door under the purple blossoms and the greedy whine of bees into the cool studio. I followed them. He looked around, putting his face up close to each painting, saying nothing—as if he knew what to look for. We hung back near the door where it was still warm, waiting for a verdict.

"You know, Chris," he finally said, in a friendly tone, "you might as well just have some more kids."

As he left the garage, he seemed lighter, looser. He waved, walked to his car, and drove away. My mother and I stood in shock at the back of the driveway.

When I went back to my father's house, Mona arrived for a visit with her husband, Richie, for a weekend. My father had a cold. He was in a dark mood. I avoided him, slipping out of rooms when he entered them, trying to stick near Mona and Richie, who were funny and warm, and feeling panicked when they went for a walk and left me alone in the house with him.

At some point I was hungry and went into the kitchen and found him there standing at the counter, eating from a bag of almonds.

"How's homework going?" he asked. I could tell he was preoccupied with something, worried.

"Fine," I said, bracing.

"The thing is, Lis," he said, in the slow voice that meant he was about to say something incisive and possibly devastating, "you have no marketable skills. Not one." He popped another almond into his mouth. The subject seemed to come from nowhere—why were we talking about marketable skills midmorning on a Saturday?

"But I'm doing all these activities," I said, "and I get A's!" And yet even as I said it—the newspaper, mock trial, the fact that I'd worked at a lab over the summer, and took Japanese—I wilted. I got his point. The confection of extracurricular activities, the flurry of self-importance—it was just a fever dream. No one hires someone for being on a debate team. I had not impressed him or fooled him. He knew all this stuff wasn't worth much, and he was worried for my future.

I assumed that activities led to other activities in a ladder ascending to adult responsibility. I wasn't supposed to be prepared for an adult job. Others seemed to think that too. At the same time, because he spoke with authority, and because I had been hoping to impress him, and because he was famous and successful and knew about the world, the remark was devastating.

"I wouldn't lose sleep over it," Mona said. "He's just being silly." I wanted her to say he was totally insane—to make him recant—in part because I worried he was right, if not about now, then about later, that I'd never be a success, never be able to get a job.

We all made allowances for his eccentricities, the ways he attacked other people, because he was also brilliant, and sometimes kind and insightful. Now I felt he'd crush me if I let him. He would tell me how little I meant over and over until I believed it. What use was his genius to me?

I was weary of going back and forth between my parents' houses. I decided to split the remaining time before college in half, six months with each. I knew my father would not like the idea. The truth is, I would have moved back into my mother's house, but I worried this would make him furious, and I didn't want to leave Reed.

I'd figured out that to negotiate effectively, you must be willing to give up the thing you want, entirely, for something else; you need a fierce apathy. Since he'd said I had no marketable skills, something had shifted and loosened inside me. Things were not going to work out with him the way I'd hoped when I'd moved in.

I waited for him to walk into the hallway after lunch that weekend, sitting on the side of the door.

"Can I talk to you for a minute?"

"Yup," he said, and sat beside me on the dark wooden bench.

"I'm sure you know how difficult it is for me to go back and forth," I said. "The two houses are polar opposites. I'd like to split the year." I was shaking. The trick was to make the request before revealing the underbelly, the girders and joists, the pylons.

"But you're already at two months," he said. "In fact, I'd like you to start coming more frequently. I don't like the way you've been doing this. If you want to be part of this family, you're going to have

to be here more. You know what? Nope," he said. "It's not all right."
Other people sought resolution, but he could sustain a dissonant
note.

He got up and started to walk away.

"If you won't let me split it," I said, as if in passing, "I'm going
to go to my mom's house for the whole year."

I watched him from the corner of my eye. He seemed to deflate,
all at once. I'd never negotiated with him and won.

"I—" he turned back. "Well, okay. Fine." The winning felt
uncomfortable, as though I'd wounded him.

I felt an obligation to be merciful. "Let me know which half
you'd like," I said.

"I'll think about it," he said, walking away.

I'd won. It wasn't much; it was a step. I would get away. I would
work toward freedom—one day, I would dangle my limbs from a
car window beneath high arching branches.

Flight

In my senior year at Paly, I was elected to the position of editor in chief of the paper. Now it would be me and three others who would edit the pages and finally deliver the paper to the press late at night. The editors in chief from previous years had seemed to me impossibly mature and knowledgeable. Now we would be the ones to look that way to others.

That year, we published articles about how the school board, amid massive layoffs, had given credit cards to staff members who treated themselves to, among other things, an expensive lunch at MacArthur Park. After the series of articles came out, the head of the school board resigned.

In the middle of one week, there were technical problems.

The computer system crashed, the screens went dark, the printer became inaccessible. If the computers no longer operated and would not reboot, days of work would be lost—all of our carefully designed pages. Josh, his dirty-blond hair the color of a sand dune worn in a thick ponytail, lay down on the floor to inspect and arrange the wires. The rest of us mulled in a daze of terror and tragedy. He always managed to fix it—the computers would sputter back to life, and the printer would aspirate and spit paper again.

"Do you want to come?" he asked me, about a trip to his house to get a missing cord. I noticed Josh more closely: dimples when he smiled, wide shoulders beneath flannel shirts. He was shy, and friendly, and had loose, complicated handwriting, like the bouncing string of a kite.

"Sure," I said, not knowing then that he lived in Portola Valley, twenty minutes away. His mother and stepfather were lawyers and had managed to get him permission to transfer to Palo Alto School District based on some provision about their commute to work.

He seemed, to me, sloppy. Too relaxed, shambolic. He could fix computers, but he was disorganized, forgetting to do his assignments for Mrs. Paugh's English class, whereas I was meticulous, a grade-grubber. He never arrived anywhere on time, and he was hopeless with a calendar, wouldn't have his homework and scrambled to do it in the minutes before class. (Later I would find out that he was taking applied mathematics and differential equations at Stanford, and he would be admitted to college at Stanford and MIT.)

He drove a used '83 Toyota Supra in incandescent teal with a pink sine wave painted along both sides. "Sorry about the paint job," he said as we got in. He'd bought it used from a female physicist in Livermore. He had nice hands on the steering wheel.

His room had a mattress on the floor and a window looking out to a yard and the forest. There were papers and books strewn around, a stack of stereo equipment and headphones. It was large enough to seem empty and cluttered at the same time. He found the cord, and we left.

On the way back we turned onto Arastradero, a two-lane road, rough and patched, that wound beside a nature preserve.

"I'm going to show you a secret," he said. "Hang on."

The speed limit was twenty-five; he began to accelerate. We advanced toward a blind corner where the road rose up and then disappeared, a hill on one side, a drop on the other. The road curled back on itself, around the hill, out of sight. Another car might be advancing toward us and smash into us at the bend; a family of deer might be walking across.

He continued to build speed, shifting up: third, fourth, fifth. The car rumbled and whined.

"Are you sure you should be—"

"Don't worry," he yelled. "I've done it before."

My mother sometimes said, There are guardian angels just for teenagers.

Oh, help me, God of Teenagers, I thought. Oh God of Teenagers.

"Hold on!" he yelled. The car scraped, the gears sang. I gripped the top of the seat belt in one hand, the door handle in the other. He shifted again, peeled around the blind curve—

And then we flew.

It was because of the uneven road—a raised portion followed by a long dip downhill. If you got up enough speed, you could catch the lip of the up and fly over the concavity, through the dots of light cast by the row of emerald trees and bushes growing alongside the road.

For me, the flight unlidded the town.

There were hidden places of freedom, and he knew them.

After we delivered the third paper a few months later, the other editors in chief—Rebecca, Nicole, Tom—and I stood together near Nicole's car in the school parking lot in the late afternoon. Most of the other cars were gone, and copper light slanted through pine trees in between the parking spaces. In the distance I saw a couple approaching, holding hands.

It was Josh, wearing a too-big white shirt and trousers that looked like harlequin pants. I found out later he'd made them himself with scraps of cloth, first mixing up the waist and the ankles and then starting again. He strolled toward us, his legs wide and bending at impact with the ground. I didn't know the girl. She was pretty and thin, with wavy honey-colored hair. They unclasped hands as they got closer.

"Hey, Josh," Tom said. "We just delivered the paper."

I felt my face muscles go slack. I had pitied him before, thinking him undesirable; now that he was with another girl, I felt shy and embarrassed and small, standing there near the two of them.

I biked home and cried to Carmen, who ran her fingers through my hair. An hour later, someone clanked open the gate. I looked over the rosebushes. Josh had never come over before, but we had friends in common, so he knew where I lived. He had a bounce in his step as he walked to the door, the white linen shirt swaying over the patchwork pants.

I invited him in and he followed me to my room. The whole thing was strange, how I hoped fervently that he'd come over, even if he'd never done so before, and now he was here.

"What's up?" I said, standing in the middle of the room under the box-shaped lantern.

"I thought you seemed upset just now." He stood nearby, his legs apart, his chest high.

"You were with that other girl," I said.

"She's older," he said. "She goes to Stanford."

"It's just—I didn't realize that I liked you and now it's too late."

"We're just friends. I don't know her that well. Anyhow the truth is—"

"What?" I asked.

"I've had a crush on you since freshman year. Since Living Skills," he said. We had been partners during the section on CPR, although I had forgotten. How was it possible that someone had liked me during those years, when I was new to the school and to my father's house and didn't have any friends?

He leaned toward me on one foot and we kissed. Everything was perfect and fluttered open. "Bye," he said, after that, and smiled. He walked out, his linen shirt rippling behind him, and I ran to the kitchen to tell Carmen.

"What are you going to be when you grow up?" my father asked Josh when they met. We were sitting with him on the floor in my brother's room, near the bookshelf—the first time I'd been alone with the two of them.

"I don't know yet," Josh said.

"I know," my father said. "You're going to be a bum."

Josh looked down.

When I told my mother, she reminded me my father had called himself a bum in high school, when she introduced him to her father, and that he sometimes used his own stories as templates for his idea of perfection.

It was a compliment, even though it didn't seem so.

Sometimes, after dark, Josh and I would drive to the Woodside house to make out. There were no lights, but you could see the white house, the white mist and silver dew on the lawn sloping down toward the significant trees.

"He said he was going to build a slide from there to there. Into the pool," I said, pointing up. "But he never did."

The bedroom and the bed were still the same as when I'd stayed with my father on Wednesday nights. The mattress was still on the floor beside the television. On a dresser was a framed picture of my father and Tina at a party, her wearing a black dress. When he talked about Tina, he said wistfully that she never wore dresses, but there she was. His suits were gone from the closet.

"Follow me," I said. I took off my shoes and ran through the wet lawn, and whooped, down the slope toward the oak trees. There was no one around. It smelled of cardamom pods, eucalyptus buttons, pepper, water, and bark. The sky was low and heavy with stars.

Some stars were dim and fuzzy, and others were pointed and bright, they were messy and close, the sky demanded notice.

"He bought the house for the trees," I said slowly, in a British accent like Laurence Olivier.

"I would have bought it for the house," Josh said. Looking back, it was all white arches covered in moonlight, white as salt. It gave me a shiver, the way it looked stark and alone.

"Me too." I said, "but he says the house is shit."

The trampoline was covered in leaves from the oak trees. We climbed on and jumped. There was no wall or guard around it. We hit each other in midair.

"What's over there?"

It was a smaller house on the property, also his—empty. From up here you could see its white outline and, past that, hills. "Seven acres," I said in the British accent.

If we didn't go to the Woodside house, Josh would drive over to the Waverley house at night, careful not to clink the ring on the gate. He would creep through the rose garden and climb through my window into my bed, his hands ice cold because he drove with all the windows down. He would stay with me until early morning, then sneak out again through the window or the sliding glass door, and drive home again.

"What if we found out Josh was coming over every night," my father asked at breakfast, "sneaking through the window." I gulped, didn't say anything, and he didn't mention it again. I managed to convince myself he might not know.

"Are you and Josh going to the Woodside house to make out?" he asked me a few days later. Josh and I had been discovered by a gardener they'd recently hired from Australia, who was staying in the house unbeknownst to me and who'd followed the sound of music and found us one night in an empty room on the second floor.

No one had mentioned the gardener was staying there. I thought
of lying, or saying we'd been there only once, but the freedom I'd
have if he said okay seemed worth the risk.

"Yes," I said. "Are you okay with that?"

"I guess so," he said.

"It happened," I said. We sat side by side on the edge of my bed.
"The final base." I was seventeen, a senior.

"Was it all right?" he asked.

"It was." I did not tell my father that at first the angle was
wrong, and so for a little while we thought sex would not be possible
for us, that we were built incompatibly, that the parts did not fit the
way they should.

Sometimes, in the late afternoon after school during the weeks
when we were not producing the newspaper, Josh and I went to
Windy Hill preserve, up above Skyline, hills wide and yellow and
soft like the humps of camels, on one side more hills like a blanket
thrown out into the wind all the way to the Pacific Ocean. The town
was a miniature below us, silent and still except for the singing,
rasping wind that flattened the tall grasses. A clear day, too much
to take in, the glassy air, and the feeling of great freedom and grace,
the world opening. I looked north and I could see San Francisco
sparkling in the distance, but clear like it was close. It was like the
way I'd seen it in the hovering dream, both close and far away,
something to do with the angle from this hill to those hills, the
refraction of the light.

That's how I felt about my parents now that Josh was around,
not that I didn't worry about how my mom would earn money, or
about my father mocking me, or even what would happen when he
realized that I was really leaving for college. I was simply hovering
above it all, so it didn't pinch or press. Now Josh was the one who
drove me to doctors' appointments or between houses. He did not

keep a calendar, forgot about homework assignments, and missed
dentist appointments and other appointments, but never the ones
with me. I was protected inside his teal Supra.

After the spring rains, when the grasses came up out of the
clods of dirt under the oak and eucalyptus trees around Stanford—
viridian fuzz like whiskers, stripes of gold light in long bright
ribbons—I thought, This is my town. I walked home after school,
and noticed the seasons change. Before this it was my father's town,
or my mother's town, or the town where I'd been placed by accident
and shifted around. Now I was in love, and the land was dimensional
and heavy and particulate; it belonged to me.

During lunchtime, I visited Paly's college admissions office, presided over by a woman with short, gray hair named Mrs. Daas. I flipped through a binder to find the names and addresses of students who'd been accepted to Harvard. Harvard, monstrous, distant, and separate from me, pulling away. It was the most legitimate organization I could think of. Also, it was one decision that seemed to eradicate uncertainty. Once I'd chosen it, I didn't have to make other decisions or discoveries. It seemed right—not for me, necessarily, as I didn't know what would be right for me at all, and hadn't bothered to think that far, but right in a general sense. There were usually a few acceptances per year. There was a space for the students to list where their parents had gone to college, and I read through all of them, trying to find an instance in which a parent had not been to college.

I paid for an SAT class, biking there on Saturday mornings. I didn't tell my parents about the process, although they knew I was applying to college. They didn't seem to understand the steps involved, or ask me questions about it.

I applied for early admission. Along with the application, we were asked to enclose a self-addressed, stamped postcard. I snuck into Laurene's office and took a fetching postcard from her book of Cartier-Bresson's black-and-white photographs. I liked these postcards; I wanted Harvard to find my application tasteful. The postcard I'd stolen would arrive back at the house—making my theft obvious. But I cared more about making an impression than I did about getting caught.

My father was away on a business trip, so I faked his signature on the application.

Over a long weekend I flew to New York to stay with Mona and look at colleges. My mother couldn't afford to take me; my father didn't have time. Mona knew more about colleges anyway.

She lived on the Upper West Side in an apartment with a line of round windows surrounded by stripped wood that looked out over Riverside Park. The radiators clanked.

Mona took me to walk around Columbia University, where she'd gone to graduate school. She took me to see Princeton, which she favored, for me, and then Harvard, where I'd arranged to have an interview at the admissions office instead of with an alumnus in California because I thought it would increase my chances of admission to be close to the source.

Two men I knew who'd been to Harvard warned me off. Dr. Botstein at the Stanford Genetics Lab, where I'd worked for two summers, said he'd been unable to join the finals clubs because he was Jewish. "I'm not going to tell you not to go," he said, "but I would give it a lot of thought." I wasn't able to believe in the possibility of my own acceptance then, let alone turning it down. The other man, Dr. Lake, said that he had been lonely there and it felt institutional, and that it wasn't until he got to medical school at the University of Chicago that he'd felt happy. I didn't believe either of them. They'd gone a long time ago. I knew what was best for me, I thought, even though I knew almost nothing about Harvard. It wasn't happiness I was after, but something they might not understand: a seal of approval, and escape. Harvard, I thought, would make me worthy of something. Of existence. I didn't think anyone could comprehend how much I wanted to go to this place I knew so little about.

It was autumn, clear and stinging cold outside, when Mona and I visited, no more beautiful or cold than Princeton or Columbia had been. The idea of it, the glamour and luck I associated with it, the brand, hovered beside the fact of it, gave it luster and dignity, the buildings, lawns, and trees.

The waiting room of the admissions office was overheated and smelled of paint, with cream-colored walls and blue carpet. Other prospective students sat in chairs nearby. I wore a black skirt with black tights.

I was nervous. It was true that I had not received a single B during high school, but I'd had to work hard for the grades. My SAT scores were good, but not stratospheric. This interview could make a difference.

"Lisa?"

I stood when I heard my name.

A tall woman with dark hair, wearing a skirt and a white sweater, said, "Follow me," and led me down a hallway and into a small, dim room. She seemed bored. She did not seem charmed by me but almost annoyed by my presence.

"Why don't you tell me a bit about your interests outside of school," the woman said. She made no reference to my application, as if she hadn't read it.

"Let's see," I said. "I suppose I do many things, like most of your candidates." I wanted her to understand that I knew I was human despite my great accomplishments, and humble, aware of, and even embarrassed by the excess of extracurricular activities I had collected for the purpose of saying them at this very moment. "I'm an attorney on our mock trial team, and I'm editor in chief of the school newspaper, with a staff of eighty," I said, glossing over the fact of the other three editors in chief. "I also take advanced Japanese, after having gone to Japan with my school, and later with my father on a business trip. He also helped me get a job at a lab at Stanford, where I developed photographs of yeast cells under the electron microscope and conducted large-scale experiments on yeast, inserting vectors of DNA into the cells." As if I were in charge of these experiments, when I only followed instructions; as if I were passionate about any of these activities besides the newspaper, or cared about Japanese or yeast as anything but a way to get into this place—if admitted, I would drop them.

I sat straight in my chair, my legs crossed. I slipped my father into the conversation like an accident.

I would use him. He was my only advantage after the grades and the activities.

"And what does your father do?" she asked politely.

I hesitated, lifting my eyebrows as if to say, "Oh, him?" I took a breath to indicate I hadn't expected the conversation to go here.

"He started a computer company," I said. "He invented a computer called the Macintosh." I said it as if she might not have heard of it.

At that, the woman stood; she looked alarmed. "Excuse me," she said. "I'll be right back." She grasped the doorknob and left the room abruptly, closing the door behind her, as if she'd realized all at once she had to attend to something urgent outside the room.

It was too obvious; I wondered if it could possibly be happening like this. Would she rush out and stop them from turning down my application? Were there other admissions officers shifting through the files of those being interviewed at that very moment?

A few minutes later, she returned. She didn't explain where she'd been, or why she'd dashed out, but seemed kinder and more attentive. She asked me a few more questions I don't remember, and the interview concluded.

When I left, my cheeks burned.

Back home, as I waited to find out if I got in, I wore corduroy for luck. I wore it top to bottom, corduroy pants with a corduroy shirt. The pants were wide wale, moss green; the shirt was a finer wale button-down with pockets, indigo blue. It felt like velvet. Usually, I wore these items singly, when I was taking or receiving the grade for an important test.

It was production week at the paper, and three of the four editors in chief had applied early to Harvard; we promised each other we wouldn't call and find out until the current issue of the paper was finished with production. Harvard had a hotline you could call to find out if you got in or not, Rebecca said, and later in the week she broke the deal, called, discovered she was in, told Nicole, and after that I started calling too, using the phone in the classroom, the line perpetually busy.

It was also possible that an acceptance or rejection letter would arrive in the mail one day that week, and so I wore the corduroy not only for the possibility of getting through on the phone, but also as a prophylactic against the chance I'd arrive home to find the letter on the counter when I was not wearing the lucky outfit. As a result, I'd been wearing the same clothes for four days straight.

On Thursday I decided I'd call the minute the phone lines opened. I set an alarm for 4:30 a.m. The admissions office call center opened at 7:30 a.m. in Boston.

The woman on the other end of the line was distant and professional. She took my last name and put me on hold.

"Congratulations," she said when she returned, her voice warm, relieved maybe—as if she, too, had been frightened of having to say no.

It took me a moment to understand what she meant. "Wait," I said.

She laughed. "You've been admitted to the Harvard Class of 2000." The words were scripted, but they might have been her own words, said with such joy.

"Thank you," I said. "Oh, thank you."

I got out of bed, put on my shoes with my pajamas, grabbed a sweater, and walked out the door into the dawn light, a blue veil over the street. The houses and lawns and cars were lit up but motionless like a stage set. Nothing stirring but me. Celebration was absorbed like the sound of a footstep on a damp lawn. The neighborhood was quiet, and I would be leaving it; that changed it, made it seem flat like a drawing. I walked past Kevin and Dorothy's house. Everyone was sleeping. As I walked, a few porch lights went off—they must have been on timers—and sprinklers began to *hish hish hish.*

I stepped back into the house and ran to my room and ripped sheets of lined paper out of a notebook. I GOT IN I GOT IN I GOT IN I GOT IN, I wrote. I taped them up on the windows that lined the hallway.

After a while I heard my father and Laurene stirring upstairs. I waited in the hallway, pacing, still in my pajamas. They walked down, first my father, then Laurene. I held my breath.

"Oh!" Laurene said.

"What is this?" my father said. "Got in where?"

"Ding dong," Laurene said. "She's into Harvard."

"Oh," he said. "Right."

Soon after, I would be moving to my mother's house.

I called out to my brother from the bottom of the stairs. For his fourth birthday I bought him a royal blue satin cape with silver stars and a ruffle around his neck. It came with a magician's conical hat and a wooden wand.

"Reed?" I called out. No response. I thought I heard a light shuffle upstairs.

"Glinda?" I called instead. This was one of the names he went by in costume.

"Esmeralda? Valencia?"

"Yes?" From a room upstairs came a thin, watery reply. "I'm Valencia."

I found him playing make-believe.

"I want to talk to you," I said, and sat him down beside me on the floor. "From now on, I'm going to live mostly with my mother." When I spoke, he was distracted, facing me but looking away.

My mother had suggested I tell him in the form of a story. "There was once a prince and a frog," I began. I wasn't sure why I'd made myself into the frog. "The prince loved the frog, and frog loved the prince more than any other prince. They were dear friends. But then, one day, the frog had to go back to his own kingdom." He listened now, rapt.

"Why did he have to go away?" Reed asked.

"There were other frogs. A land of frogs. He'd been away for a long time. But, you see, the frog still loved the prince. He wasn't leaving because he didn't—he just had to leave for his own reasons." The story was undeveloped, no real plot, leaden, but he didn't seem to mind, and wanted more.

"But he had to leave?"

"Yes," I said. "Because he needed to go home to the other frogs."

Later that year, my sister Erin was born, after I'd moved to my mother's house. She had dark hair and a widow's peak and large, soulful eyes. If she was still awake when I visited, I would hold her and stroke her forehead up toward her hairline. At just one stroke she would fall, miraculously, fast asleep. In the months leading to her birth, my father traveled in Europe for work, his company Pixar, which was on the verge of going public, and he returned from these trips with baby dresses from expensive shops, so that by the time she was born she already had many in plum and jute and white, hanging on a rail.

Harvard sent a form we were supposed to fill out to determine who our roommates would be. I wanted to sound cool and easygoing in order to attract cool, easygoing roommates. I concluded an autobiographical paragraph with the line "And, occasionally, I like to pick up a guitar and play a song." This did not capture me at all, as uptight as I was. I'd once been able to play a couple of songs but had since forgotten, and even when I could play, I had been mortified to play in front of other people.

The summer before I left for college, when I was living at my mother's house, my father took me to San Francisco to get a coat. It was his idea, and if I'd known he'd get me a coat, I might not have collected the others. We went to Emporio Armani, located in a converted bank with a towering ceiling and a café inside an internal balcony. We stopped at a rack of ties my father inspected and held with his thumb and index finger. I liked the way he held things. He looked at them with such intensity, but then he didn't bother to buy any. I worried, as I always did when shopping, that my size would be sold out.

On the far wall below the balcony of the café were the coats. These were not coats for California but for another kind of life. "How about this one," he said. Black wool with a collar and a double row of buttons that ran down the front. It swung out at the bottom, like a dress. We would have to get it adjusted, the sleeves, the length. "It's nice," he said. "Quite nice." I agreed, but I wondered if it was too unusual. And what others would be wearing when I arrived. It looked like a dress for a French mime. He bought it for me.

On the day my father bought me the coat, on the way back to Palo Alto along Highway 101, the coat left with the tailor for alterations, he and I hardly spoke. He didn't joke about Ruby's when we passed it. It didn't occur to me that he was silent because he was considering the fact that I was leaving—that he might miss me after I'd gone. Or he might have been thinking about work, about NeXT and Pixar. The silence between us would grow over the next years. Soon he would no longer write or call back; I wasn't sure how it started or why. That day he looked ahead, both hands on the wheel, moving his shoulder in its socket, brushing his thumbs back and forth, and clenching his jaw, the rhythms continuous but not exactly the same, like a mechanical man.

"I'm going to teach you to clean a toilet," my mother said at her house a few weeks later. I'd shown her the coat, back from the tailor, and this was her answer to it: what she would give me in preparation for Harvard.

"I won't be cleaning toilets where I'm going," I said.

"Maybe not," she said. "But you will someday." She was right.

Coda

If you still desire a thing, its time has not yet come. And when you
have what you desired, you will have no more desire, instead you will
have time. Weak desires protect you from disappointment. But nothing
keeps you safer than being a visible ruin.

—Fanny Howe, *Indivisible*

I arrived at Harvard alone the week before school started to join the First-Year Outdoor Program. It was hot and humid. I waited in the registration line under a white tent, but when I got to the front and said my name, a woman pulled me aside to say my tuition had not been paid. She seemed skeptical of my right to be there. I told her there must be a mistake, but I was embarrassed, and felt exceptionally alone. My dorm assignment and registration packet were delayed. I found a pay phone and called Jeff Howson, my father's accountant, who said he would do his best to set it right. The following week, when I returned from camping, my tuition had been paid, and I was given a dorm assignment.

In the first three months of my freshman year, before my father stopped responding to my calls and emails, I complained to him on the phone about how I couldn't *see* since I'd arrived in Boston. Everything was flat and close; there were no vistas; my eyes ached; the buildings were smashed up against the sightlines. "All I see is the building in front of me, everywhere I go."

"It's a metaphor for the East Coast mind," he'd said.

When fall arrived, I was cold in my new coat. I'd brought only a few pairs of cotton socks. I did not yet understand the importance of wool.

I worried about my mother. How would she afford to pay the rent?

"I'll figure something out," she said when I asked. "You don't need to worry about me. I always make things work."

She would be the one I'd call for hours every night during my first year in college, for her insights and care, when I found a culture far more alien than I had expected, and after I experienced my first heartbreak when Josh and I broke up, for which neither a fancy coat nor a skill at cleaning toilets had prepared me.

I was floored by grief.

About heartbreak my parents gave, separately, the same advice: "You've got to feel all your feelings. That way, next time, when you fall in love again, it will be just as meaningful and profound."

"The first heartbreak brings up the pain of the past," my father said. "The first big loss. Harness it."

"If something is really painful, it's the undertow of a big, beautiful wave," my mother said.

Other people said, "Get over it," and "Go out."

I took only what interested me: a class on anthropology that was held in the back of a wooden building filled with bones; a film and literature class; a class about the laws protecting children; and an art class in which we had to draw one hand with the other. I joined the paper, the literary magazine, and did community service at a local school.

My father came to visit me once that year. Walking behind me up the stairs to my dorm, he'd said, "You need to lose some weight." He told my new suitemate that her artificially flavored microwave popcorn was "shit." Despite his temper, he'd had an air of melancholy, even offering to buy me a leather jacket at a nice clothing shop called Agnès B. I refused because it seemed too expensive, it seemed weighty, as if it really meant something else but I didn't understand what, or what to say to him, being sad myself, lonely again without his company in this strange place I was supposed to like.

That summer, when I returned, my father treated me strangely, not talking with me unless he snapped at me with contempt. I was too thin. Laurene told her friend I was anorexic. I wanted to eat, but store-bought food tasted like cardboard, and I didn't know how to cook. Laurene kept buying me sandwiches.

When I went to see Dr. Lake, I discovered my father had decided not to pay the bill anymore. Dr. Lake said, "No one has the right to refuse you medical care," and reduced his fee to twenty-five dollars per session, which I paid myself.

Over the summer I worked at Hidden Villa where my mother had taught the art class years ago. I was a camp counselor for groups of children who came to learn about the animals and the farm.

Since I'd left for college, the checks from Jeff Howson that helped pay her rent had stopped coming, and my mother could not afford to stay in the house on Rinconada and would have to move.

My mother was now dating the software engineer with a black belt in karate she'd met in yoga class. She would move in with him until she could find her own place. He owned a small house in unincorporated Menlo Park. Unincorporated, as far as I could tell, meant that there were no sidewalks, just gutters, and the trees were bushy and more abundant, not planted in orderly rows. He said she could stay until she found another place, but his house didn't have enough space for me.

She was in the midst of packing up the house on Rinconada one Saturday, with the help of some friends. I was supposed to help too. She was directing traffic, moving quickly on the path under the wisteria bush between the garage and the house through the spots of sunlight. "C'mon, Lisa," she said. I found myself standing over boxes and stacks of books and clothing and dishes, all the things of our lives, our past together, unable to move.

"Pack," she said, "please," but I could no longer distinguish between items to discard or keep, or what boxes they went in, and my legs were paralyzed. Soon she gave up on me.

In the late afternoon, after the others had stopped packing, I sat at my mother's desk as she cooked for me and I was comfortable for the first time in days. I knew I would soon eat and be nourished. I didn't want to leave the circle of her care.

But that night my father had tickets to Cirque du Soleil. Even though he had hardly talked to me or looked at me since I returned from college, he wanted me to go to the circus, and had become fixated on my attentions to my little brother. I was thin and depressed, like a rag doll, unsure of myself, trying but unable to please him. I decided I wouldn't go.

"I can't go tonight," I said to him on the phone at my mother's house. "I'm sorry."

"You have to go," he said. I was not sure why my presence could be so important to him, unless it had to do with watching my brother, who might need to be walked around the circus tent.

"I need to stay, I need to eat. Mom's cooking for me," I said. My mother was looking at me from the kitchen with concern.

"Lis, you're not being part of this family," he said. "Frankly, we think you're being really selfish."

"I want to be part of the family," I said.

"If you skip the circus, you'll need to move out."

"Fine," I said, and hung up, because at his words I was filled with an unexpected wave of relief, as if I had stepped from a small dark room into a bright open field.

Right away I called Kevin, the neighbor.

"He told me to move out," I said, "that if I didn't go to the circus tonight, I was supposed to leave." I liked the feeling of openness it gave me, the permission. "What do you think I should do?"

"Let's move you out," Kevin said.

"When?"

"Tonight. While they're at the circus." Years before, he'd also moved Dorothy out of her father's house. He'd saved her from her own father, and they'd married young.

"And then?" He knew my mother was moving and I didn't have a place to stay.

"You can live with us," he said.

This was the answer I had wished for.

◆   ◆   ◆

That night, I met Kevin at his house at dusk and we drove a block to my father's house to gather my things. I took most of my clothing and shoes, my toiletries, some of my personal letters, left my CDs. Even though I knew my father must be at the circus, which was at least a thirty-minute drive away, I kept on feeling he could come back at any second and catch us. Kevin was also not in a mood to dawdle, more serious than usual. I threw my things into a bag.

What would it be like when my father returned and found me gone? It seemed incredibly sad, then, in a way it hadn't been when I imagined how it would be from the conversation before: the shock. It was possible that he did not want me to leave, that he helped cause the very losses he didn't want, that he wasn't able to keep in his life the kind of people who might explain this pattern to him. Had he kept them, he wouldn't have listened to them anyway.

It was only much later that I had the audacious idea that with my departure for my mother's house for the second six months before I left home, and then for college far away, he had felt abandoned, and even betrayed. It wasn't fair, but may have been true nonetheless: he had been negligent about spending time with me and caring for me, but now that it was time for me to go, he was angry at my departure. At the time, I would have told you that he hated me and that he must have hardly noticed my presence, that it could not possibly be missing me that had stirred him to such a fury. I was not *enough* to miss. It wasn't until my early thirties that I realized that the loss of me might be what he was mad about. Many parents spent time with their children for years, and had learned to abide loss in smaller increments—but he was new at it.

My father had come to visit me in London when I was in my mid-twenties, and we had walked to Green Park, found a bench, and sat side by side. "If I was an old man, I'd be out here all the time, sitting on one of these benches," he said, looking around, but there were no old men out that morning and the other benches were empty.

"You know," he'd said then, "those years you lived with us—those were the best years, for me." This was news—I didn't know what to say—for me they'd been difficult, and I'd thought for him they were some of the worst.

"Take just what you need," Kevin said. "And leave a note."

I wrote, "Dear Steve, I've moved out, as you said I should if I didn't go to the circus. I hope you will call me tomorrow." Write where you're staying, Kevin said. "I'm staying at Kevin and Dorothy's house," and I wrote their phone number, and "I love you." It seemed less real now that we were doing it than it had seemed talking about it this afternoon. I kept on hoping to relax, but not to relax so much that I gave Kevin the notion I was accustomed to my salvation.

Why did the neighbors choose to help me? For years they were aware of how my father treated me and they were profoundly uncomfortable with it. Dorothy's father, also a prominent, charismatic man, had been cruel to her. They had enough money to help me. They didn't like the idea that because my father had money and was surrounded by people who pandered to him, he could get away with being cruel to a child. When I asked many times over the next few years how I could possibly repay them, they said I should pay it forward, when I could. Help some other kid.

"Let's keep it moving," Kevin said.

On my bed at their house that night, Dorothy had left a tray with Russian tea cookies dusted in sugar and wrapped in plastic, a thermos of herbal tea, and a welcome note. In the morning, before work at the farm, I cracked my neck, pulling the tendon across the bone, and gave myself a crick. I couldn't move out of the contorted position all day.

My father did not call or return my calls.

The rest of the summer continued in a similar way, living with the neighbors, working at the farm, seeing my mother, speculating about my father and what he was thinking. Dorothy cooked for me. I decided not to take drugs for depression, as my therapist had recommended at the beginning of the summer, but kept telling myself positive things for all the negative ones that seemed to pop into my mind, at first very frequently and then less frequently, and by the end of the summer most of the cruel and knifing voices had gone away, and I was not depressed anymore, or too thin.

◆

"I'm going to ask Steve to buy me a house," my mother said on the phone, during my sophomore year of college.

She was still living with her boyfriend; I stayed with the neighbors during school breaks. "He'll never do it," I said.

"I'm going to keep on asking until he does."

She had never owned a house. In all the years I was growing up, he had not bought us a house; we had never lived in a house we owned. Surely, if he had been willing, he would have done it then. I wondered why she thought she could get it now, especially now that I had already left home—and he wasn't even talking with me—and why, if she could convince him to do things, she hadn't done it sooner.

The idea that it was possible, that it might have even been possible before, enraged me, even if I wanted her to have it.

In fact, several months later, he agreed. She found a house for sale in Menlo Park that met his criteria: within a certain radius of his house, and less than four hundred thousand dollars. It was a thin-walled, two-bedroom wooden house on the busy Alameda de las Pulgas, with a nice back garden. He'd said it had to be close to his house so that he could see it before buying it, but in the end he didn't even come to look before he bought the house in her name.

The summer after my sophomore year at Harvard, I got a job working at the Stanford Genetics lab, as I had done during high school. This would be the last time I lived in Palo Alto.

My mother made us salads with fresh tarragon leaves mixed in with the lettuces. She made curtains with French seams. She grew tomato plants in the garden in the back, forgetting to water them

until the leaves wilted and browned, her neglect making the fruit
the sweetest.

That summer, my father would not talk with me but insisted that I
babysit my brother, who had been missing me. I'd been over to his
house several times to babysit, hoping to talk with him, but he had
ignored me. After that, I told my father I would need to talk with
him *first*, and that I wouldn't babysit unless he agreed to talk with
me, but he refused, and said I had abandoned my brother.

One afternoon, Kevin and Dorothy came over to my mother's
house when my mother and I happened to be in a panic. My father
had just called me, yelling that I had to babysit my brother, and then
sent my mother an angry email. I was horrible and selfish, he wrote,
shirking my responsibilities toward my brother. My mother and I
were upset, not knowing how to respond. I suspected that, in some
way, I must be wrong. I kept repeating to my father, on the phone
and then over email, that I would *love* to see my brother, but would
simply need to talk with *him* first.

"I don't want to talk to you or see you," he said to me on the
phone. "You won't see Reed, and I love Reed, and I don't want to
spend time with people who won't spend time with the people I
love," he said.

Dorothy stood over my mother and dictated a response that
began, "Cut the sanctimonious bullshit, Steve." My mother typed it
out. Dorothy spelled out *sanctimonious*. I was thrilled about Dorothy's
response, and the new word.

At Harvard, I decided to major in English. During my junior year, I took a seminar on Chaucer's *Troilus and Criseyde*, taught by a Chaucer scholar from England with charming, uneven teeth and tufts of white hair in his ears. At some point, Criseyde has left Troilus, but Troilus can't seem to forget her.

"It makes Troilus seem so pathetic," I said confidently during the seminar, "that he can't get *over* her."

"No," the professor said, looking at me with a kind gaze. "His *strength* is that he can *hold on*."

That spring, soon after I wrote what I took to be a rather poignant villanelle about my eyebrows and entered it for submission in the college literary magazine, I went to see a free campus therapist, writing my name on a sign-up sheet to reserve an hour. She was a thin woman with a thin voice, and thin hair, a thin face, and a thin nose, like a Modigliani woman, with a peaceful expression and a sense of calm around her.

I went to see her a few times over the course of the next few weeks, and before the last session, at the end of the year, I told her about a dream I'd had the night before: I was sitting on a cliff, looking out over the vast ocean, where my father was sitting at his desk under a cone of light. The desk was like a raft, and the whole work raft was drifting out to sea as he concentrated on the screen.

"He'll go away," she said, a sad note in her voice, "and then maybe someday he'll realize that he did the same thing to you that was done to him." I was surprised that she could make such a quick summary, and I assumed something so quick and short must be wrong. But later, when I thought about it, it seemed true. I thought of my family as unique, but it must not have been, and I was surprised that it could be so obvious.

This was around the time my father had started working at Apple again. I read about it in the papers, and before I left to study abroad in London during my senior year, the first advertisements of the colorful new iMacs appeared, shrink-wrapped around the buses in Harvard Yard.

Over the next summer, I stayed in Cambridge to work at the Harvard travel-guide company, Let's Go, as an assistant editor for the Southeast Asia guidebook. Halfway through the summer I received a notice from Harvard in the mail saying that my tuition for the following year hadn't been paid.

After I moved out on the night of the circus two years before, my father had stopped paying for other expenditures besides tuition—flights to and from college, books, and spending money. I'd been paying for these with money from work and help from Kevin and Dorothy.

The next day, I wound my way down a dark basement corridor for a meeting with a Harvard financial aid officer. The man sat at a desk facing the door. Behind him, in the corner of the room, a ceiling tile was missing and piece of insulation had started to come loose.

I explained that my father had decided not to pay my tuition, even though he could afford to do so.

"You'll have to drop out until the age of *majority*," he said.

"What's the age of majority?" I asked, hoping it was twenty-one.

"Twenty-five," he said. I deflated.

In college, I had two jobs, one as an ESL teacher and one in the University Development Office, where the word "development" meant raising money for the college through fundraisers and advertising.

I had assumed the financial aid office would look something like the development office—money in, money out. In fact, this office, and this man, seemed beleaguered, as if to communicate that Harvard didn't have the money one might think it had. I was furious at this man for his no-nonsense talk; there *must* be a way to make it work. Surely Harvard would want to help me, to keep me, I thought, when, in fact, it was this man's job to inform me that it did not.

"Harvard financial aid is need-based," he said. My father's status rendered me ineligible for any aid.

"So I just have to drop out? There's nothing Harvard will do to help me stay?"

"That's correct," he said. "Absolutely nothing."

When he came to Boston for business, Kevin took me for dinner. I liked these dinners because they made college less lonely, and made me feel like other people who sometimes went to dinner with their fathers, even if he wasn't my father. Sometimes he seemed competitive with my father—"He might have nice cars," Kevin said, at dinner, "but he doesn't really know how to *drive*." Good driving, as Kevin defined it, involved making the passenger comfortable, unaware of the speed and acceleration of the car. If this was true, my father did not have that skill; his driving was like a wire in my stomach. He fishtailed through curves. Before my father's success at Pixar and his new job at Apple, Kevin talked about my father's poor business acumen, how NeXT was doing poorly, worse than other people might know, which you could tell because he had stopped buying things, Kevin said. I listened and nodded. But my father had rarely bought much, compared with other rich people, and none of these attributes made me care about him less, or diminished his importance to me. He could have been the worst executive and the worst driver in the world.

"He doesn't love you," Kevin said to me. "Love is what you *do*."

"Maybe you're right," I said, and contemplated the idea. It was a stab at first, but after that, it felt almost like a relief to say it like it was.

"How dare Kevin say that. He *does* love you," my mother said on the phone when I told her.

"But *love* is a verb," I said. "So what does it matter?"

"It matters," she said.

I thought maybe she didn't know. I experimented with the idea as I walked around. He doesn't love me and that's why he's like this. The plain truth.

Kevin and Dorothy paid my tuition for my final year.

My mother said she had tried to sell her new house to pay for it, but there wasn't much time, and she couldn't find a buyer. She also said she had a vision of an enormous, brilliant gold angel towering behind the neighbors. It was impossible, I knew, but the image made the gift easier to receive, if I could imagine the money came from an angel and not just from them, whom I worried I could never repay. The gift was unfathomably big.

At times, I wished that these stable, responsible neighbors were my family instead, and if I yearned to be good enough for a family like this, they might have liked being an example to me, and delighted in how I saw them heroically. They were often cracking jokes and giving me ideas about how people lived, and how families interacted, and how I shouldn't interrupt, and what questions were rude, and how to defend myself with my words, and how to think about the people who fawned on my father and stepmother and did not notice or care about me. I flipped back and forth between wanting to be exactly like them and wanting to be myself, with them as my doting parents. For a while, perhaps, all of us were caught up in the wish that we could be a family.

My mother called a friend to ask him what he thought would come of all this.

He said, "Lisa's going to find out she can't replace her parents, and Kevin and Dorothy are going to learn they can't buy a daughter."

I had already committed to study abroad at King's College in London for my final year of college, and Kevin and Dorothy insisted that I go.

That year, near my dorm, the London Eye was lifted from the surface of the water.

Toward the end of my year abroad, I dated an English lawyer with a high-standing blond ruffle of hair.

"You should invite your father to your graduation," he said.

"No way," I said. I told him everything my father had done wrong.

"But he's your *father*," he said. He kept pressing, saying that it didn't matter what one's father had done; he was still one's father, that fathers had done worse things and still should be invited to momentous events, and if I didn't invite him, I'd regret it later when it was too late to fix. I was ambivalent, but in the end I sent my father and Laurene two tickets and a note.

Kevin and Dorothy, whom I invited and who planned to come, were deeply hurt that I'd invited my father, after all they had done for me when he had not, and decided not to come.

My mother was worried she wouldn't be able to afford the trip, but at the last minute she got a consulting job with Hewlett-Packard, bought a flight, reserved a hotel room, and bought a stunning black cotton dress that was ruched up at the bottom like a parachute.

Later, when my father talked about that day, he said, several times, "Your mother was so graceful." He did not know what I knew—that she'd carefully rationed her words to him, giving him a maximum of twenty-five. To him she spoke deliberately and carefully, to protect this economy.

My father and Laurene had slipped through the river gate of Winthrop House to watch me walk down the line and receive my diploma. When I came to join my mother, I found them standing beside her. "I don't believe in genetics," my father blurted out after we'd exchanged hellos. He sometimes made pronouncements like this. At other times he had talked about how powerful genes were. I didn't know how to respond.

"What are you going to do next? Do you have a job?" he asked.

I was almost too embarrassed to say, because I knew he didn't respect banking, or what he called "the straight and narrow," and neither did I, and I withered under my imagination of his judgment.

"Tell him," my mother nudged me, and I mumbled it. I would be starting work as an analyst at a bank in London. It was the wrong kind of job for an English major, and I felt foolish to have joined the normal hubbub of the world, and for being one of the people my father sometimes mocked, but Schroder Salomon Smith Barney would get me a visa so that I could live and work in London. I would be able to support myself.

After graduation, I would see my father once a year, if that. My younger sister, Eve, was born when I was away at college, but in a few magazines I came across in the following years and on his bio on his company website, he said he had three children, not four. Sometimes, he would be wonderful, but then he would say something unkind, so that I found myself guarded around him, happy to stay away.

A few weeks after graduation, my mother asked Kevin and Dorothy to provide a sheet with a detailed accounting of everything they'd spent on me, including the flights, books, vacations, and clothing for school. She sent this piece of paper to my father and, shortly after, he paid them back.

◆

When I was twenty-seven, no longer at the bank but working at a graphic design company in London, my father invited me to join a yacht trip that he, Laurene, my siblings, and the babysitter were taking in the Mediterranean. He invited me for a weekend, but then implored me to stay for a few more days when the weekend was up. After those days were up, he asked me to stay longer again, until I had stayed as long as I could, for more than two weeks. Off the coast of the South of France my father said we were going to make a stop in the Alpes-Maritimes to meet a friend for lunch. He wouldn't say who the friend was. We took a boat to the dock, where a van picked us up and took us to a lunch at a villa in Èze.

It turned out to be Bono's villa. He met us out front wearing jeans, a T-shirt, and the same sunglasses I'd seen him wearing in pictures and on album covers. He seemed plain, and he was kind, without the awkward distance usually affected by famous people.

He gave us an exuberant tour of his house, as if he couldn't quite believe it was his. The windows faced the Mediterranean, and the rooms were cluttered with children's things. In an empty, light-filled octagonal room, he said, Gandhi once slept.

We had lunch on a large covered balcony overlooking the sea. I sat a few seats away from my father, who sat beside Bono at the head of the table. Waiters delivered food.

Bono asked my father about the beginning of Apple. Did the team feel alive, did they sense it was something big and they were going to change the world? My father said it *did* feel that way as they were making the Macintosh, and Bono said it was that way for him and the band too, and wasn't it incredible that people in such disparate fields could have the same experience? Then Bono asked, "So was the Lisa computer named after her?"

There was a pause. I braced myself—prepared for his answer.

My father hesitated, looked down at his plate for a long moment, and then back at Bono. "Yeah, it was," he said.

I sat up in my chair.

"I thought so," Bono said.

"Yup," my father said.

I studied my father's face. What had changed? Why had he admitted it now, after all these years? Of course it was named after me, I thought then. His lie seemed preposterous now. I felt a new power that pulled my chest up.

"That's the first time he's said yes," I told Bono. "Thank you for asking." It was as if famous people needed other famous people around to release their secrets.

◆

A few years later, I was living in New York. I went to visit my father in Palo Alto, and he wanted to go out for sushi, just the two of us.

By this point I knew he was sick with cancer. He was very thin.

Over the past month in New York it occurred to me that I should say the good things to him before it was too late, even if I had no sense of how sick he was. I believed he might soon recover.

"You know, in many ways you were good about sex," I told him. Sex was our easiest subject. "When you put in a diaphragm," he'd lectured me in high school, "you have a moment all to yourself to decide again what you want to do." He had not insisted I take the pill, or worried openly about my becoming pregnant, instead giving the sense he trusted me, and knew me to be reasonable, profound even.

"You didn't try to make me feel ashamed," I said.

"Yes. Yes!" he said. He was hardly able to contain himself, bobbing his thin legs up and down in the seat beside me. We were in the car with the engine off because we had arrived at the sushi restaurant in the mall. "That's what I was *trying* for," he said. "And do you know what? I was the first person you talked to after you lost your virginity!" he said. "It was so great. It meant so much to me." I'd forgotten this before he mentioned it.

"I know you better than I know the girls," he said, as we got out of the car and walked toward the restaurant. I didn't know what to say back; this was a shocking claim, considering I'd met him so late and they'd lived with him their whole lives. It couldn't be true, I thought.

That night, I walked into his bedroom upstairs when he was watching old episodes of *Law & Order*. He'd asked me, abruptly, from bed, "Are you going to write about me?"

"No," I said.

"Good," he said, and turned back to face the television.

My mother became sick, a sinus and bone infection that we couldn't diagnose at first, leaving her unable to work and unable to pay her rent. She had sold her house on Alameda de las Pulgas a few years before, against my wishes, and had used the money to travel and live for several years until the money ran out. Desperate, I called the parents of a friend from Nueva who offered her a place to live for a few months in their extra house in San Francisco. Another set of friends loaned me money to help her pay for oral surgery that made her cheek balloon out as if it had been stung by a bee.

A few weeks later, I went to visit my father in the hospital in Memphis after he'd had a liver transplant. He'd gone to Memphis because that's where a liver became available, he and my stepmother flying there in his private jet late at night. Once, when he had to urinate, a nurse had tried to usher me out of the room.

"She can stay," he'd said, and then proceeded to pee in a plastic jar under his gown while I stood there, talking to me as he peed, as if he couldn't be away from me for even one second. He'd had two rooms at the hospital, a room with his hospital bed and a small anteroom, and in the anteroom were a couch and chairs, like the kind at elementary schools, with melamine bodies and metal legs, and in order to visit we had to move the chairs around, pushing the extras out of the way, making them clack. At one point, sitting in the anteroom with me and my aunt and stepmother, he started gasping for breath and turning purplish, and we all panicked, trying to find out what was wrong. I glanced down surreptitiously and noticed with dismay that the leg of my chair was crimping his oxygen tube. I moved my chair as quickly as I could, and he started to breathe again.

Less than a year after the transplant, back at the Waverley house, the cancer had spread to the top of his femur and the outside lining of his gut. "What's it called?" I asked the nurse, Elham.

"It's called the superficial fascia," she said. I imagined it, the pouch holding his intestines together, and for some reason in my imagination it was a phosphorescent skein like a jellyfish or like city lights seen at night from an airplane. Inside the glowing outlines, it was dark. He was called Johnny Eight on the papers in the hospital. Sometimes he sucked on morphine lollipops. In the bed sleeping, at certain angles, he looked like a pile of yellow bones. He couldn't walk anymore. "He's not in pain," Elham reassured me. His brain, according to the MRI scan, was cancer-free.

During my previous visit, he was still eating a little. (He remained picky; if one type of mango touched another type of mango in the bowl, he turned away and would not eat.) This time he took only liquid food, called TPN, intravenously at night, never long enough to gain weight; the process gave him 150 calories per hour.

Only a few months after the visit when he'd said I smelled like a toilet, I was still stealing small objects from around the house. I called my mother to tell her about what I was doing. I wanted her to absolve me. I wanted her to make an exception to the no-stealing rule just for me, just this time. I wanted her to say, Honey, you can keep *everything*.

But she said, "You've got to return their things. It's important. You must not steal—it's like Persephone." It was like her to make this mythical. "You know, the one who ate the pomegranate seeds?"

I remembered she'd gone to the underworld, where she wasn't supposed to touch anything, but she couldn't resist and she ate the seeds. Then as a punishment she had to stay down there for part of the year. That was supposed to be why we have winter. I tried to remember how many seeds she took.

"It doesn't matter how many," my mother said. "The point is, because she took the seeds she was stuck there. She stole from the underworld, she partook of it, and then she was *bound* to it."

"And?"

"If you keep those things, you're bound to that house. It doesn't free you; it *ties* you to it." Of course the story of Persephone was also a story of a mother and daughter, a mother making the land barren because of her grief during the months her daughter was gone.

I took the stolen items back in shifts because there were too many to take all at once. I wrapped the bowls in the pillowcases so they wouldn't clink. I put the lip gloss back on the shelf in the bathroom, the cream in the cabinet upstairs, the shoes in the closet. It turns out that to return stolen things and not get caught is just as difficult as stealing them in the first place.

During this visit my father did not seem particularly interested in seeing me; he asked me to leave the room so he could watch a movie with my brother. He could no longer walk, or eat, but I believed in a delusional way that he'd live for a long time yet. He'd been sick for such a long time that I didn't notice when this changed into dying. I avoided his room, only forcing myself to go in sometimes and hoping that he'd be asleep when I did. At the end of the visit I thought I might not return to see him again because it felt hollow and unsatisfying.

But a month later he texted—he didn't usually text me—asking me to visit during a weekend when Laurene and my siblings would be away. I took a train to Palo Alto from the San Francisco airport.

The air was crisp and the light was sharp on the platform pilings. In New York the air was flat; it rarely smelled of anything, or it smelled of one thing: garbage or rain or perfume or smog. Here, the wind was cool; it carried water in it. Fog curled over the hills like other, softer hills. The air smelled of eucalyptus and grasses, spice cake and menthol. Wet dirt, dry dirt.

I was skeptical that this trip would be different from the others. Mona had named me Ye of Little Faith a long time ago, and my mother called me that still, to tease me.

I got off at the California Avenue stop. The town had the look of nothing going on, the road straight like a runway to the deep green hills. I took the underpass below Alma Street that emerged in the golden light on the other side, and walked past the park and the pine trees. The houses around here hugged the ground.

For the previous six months, I'd been taking a small dose of clonazepam, an antianxiety drug that allegedly reduces the amygdala's fight-or-flight response, 0.25 milligram per day. It was despite, or perhaps because of, my father's insistence I try weed or LSD that drugs had seemed unappealing before—I'd never done any—but flying back and forth to see him every month, finishing graduate school, my mother sick and low on money, I had found myself unable to focus. Instead, I moved and talked faster and faster. I had a frantic quality, hoping to distract others and not expose myself. I was jittery and defensive and self-conscious, terrified my father would say something awful and then he would die and nothing would be resolved.

In movies, there is the scene when the dying person apologizes—but this was life.

I walked through the house and paused at the threshold of my father's study that had become his bedroom. There was a photograph by Harold Edgerton of an apple being shot through by a bullet, the skin fraying around the edges of the hole.

I rounded the corner to his room. He was propped up on pillows, his legs pale and thin, like knitting needles. There were framed photographs covering the surface of the chest of drawers, each tilted to face his bed. The chest had drawers of equal widths, and later I would see that inside he'd organized the art and photographs in each one. He was alone, awake, and seemed to be waiting for me. He smiled.

"I'm so glad you're here," he said. His warmth was disarming. Tears fell down his face. Before he was sick I'd seen him cry only twice, once at his father's funeral, and once in a movie theater at the end of *Cinema Paradiso*, when I'd thought he was shivering. "This is the last time you're going to see me," he said. "You're gonna need to let me go."

"Okay," I said. But I didn't quite believe him, and I wouldn't have believed he'd die about a month later. I had fuzzy, indeterminate thoughts about how long he'd live. I sat on the bed beside him.

"I didn't spend enough time with you when you were little," he said. "I wish we'd had more time."

"It's fine," I said. He was so weak and fragile. I lay down on my side in his bed, facing him.

"No, it's not okay. I didn't spend enough time with you," he said. "I should have spent the *time*. Now it's too late."

"I guess our timing was off," I said, not convinced of it even as I said it. In fact, I had recently realized my luck: I got to know him before he became hugely famous, when he was healthy enough to skate. I'd imagined he'd spent a lot more time with everyone else than he had with me, but I wasn't so sure about that anymore. He looked into my eyes and teared up. "I owe you one." I was not sure what to make of this phrase. During that weekend, he repeated it over and over: "I owe you one, I owe you one," he said, crying, when I went to visit him in between his naps. What I wanted, what I felt owed, was some clear place in the hierarchy of those he loved.

He and I were alone in the house, except for the nurses who rotated every six hours. A few other people came to visit—people he'd worked with. A few people he didn't know came to the doors wanting to see him too, wandering into the garden with packages, or empty-handed. A stranger in a sari begged to talk with him. A man came in through the gate and said he had flown in from Bulgaria just to see my father. A cluster of people gathered at the side door, talked among themselves, and then dispersed.

"Do you remember your dreams?"

I was lying on my side in his bed. He was drifting in and out of sleep.

"Yup."

"Have you always remembered them?"

"Most of the time."

"What do you dream about?"

"Work, mostly," he said. "Trying to convince people of things."

"What things?"

"Ideas."

"Ideas you thought of while you were dreaming?"

"Sometimes. But usually in my dreams I can't convince them. Usually, they're too much of a bozo to get it."

"Did you come up with a lot of ideas that way? In your dreams?"

"Yes," he said, then fell asleep again.

The next day I went to the hospital with him for a blood transfusion. This took up most of the day because he was too weak to walk and had to be transported from chair, to car, to chair, to hospital, to chair, to car, to chair, and back into his bed again. The blood was thick and dark in the bag. It looked like fake syrup Dracula blood. The hospital brought him heated blankets that came out of a machine that looked like a refrigerator. He was cold and then hot and then cold.

I sat on a chair in the room with him, hearing the mechanical whoosh of the machine. I wondered whose blood he was getting. I wanted to ask, but I didn't want to call attention to the bag. He had a transfusion every ten days or so. It took several hours. Afterward, he had more color.

"He's cold, I think," I told one of the nurses toward the end of the transfusion.

"I'm fine," he said. I sat on the chair in the corner to wait for him.

"I think he might be cold," I said again, a few minutes later. I could feel gusts of cold air blowing through the vents.

"I'm fine," he said, and I had to leave the room for some reason, and when I was called back in, to sit on the chair in the corner, the nurse brought me a blanket.

"He said you were cold," she said. I hadn't noticed I was.

"I'm sorry I didn't spend more time with you. I'm so sorry," he said from the bed.

"I guess you were working really hard, and that's why you didn't email me or call me back?" He'd rarely returned my emails and calls, did not mark my birthdays.

"No," he paused. "It wasn't because I was busy. It was because I was mad you didn't invite me to the Harvard weekend."

"What weekend?"

"The introductory weekend. All I got was the bill," he said, with a catch in his voice.

Matriculation. I remembered later how when I was eighteen I'd been carefully juggling my parents, who didn't want to come at the same time, and we'd decided, with the help of my therapist, and the agreement of both parents, that she would come that weekend, and he'd come a few weekends later. At the time he'd agreed this was best.

"Why didn't you tell me?"

"I'm not too good at communication."

"I wish I could take it back, or change it," I said. It seemed unlikely, and possibly insane, that our relationship was pinned on one weekend. I didn't believe it. I'd ascribed some sort of overarching wisdom to him, but people who are dying and trying to set things right aren't necessarily reflective and profound. I didn't buy the idea that one invitation, one weekend, could have justified his ten years of almost silence, and the withholding of money for college tuition in my final year.

All through those years I'd been looking at my palm. I was meant for a good life—that was what the lines meant.

I remembered how, a year before, my mother had come to visit me in New York. She was getting over the illness that had left her fragile and her ears clogged. We went for a walk in the late afternoon.

West Fourth Street intersected Charles Street at a brick row house covered in light. My mother and I stopped to gaze at it together. Those days we had started to have the feeling that we had survived, we had made it through, we would be happy.

"And the palms? Do you even know how to read palms?" I'd built up the courage to ask.

"Sort of," she said, a slight smile that meant she was lying.

"I mean, do you have *any* expertise?" What I wanted her to say was she'd met someone in India or she'd read a rare book.

"You needed the right stories. We needed to get to a radically different place from where we were. I didn't know how else to get us there, besides stories. And anyway, the things I was saying—they were true."

That evening, back at the house, he called me in with the weak voice he used to call the nurses. "Lis." The backpack that held the bag of TPN was whirring its motor, ticking like a toy train around a track, the milky fluid going into his veins. He was lying on the bed with his knees up, propped up on pillows. He was freakishly thin; it was hard to look at him and think of anything else besides his limbs, his gaunt face.

"About what we said earlier—" he said. It struck me how he referenced a previous conversation about emotions, something he'd never done with me before. "I want to say something: You were not to blame." He started to cry. "If only we'd had a manual. If only I'd been wiser. But you were not to blame. I want you to know, you were not to blame for any of it." He'd waited to apologize until there was hardly anything left of him. This was what I'd been waiting to hear. It felt like cool water on a burn.

"I'm so sorry, Lis," he cried and shook his head side to side. He was sitting up, cradling his head in his hands, and because he had shrunk and lost fat, his hands looked disproportionately large, and his neck too thin to hold his skull, like one of the Rodin sculptures of the burghers of Calais. "I wish I could go back. I wish I could change it. But it's too late. What can I do now? It's just too late." He cried and his body shook. His breath caught on his sobs and I wished he'd stop. After that he said again, "I owe you one." I didn't know what to say. I kept sitting beside him on his bed. Even now I didn't quite trust it: if by some miracle he recovered, I imagined he'd snap back to his old self, forget this happened, go back to treating me as he had before.

"Well, I'm here now," I said. "Maybe, if there is a next time, we could be friends?" It was also a gentle jab: *just friends*. But in fact, in the weeks following this visit and after he died, it was our missed chance at friendship I grieved about.

"Okay," he said. "But I'm so sorry. I owe you one."

Since returning the stolen objects, I hadn't taken anything else, but I'd still noticed other things I wanted. Now the wanting dried up. I never felt like stealing again.

The family returned and the house was bustling. In the evening after dinner, Laurene and I were alone at the kitchen table together. On other visits I would have hopped up to wash the dishes, but this time I stayed where I was. "He talked to me," I said. "We exchanged important words. Momentous words. I feel better." I thought she would ask me about it, but instead she got up to wash a dish at the sink.

"I don't believe in deathbed revelations," she said.

◆ ◆ ◆

My younger sister Eve was having a birthday party. I wandered out into the garden that smelled of succulents, geraniums, and water. A cluster of girls stood on the darkening lawn, with some light still in the sky, like a Magritte painting.

My sister had tied low strings like trip wires over the surface of the large outdoor trampoline to imitate horse jumps, and she and her friends did jumps on arms and legs across the surface. Birds flew into the eaves of the house, and the pug grunted and rooted around beside the trampoline legs.

"Who are you?" one girl asked me. She was a few inches taller than my sister, up to my nose, hair like straw. My sister climbed off the trampoline and stood nearby.

"I'm the sister of the birthday girl," I said. The friend looked confused, maybe because we are twenty-one years apart. "I'm much older because we have different mothers," I said, to explain.

"Oh," the girl said. "It's nice to meet you."

"She was daddy's mistake," my sister announced.

I grabbed her shoulders for a minute to steady myself, her back against my chest. "You shouldn't say that," I whispered in her ear, and then walked back into the house through the dark.

Inside, there was a honey jar on the kitchen table, and I leaned closer to inspect the label. On it were five illustrations of bees with the names of the family members written underneath each: Steve, Laurene, Reed, Erin, and Eve. Above them was the title "Jobs Family Farm."

The next day, in a drawer below the napkins, I found a cluster of many of these labels, each with an adhesive back. They were for gifts, I figured. There were so many labels that they clung together and fanned out like the fall leaves raked into tight piles on the streets around here. I kept looking at the labels, searching for my name among the bees, as if it might appear there. In the dining hall in college, a girl had said, half-joking, "The trick must be to marry rich. How do we marry rich?" and I'd felt the same heaviness of being outside the circle of fun.

In the past couple of years, I'd moved to New York, finished an MFA at Bennington College, started a consulting job at a graphic design firm editing and designing a section of the MoMA website, and moved in with a man I loved and hoped to marry. I had grown up, I had moved on, so it surprised me, returning to see my father when he was sick, how painful it still was not to be included in his life.

Visiting reminded me that while I'd lived at this house, I'd wished to be someone else. But around this time—during one of these visits during these strange years flying here to visit my father every month or so—I had a moment of revelation, a moment of lightness, as if a huge burden I'd been carrying around had been lifted all at once as I was standing under the frill of jasmine around the front door: It was irrelevant that I wasn't named on the honey-pots. I had *not* been a mistake. I was not the useless part of something meaningful. I heard from someone that the pattern of our breath isn't supposed to be even, regular. Humans are not metronomes. It goes long and short, deep and shallow, and that's how it's supposed to go, depending at each moment on what you need, and what you can get, and how filled up you are. I wouldn't trade any part of my experience for someone else's life, I felt then, even the moments where I'd wished I didn't exist, not because my life was right or perfect or best, but because the accumulation of choices made had carved a path that was characteristic and distinct, down to the serif, and I felt the texture of it all around me for just a moment, familiar, like my own skin, and it was good enough.

At the memorial service and in the years since, people want me to know how close they were with my father.

"He liked giving special advice to my son," someone said. "They were *very* close."

"They had such a tight relationship," another said of her son and my father.

"He was like *a father* to me," said a man, tearing up.

These conversations have a particular quality in which I feel I am supposed to be, more than a participant, a witness. These people do not ask about my father, but talk fervently *at* me, as if my listening is the missing ingredient, the yeast, that gives their stories life. They recite anecdotes like speeches, and walk away.

Do they want me to feel deferential? He'd been like a father to them too. They're asserting a claim and I'm supposed to confirm him as the ur-father. His great greatness.

When people speak and write about my father's meanness, they sometimes assume that meanness is linked to genius. That to have one is to get closer to the other. But the way I saw him create was the best part of him: sensitive, collaborative, fun. The friends he worked with got to see this more than I did. Maybe the meanness *protected* the part that created—so that acting mean to approximate genius is as foolish as trying to be successful by copying his lisp or his walk or the way he turned around and wagged his hands around his back and moaned to pretend he was making out.

"Look at those clouds," he'd said once when he was sick but could still walk, in a sweet mood, pointing up out of the window on a sunny day. "Those clouds are approximately ten thousand feet up.

That's about two miles. If we wanted, you and I, we could walk—let's see, a twenty-minute mile.

"We could be there in forty minutes," he said.

Rinpoche, the Brazilian monk, said to my mother that if he'd had two more months, just *two months*, he could have achieved a better resolution between my parents.

But who knows?

When I see my mother now, the more time we spend together, the more I feel attached. When I have to pee, I leave the door open, so we can keep talking. We are like suction cups: once together it's difficult to pry us apart. Sometimes we fight. When we're apart—she on her coast and me on mine—I forget how it is to be together, how it's exhilarating, and up and down. When she visits New York, we go see art. At the Agnes Martin exhibition at the Guggenheim, we start at the top and corkscrew to the bottom, against the traffic of people walking up, looking at stripes. For us, Agnes gets younger and younger. After that, we walk out into the day. We cross Fifth Avenue to Central Park and she says, "Look!" and points to the thick white lines against the dark asphalt. "There's another one!"

There was one picture of my parents together before I was born. They are standing at the train station one morning when my father left to return to Reed College. My mother's cheeks are round and full. She's wearing jeans. My father's face is pale and sweet. They look incredibly young. I thought it was my mother who lost things—houses, objects, my father. But she had kept this picture for many years, and she gave it to me, and I moved, and I left it somewhere. Recently she gave me a painting she'd made in high school for which she'd won a prize.

"He's following you around, your father," she said, when she came to visit me after he died.

"A ghost?"

"Him. I don't know how else to say it. I can feel him here. And you know what? He's overjoyed to be with you. He wants to be with you so much he's padding around behind you. I mean, he's delighted just watching you butter a piece of *toast*."

I didn't believe it, but I liked thinking it anyway.

Acknowledgments

Thank you to Grove Atlantic: to my excellent editor Elisabeth Schmitz, and to Katie Raissian, Deb Seager, Julia Berner-Tobin, Sal Destro, Judy Hottensen, and Morgan Entrekin. Also to Bettina Abarbanell and Eva-Marie von Hippel at Berlin Verlag. Thank you to my honest, smart agent David McCormick, who thought I might give up, and to Susan Hobson and the rest of the team at McCormick Literary.

I wrote for two extended, productive periods at the residency at Art OMI: Writers. Before that, I am grateful to have attended the low-residency MFA program at Bennington College.

Thank you to Caterina Fake, Bryan Burk, Claire Sarti, David Boaretto, Stefanie Kubanek, Brandon Lussier, and DW Gibson for encouraging me to write. Thank you to Ann Godoff and Ginny Smith-Younce at Penguin Press, and to Uschi Weissmueller and Pascale Kramer, and to readers Ellen Graf, Hannah Blumenthal, and Mona Simpson. Thanks to Finn Taylor, Christina Redse, Linda Brennan, Jamie Brennan, Ron, Ilan, Debbie, and David for stories and thoughts about the past.

I am grateful to Lawrence and Hillary Levy, who helped with everything at every stage. And to Phillip Lopate, Susan Cheever, Kai Barry, and my mother—all of whom offered many years of support as I wrote this. I am also profoundly grateful to Jamie Quatro, who expertly and sensitively helped extract this book from a very long draft, and then found me my publisher.

Finally, thank you to Bill for his joy, optimism and care, and to wonderful Bodie and Julie, and to little Thomas for providing a deadline and even more joy.

GROVE PRESS

Reading Group Guide

SMALL FRY

LISA BRENNAN-JOBS

ABOUT THIS GUIDE

We hope that these discussion questions will enhance your reading group's exploration of Lisa Brennan-Jobs's *Small Fry*. They are meant to stimulate discussion, offer new viewpoints, and enrich your enjoyment of the book.

More reading group guides and additional information, including summaries, author tours, and author sites for other fine Grove Atlantic titles may be found on our website, groveatlantic.com.

QUESTIONS FOR DISCUSSION

In an interview with the *New Yorker*'s editor David Remnick, the author says she wrote this book in spite of her father's fame: "I wanted to write a coming-of-age story about a girl growing up in California in the 80s and 90s because I felt like ... if I got deep enough into it, it was a universal story." As Sven Birkerts writes in *The Art of Time in Memoir*: "Done well, any writer's presentation of her coming-of-age puts us into active contemplation of the passages we endured in our own younger years. Specificity allows the scenes to come alive, and as they come alive they inevitably activate certain archetypes, whether these have to do with rebellion, sexual longing, friendship, betrayal, leave-taking ..." How much of the story depends on its situation—its characters and its Silicon Valley setting? How does Brennan-Jobs reach the universal? What archetypes are activated in this book? Where do you recognize your own experience?

In that same interview, Remnick asks the author why she begins the book with the story of her thefts, and she responds: "One thing that happened when I started writing is that I was disappearing in the pages ... At some point I read *This Boy's Life* again, and I realized that every time the author was devious, I loved him more ... with that new idea, I found a new freedom to try and figure out where I had participated in my own life, and more—where I'd been kind of bad." Is beginning with this unflattering view of herself audacious or humble? Why, rather than mistrust and judge her, do we as readers do the opposite? What compels her to steal? Though the author is concerned with showing herself as a person with agency in the book, how does she exert a strong presence through her narration of the story alone?

How does the author create a persona for herself on the page? Describe her voice. How do the things she notices and her manner of describing them tell us what sort of person she is? How does she win our trust and interest? She often provides a number of possible interpretations of a given event (as on p. 51, where she guesses at what's motivating her mother at the Humane Society)—what does this narrative strategy say about her?

On the surface, the parent/child dynamics in the book could be stereotyped: the absent father, the overbearing mother. How does the story complicate these oversimplifications? Is Steve Jobs ever absent from his daughter's psyche? Are there times when Lisa craves closeness with her mother? What tactics does each parent deploy to demand Lisa's loyalty? Does she ask different things of each of them? What does she admire about each? What does she learn from them? Though they may easily be seen in opposition, what attitudes unite them?

"Values" are referenced throughout the book. At his own wedding ceremony, Steve delivers a speech in which he says it isn't love but shared values that brings people together and keeps them together (p. 208). What values does Steve profess? Does Steve apply this philosophy to his relationship with Lisa as well? Does he treat her in ways that are similar to how he treats his romantic partners?

When Lisa sees Steve's New York apartment, she describes it as "the opposite of the counterculture ideals he talked about, a showcase made to impress" (p. 202). What other discrepancies do you see between Steve's professed ideals and his actions? What do our contradictions reveal about us? Which do you think reflects our truer self: our actions or our words? How does the book interrogate the privileging of one over the other?

For the most part, the photographs included in the book appear to depict positive family interactions (with the possible exception of the one of Lisa with her mother at the start of the section titled "Runaway" on p. 179). How did you read the photographs as you went along? Do they argue with the text or complement it? Reread the author's description of her time on the trampoline with her father (pp. 71-2) and then revisit that photograph. Are there photographs in your own life that have shaped or challenged your memories?

Discuss Lisa's mother's character, her mothering style, and the vicissitudes of Lisa's relationship with her. What gives Lisa the self-possession to finally stand up to her, leaving the house and returning to say, "You shouldn't have yelled at me" (p. 222)? Later, walking home after leaving her mother at a restaurant, the author writes: "I felt a strange sort of calm, too calm; I was a girl walking and a girl who watched a girl walking" (p. 269). Is this division of self a necessary part of Lisa's growing up? Is it only by separating from her mother that Lisa is able to mature fully, accepting her mother's flaws and valuing her strengths?

How does Lisa construct and reconstruct her identity throughout the book? How do her goals and yearnings change? Consider how the following women serve as role models for Lisa: her mother, Mona, Laurene, Steve's girlfriends. Lisa's mother and father both tend toward fierce self-definition, as when Lisa's mother responds to Lisa's suggestion that she clip coupons like Debbie with: "No way. It's not the kind of person I am. Or *ever* want to be" (p. 56). How is identity formation based on identification with others different from one based on opposition to them? At the end of the book, the author writes: "I wouldn't trade any part of my experience for someone else's life … the accumulation of choices made had carved a path that was characteristic and distinct, down to the serif, and I felt the texture of it all around me for just a moment, familiar, like my own skin, and it was good enough" (p. 378). What enables us to accept our own experiences, no matter how negative? Is Lisa's ability to do this—to deem her experience "good enough"—her ultimate act of self-affirmation?

The fragility of Lisa's own sense of existence runs throughout the book and is intimately tied to her relationships with her parents. After spending more time with her father, she says: "I was starting to disappear. I noticed details about him with exact focus, but had difficulty locating myself" (p. 95). Later, she writes in her journal: "When I tell him events, they come alive. When I don't tell him, they don't exist" (p. 229). And when she listens to her mother's life stories, she inhabits her mother's perspective rather than her own (p. 58). How does this sense of her negligibility affect Lisa's relationships? How does her relationship with Josh help her toward the sense of ownership of her experience she expresses on p. 338?

Lisa says of her father's house: "For the years I lived there, I longed for more furniture; the longing would grow into a feverish craving for the furnished rooms I'd seen in other houses" (p. 240). Is longing for material things always a stand-in for an immaterial longing? Revisit the epigraph to the final section, "Coda," from Fanny Howe about desire (p. 347). Do you agree with her assertions? How have Lisa's desires been a positive and motivating force in her life, and how have they been destructive or unhelpful? Are we doomed to be helpless victims of our desires, or can we school them or harness them?

Throughout the book, the author is critical of her childhood self, as when she feels disappointment over her father's failure to say good-night to her: "What did I want? What did I expect? He didn't need me the way I needed him" (p. 264). Later, when Steve and Laurene do come tuck her in, it's awkward and never happens again. Where does the author's judgment seem ultimately to fall? Do you think she's overly critical of herself? Does she have to be self-critical to avoid alienating readers? Do adults ever need to apologize for mistakes made in childhood? When do we become fully accountable for our actions?

Revisit the two epigraphs at the start of the book from Shakespeare and Saul Bellow. How do you interpret them? Do they speak to each other? Do they implicate us as readers? Could we be seen as devourers of Lisa's story? As observers whose gaze has the capacity to do harm? Do we have different obligations as readers (and as judges) of memoir than we do as readers of fiction?

How would you characterize the experience Lisa has on the Hawaii trip when she sees a fish illuminated by starlight and says: "In that moment I saw—sensed, really—a cord strung between the fish and the star, connecting them . . . There was no unimportant, no negligible, being, I felt, just then; something as small and seemingly insignificant as one fish in the slapping ocean was connected to the galactic immensity" (p. 315). Do you think this epiphanic moment of understanding comes from within Lisa herself, or is it something she's gifted with from outside herself? Have you had similar flashes of new understanding?

After she tells her father she'd like to split the year between his house and her mother's, she says: "I would work toward freedom—one day, I would dangle my limbs from a car window beneath high arching branches" (p. 327). Later, when she and Josh fly in his car over a dip in the road, she says: "For me, the flight unlidded the town. There were hidden places of freedom, and he knew them" (p. 333). Discuss these two images of freedom: as something to work toward, and as something waiting to be discovered. Consider others' gestures toward freedom in the book: the hippies, who eschew convention; her father, who doesn't want to be "bound by time" (p. 102) or laws (p. 280); her mother, a freethinker who defies even orthodontal authority (p. 173). What kind of freedom does Lisa seek by comparison?

When her mother visits the adult Lisa in New York, she confesses she never knew how to read palms and justifies her deception: "We needed to get to a radically different place from where we were. I didn't know how else to get us there, besides stories. And anyway, the things I was saying—they were true" (p. 375). Does it matter whether family stories are factually true so long as there is good intention behind their telling? Lisa's mother's stories are instrumental in shaping Lisa's idea of herself and her family. Is her mother a reliable source? Is there such thing as a reliable source? How does the book explore the way in which stories do not contain fixed meanings for our passive reception? Consider the story about the orange hitting Lisa's mother in India (pp. 25–6). How does Lisa interpret this and other stories for her own use?

How do you receive Steve's final conversations with Lisa—his regrets, tears, apologies (pp. 372–6)? Do they require Lisa to reevaluate his previous behavior? If the progression of events were reversed—if Steve had been a supportive and present father and had then made cruel declarations on his deathbed, would that be more unsettling? Is redemption at the end what we long for most in a life story? Is a life ever irredeemable?

Lisa observes that when Laurene talked, "she used a group of words I'd never heard people use in speech before—*gratify, garner, providence, interim, pillage, marauding*—slipping the words into her sentences like jewels" (197). Where else do we see Lisa's aliveness to language growing up? One of the great pleasures of reading the book is the author's skillfulness in bringing scenes so vividly to life—what are some of your favorite word choices, descriptions, uses of metaphor and simile? To take just one example, how does the author's use of metaphor in the description of her father at the parent-teacher conference (where he "seemed to carbonate the meeting with his presence, both teachers becoming giddy near him" [p. 191]) resonate beyond the sentence itself, amplifying our understanding of Steve and his effect on others?

When Lisa confesses to her mother that she's been stealing from Steve and Laurene, her mother reminds her of the myth of Persephone, the Greek goddess who goes to the underworld and eats pomegranate seeds that are forbidden to her. Her mother tells her: "She stole from the underworld, she partook of it, and then she was *bound* to it" (p. 370). What do you make of her mother's admonition? Does it surprise you that she doesn't counsel against the dishonesty of stealing but focuses on the tie it forms between thief and victim? Look at the situations where Lisa is witness to her father's ill treatment of others (such as the incident with the waitress on p. 310 and with Lisa's cousin on pp. 139–41). What is the psychological effect of her staying silent out of fear? Do witnesses become involved in Steve's cruelty—bound to it, in some sense?

Lisa's mother offers this guidance to the second graders in her weekend art class: "Don't draw the tree you *think* you see. Draw the tree. Trust your eyes" (p. 44). How do we see Lisa attempting to achieve this clarity of vision toward her own life? What does she need to brush aside to trust her own eyes? Elsewhere, her mother advises: "There's no such thing as a color without a color around it. Even the color of the paper is not nothing. Everything matters, not just of itself, but in relation to everything else" (p. 46). Consider how these insights describe the way in which the author has presented her life story.

SUGGESTIONS FOR FURTHER READING:

Why Be Happy When You Could Be Normal? by Jeanette Winterson; *Patrimony* by Philip Roth; *The Memory Palace* by Mira Bartok; *Famous Father Girl: A Memoir of Growing up Bernstein* by Jamie Bernstein; *This Boy's Life* by Tobias Wolff; *Reading My Father: A Memoir* by Alexandra Styron; *The Glass Castle* by Jeannette Walls; *The Wine Lover's Daughter: A Memoir* by Anne Fadiman; *Safekeeping: Some True Stories from a Life* by Abigail Thomas; *Lying: A Metaphorical Memoir* by Lauren Slater; *The Boys of My Youth* by Jo Ann Beard; *The Mother Knot: A Memoir* by Kathryn Harrison; *Wild* by Cheryl Strayed; *Dog Years* by Mark Doty; *Blood-dark Track* by Joseph O'Neill